Mario Glowik
Market Entry Strategies

D1665000

Mario Glowik

Market Entry Strategies

Internationalization Theories, Concepts and
Cases of Asian High-Technology Firms

2nd, revised and updated edition

DE GRUYTER
OLDENBOURG

ISBN 978-3-11-042592-5
e-ISBN (PDF) 978-3-11-043987-8
e-ISBN (EPUB) 978-3-11-043988-5

Library of Congress Cataloging-in-Publication Data
A CIP catalog record for this book has been applied for at the Library of Congress.

Bibliografische Information der Deutschen Nationalbibliothek
The Deutsche Nationalbibliothek lists this publication in the Deutsche Nationalbibliografie;
detailed bibliographic data are available on the Internet at http://dnb.dnb.de.

© 2016 Walter de Gruyter GmbH, Berlin/Boston
Cover illustration: zhu difeng/iStock/Thinkstock
Printing and binding: CPI books GmbH, Leck
♾ Printed on acid-free paper
Printed in Germany

www.degruyter.com

MIX
Papier aus verantwor-
tungsvollen Quellen
FSC
www.fsc.org   FSC® C083411

Contents

Introduction

What differentiates *Market Entry Strategies* from other publications on the subject? This book serves the reader through its unique integration of internationalization theories with real-life global business practise. Complex issues are explained in a manner that results in understanding, and relevant topics are applied in authoritative industry and firm case studies. The focus on Asian firms in the case studies delivers interesting insights into modern high-technology industries and changing global business dynamics. Various illustrations and tables enable comprehension of the points being discussed.

Questions at the end of each chapter help the reader review the core content of the chapter topics. The review questions are suitable both for students' self-assessment of understanding and for team exercises. Questions can be assigned either as written homework or for class discussions or presentations. The case studies are of different lengths, giving instructors flexibility in terms of the timing and scheduling of the content to be taught in each class session.

Supporting the book's pragmatic and goal-oriented philosophy, the publication is divided into three main chapters: 'How to Combine Theory and Business Practise', 'Internationalization Theories', and 'Market Entry Strategies'.

Chapter One introduces and explains the importance of solid theory in academic work. Qualitative and quantitative research approaches as well as mixed-research methods are described, and the relevant strengths and weaknesses of each method are compared. Particular attention is paid to case study methods because the firm case studies presented in this book provide the reader with a window to international business reality. At the same time, the reader gains knowledge of case study design, which is helpful when developing his or her own case studies – whether required at a university (e. g., homework, thesis writing) or in business (e. g., competitor analysis). The case study of *Panasonic*, which completes chapter one, invites the reader to develop scenarios in terms of Panasonic's business future.

Chapter Two is devoted to the most important theories of internationalization, including Product Life-Cycle, Internalization, Location, Eclectic Paradigm, Uppsala, Network, and International New Venture (Born Global). These models are grounded to a considerable extent in the Transaction Cost Theory and the Resource-Based View as explained and illustrated in the chapter. While writing this part, I emphasized the main contents of the theories, which necessarily includes a review of their conceptual weaknesses. The case study of *Sharp* illustrates rapidly changing technological industry dynamics. The industry case study titled *Market Entry of Asian High-Technology Firms in Europe* reviews and applies the section dealing with Location concepts. The *Sony* case serves to apply important elements of the Resource-Based View and how crucial firm resources, as a result of management decisions, change over time. The case study of *Haier* delivers insights to the firm's learning by imitation capabilities. Finally, International New Venture (Born Global) concepts are illustrated in the *Xiaomi* case study.

Chapter Three starts with the introduction of the terms *strategy* and *internationalization*. It continues with a discussion of relevant market entry strategies, including exporting, franchising, licensing, contract manufacturing, international joint ventures, and foreign direct investment, among others (e.g., greenfield and acquisitions). Each market entry strategy is discussed in depth; thus the reader becomes aware of the strategy-specific advantages as well as the potential risks. All relevant strategies for market entry are explained and categorized in light of the crucial determinants of international business decision making: hierarchical control of operations, the firm's proximity to the foreign market, the investment risk, and the factor of time. The theoretical discussion of relevant market entry strategies comes alive through the cases studies of *Samsung* (strategy and internationalization), *Foxconn* (contract manufacturing), *LG Electronics* and *Philips* (international joint ventures), *Lenovo* (acquisitions), and *TCL* (incremental takeover of control in the course of international joint venture operations).

I sincerely thank all the readers, students, instructors, scholars, and business executives who, through their valuable comments, contributed to various improvements to the 2009 first edition of the book. I would also like to thank Corinna Hlozek and Irina Fensky for their tremendous assistance as I developed my manuscript. I sincerely thank Margie Dyer from the US for her very professional and reliable support proofreading my final manuscript. For her outstanding expertise and ongoing assistance in the course of realizing this second edition of *Market Entry Strategies*, I wholeheartedly thank Anja Cheong from the De Gruyter Oldenbourg publishing house.

Berlin, Germany, January 2016   Mario Glowik

1 How to Combine Theory and Business Practice?

1.1 About Theory

'There is nothing more practical than a good theory,' wrote Lewin (1952: 169). In other words, theorists should develop new ideas for understanding and conceptualizing a challenging research issue, ideas that may suggest potentially fruitful and practical avenues for dealing with the issue in the real world (Vansteenkiste & Sheldon, 2006: 63).

Wacker (2008: 7) describes a theory as a set of conceptual relationships that mainly comprises four properties: definitions, domain, relationships, and predictions. The first property, 'definitions', refers to a clear terminology and description of the target subject. 'Domain' means that a good theory provides generalizations and abstractions of the phenomena observed in reality. The third property, 'relationships', focusses on the consistency of the entire theory and the possibility of verification of the variables in the theory. Finally, a well-grounded theory allows valuable 'predictions' for the future (Wacker, 2008: 7–8).

Eisenhardt (1989: 532) defines the development of theory as a central activity in organizational research. Theory is developed by combining observations from literature, common sense, and experience. The goal of explanatory (academic) research, including inductive theory building and hypothetical deductive theory testing, is to develop an understanding of an existing phenomenon as well as to develop theoretical explanations for and predictions regarding the phenomenon (Holmström, Ketokivi, & Hameri, 2009: 68–69).

There are concerns that academic research findings are, to some extent, not useful for business practitioners because a theory necessarily reduces the multifaceted and complex issues of a firm's environment to a generalized and simplified model. Thus, a theory provides only limited potential for specific recommendations to managers. The gap between theory and practice is known as the knowledge transfer problem. Knowledge transfer is based on the assumption that practical knowledge (knowledge of how to do things) in a professional domain is derived, at least in part, from research knowledge (knowledge from science and scholarship) (Van de Ven & Johnson, 2006: 802). It is necessary to reconcile theory building and business practice, with the aim of generating theory and academic research findings that are relevant and applicable in practice (Anderson, Herriot, & Hodgkinson, 2001: 392; Slack, Lewis, & Bates, 2004: 385). Research should conceptualize and generalize new developments of use to business practitioners, while, simultaneously, new knowledge derived from practice should stimulate new directions for research and theorizing (operationalizing theory). Van de Ven (2011: 44) proposes a 'diamond model' to link theory with reality, which suggests a process of

- problem formulation, in which the phenomenon is grounded on concrete details;
- development and testing of alternative models to address the research question;
- collection of evidence that allows comparing existing alternative models; and
- communication and application of the findings in ways that encourage their use in the real world, for example in business practice.

Researchers should locate themselves in both the theoretical and the practical perspectives in the research cycle at different times. They cannot stay fixed in either the world of practice or the world of theory. Researchers should keep in mind Poole and Van de Ven (1989: 562), who argue that 'even a good theory' is a limited and 'fairly precise picture' as it attempts 'to capture a multifaceted reality with a finite, internally inconsistent statement' and is, therefore, essentially incomplete. Thus, the challenge addressed by international business and management research is to profoundly develop an interaction between the world of practice and the world of theory, rather than focussing on either one of them alone (Tranfield & Starkey, 1998: 353).

1.2 Qualitative, Quantitative, and Mixed Research Methods

Qualitative and quantitative research methods have in common that researchers systematically collect and analyze empirical data and carefully examine the patterns in it. However, the two approaches differ in some ways that mainly depend on the research subject and the availability of reliable information and data. Qualitative research methods describe and interpret a research object if a reasonable amount of quantifiable data is not available and, therefore, hypothesis testing is impossible. The main circumstances in which qualitative research approaches are recommended are, for example, when the research subject

- is new and, therefore, reliable data sets in larger numbers are not available yet;
- tends to be complex and needs to be described in depth;
- is based on variables that are difficult to quantify; and
- requires an analysis aimed at formulating specific recommendations instead of deducing general models.

Because qualitative research is usually done in exploratory settings, that is, in studying topics that are new to the field and hitherto under researched, it is of vital importance to make sure the subject matter is truly novel and merits attention (Birkinshaw, Brannen, & Tung, 2011: 579).

The qualitative researcher views the social phenomena of complex social networks holistically (Orum, Feagin, & Sjoberg, 1991: 6–7). This explains why qualitative research studies appear as broad, with panoramic views of an object, rather than as a micro-analysis. The more complex, interactive, and encompassing the narrative, the more desirable qualitative study approaches are. Qualitative researchers often rely on interpretative data and apply 'logic in practice' by following a nonlinear research path. 'Logic in practice' is based on an apprenticeship model and the sharing of implicit knowledge about practical concerns and specific experiences. The researchers speak a language of 'cases and contexts' (Creswell, 2009: 182; Neuman, 2006: 151).

In heuristic qualitative research, the data analysis tries to find similarities, which help with formulating propositions, research questions, and hypotheses, instead of simply testing a hypothesis, which is done at later stages of research when more information and datasets relevant to the target subjects are available (Kleining & Witt, 2001: 12). Qualitative research methods are particularly well suited to theory development, which means both framing a study in terms of the existing debates in the literature and being explicit about what body of theory(ies) it is building upon and why (Birkinshaw et al., 2011: 579).

In order to explain outcomes in particular cases, qualitative researchers think about the factors that may be causal related to a research subject. Thus, with this approach, scholars seek to identify the main variables (causes) and their combinations that influence the research phenomena (outcomes). The approach assumes that there are multiple causal paths (equifinality) to the same outcome. Research findings can be formally expressed through Boolean equations such as the following.

Outcome (Y) = Causing Variables A $_{(t1, t2 \dots tn)}$ and B $_{(t1, t2 \dots tn)}$ and C $_{(t1, t2 \dots tn)}$

Because the causing variables (A and B and C) may change over time, it follows that the researcher must make a number of observations over time. This might involve a very long period of time (e. g., years, decades) or multiple observations taken over a short period (e. g., an hour, a week) of time (t_1, t_2 ... t_n). To say that A and B and C cause the outcome Y presumes that all other things are equal. In other words, any temporal variation in Y observable from t_1 to t_n should be the result of temporal variations in A and B and C (the causal factors of interest). This ceteris paribus assumption must hold; otherwise, causal argumentation within a qualitative research project, such as a case study, is impossible (Gerring & McDermott, 2007: 690).

In order to figure out critical A and B and C variables, for example in a field study with interviews of experts, semi-structured questionnaires that include 'open questions' and 'closed questions' are often recommended. Open questions aim to elicit a free flow of thoughts and storytelling by the interviewee. 'Closed questions' are aimed at ranking the interviewees' answers, usually in a 'Likert scale', ranging , for example, from 'strongly agree' (+5) to 'strongly disagree' (-5) (Baker, Thompson, & Mannion, 2006: 40). It is always very important 'to leave the door open for the interviewee': thus, to let her or him have the chance 'to escape from answering' by providing an option to indicate that the interviewee does not know or chooses not to answer; for example titled 'I have no opinion / I don't want to answer 'etc. This neutral value box avoids that the research outcomes are biased because the interviewee feels forced to answer in a certain category (e. g. interviewee does not have the appropriate knowledge or feels uncomfortable to clearly positioning its opinion in the Likert scale, for what reason ever).

Various kinds of information sources, including media, annual company reports, industry surveys, and others should be explored to gather ideas about the relevant opinions and practices of the interviewee to guide the development of the interview questions. Prior to conducting the interview phase of the study, a pre-study period should be scheduled, where the researcher should hold mock interviews and fine-tune the research design and the interview questions (Wahyuni, 2012: 74).

Quantitative research, in which the analyst typically seeks to identify the values of variables and figure out the standardized relationships among them, differs from qualitative study (Mahoney & Goertz, 2006: 232). Quantitative research necessarily assumes that standardized and reliable data in larger quantities are available for statistical testing. In consequence, quantitative researchers apply 'reconstruction logic' and follow a linear standardized research path. 'Reconstruction logic' is based on reorganizing, standardizing, and codifying research knowledge, using explicit rules, formal procedures, and research techniques. Quantitative scientists tend to speak a language of 'variables and hypotheses' and emphasize measuring linked variables precisely and arriving at general causal explanations (Neuman, 2006: 151).

Thus, the vital requirement for hypothesis formulation in the course of conducting quantitative research is that reliable datasets in appropriate numbers are available. These data are collected either from secondary or primary sources or both of them. The main aim of quantitative research is hypothesis testing (null-hypothesis versus alternative hypothesis), which is carried out through analysis of the relationships among model-relevant variables. Therefore, quantitative research methods are particularly suitable for testing the validity of a theory and further development of a theory. Common statistical methods of quantitative research are located within the field of descriptive statistics (e. g., frequencies, mean, median, analysis of correlations among variables) and inferential statistics (t-test, Analysis of Variance (ANOVA), regression analysis, etc.) (compare: Brosius, 2013; Schendra, 2008). Based on the discussion above, Figure 1 provides a comparative overview of the strengths and weaknesses of quantitative and qualitative research methods.

Mixed research methods, as the term indicates, combine both qualitative and quantitative forms of analysis. Instead of simply incorporating both methods, mixed research approaches are rather applied in *tandem* in order to maximize research outcomes (Creswell, 2009: 4). The tandem approach alleviates the conceptual weaknesses of using only qualitative approaches (e. g., limited generalization of study outcomes) or only quantitative approaches (e. g., less in-depth understanding of the research phenomena). Combining qualitative and quantitative methods supports the identification of causal variables and the interpretation of the results (qualitative methods). On the other hand, statistical analysis (quantitative methods), such as frequencies and correlations among crucial variables, contributes to the ability to

Comparison of the Strengths of the Research Methods	
quantitative	qualitative
– appropriate method for hypothesis testing – particularly useful for theory validity testing – high representativeness due to larger sample – statistical robustness by measuring the correlation among variables and the probability that the analysis reflects the population – data objectivity because data are quantifiable – generalization of research outcomes – data comparability and transferability – reasonable in cost and time	– appropriate method for hypothesis development – particularly desirable for exploration of a new phenomenon – explains 'cause and effects' of individual cases – tests whether a theory is applicable – aids understanding of research subject causalities – reflects specificity/complexity of business reality – flexible research method – better contextual validity of the research subject

Comparison of the Weaknesses of the Research Methods	
quantitative	qualitative
– generalized model assumptions – availability of aggregated data sets in larger numbers – limited ability to determine causation from research results due to quantifiable/fixed questions approach – rather less method flexibility – limited potential for specific individual recommendations	– study tends to be time-consuming and therefore costly – limited potential for generalization – interviewer needs profound knowledge of the research subject (e. g., industry expertise) – minor numerical indications – risk of subjective interpretation of research results by the interviewer

Figure 1. Comparison of quantitative and qualitative research methods

generalize research outcomes (Dobrovolny & Fuentes, 2008: 10). For decision makers in policy, business, and management, study outcomes from mixed research approaches are more useful if they provide quantifiable information about effects but also about the variables' causation mechanisms that lead to certain effects (Obermann, Scheppe, & Glazinski, 2013: 255).

1.3 Cases Studies: Why, How, and What?

Case studies, which were initiated and developed at the Harvard Business School during the 1920s, are a useful tool for research and teaching that provide a transition between theory and practice. Formal case study structure includes identification of a problem, development of initial research questions, and conducting research by collecting information and making observations. Like other research approaches, there are methodological drawbacks: case studies do not deliver evidence about the perfect solution to an existing problem. The vital strength of case studies is that they connect students, scholars, and researchers to social phenomena and real-life situations in a way that helps to develop solution scenarios and, as a result, sharpen complex thinking and decision-making behavior (Breslin & Buchanan, 2008: 36–38).

Case studies are generally described as useful for theory development (Aaboen, Dubios, & Lind, 2012: 236) because they are exploratory and descriptive by nature, identifying a new and often complex research phenomenon (Breslin & Buchanan, 2008: 38). A case study serves as a research strategy that examines, through the use of a variety of data sources, an event or subject in its naturalistic context, with the purpose of confronting theory with the real world (Piekkari, Welch, & Paavilainen, 2009: 569). Yin (2014: 16) describes case studies as an empirical inquiry that investigates a contemporary phenomenon in depth and within its real-life context, especially when the boundaries between the phenomenon and the context of research are not clearly evident. Built on a profound and solid literature review, a case study relies on multiple sources of evidence with various variables of interest and data including archival data, annual reports, market survey data, statistics, press releases, interviews, and observations (Eisenhardt & Graebner, 2007: 27–28). A case study approach can also be used to demonstrate whether a theory is applicable or rather lacks applicability under certain conditions not previously investigated. Thus, a case study can impose restrictions on a theory's generalizability or can lead to totally disproving a theory. In addition, a case study can provide 'a high degree of control for testing a new theory or comparing multiple competing theories' (Dowlatshahi, 2010: 1365).

It is of vital importance that the research questions guide the choice of methods and not vice versa. The researcher should clearly articulate in his or her paper why a particular qualitative or quantitative method or a combination of methods is appropriate for the objectives of the study (Birkinshaw et al., 2011: 579). Defining the research questions serves as the most important step to be taken in a research project.

'Why' and 'how' research questions are posed by the researcher because such questions are more explanatory and can better analyze complex dynamics in real-context reality. Thus, 'why' and 'how' questions are likely to lead to the use of a case study or experiment as the preferred research method. These questions deal with the operational links and relational causalities of variables, which need to be traced over time, rather than mere frequency observations (Yin, 2014: 10). Van de Ven and Engleman (2004: 355) claim that 'how' questions describe and explain temporal sequences of events studied over time.

Yin (2014: 10) distinguishes between two types of 'what questions'. There is a category of 'what' questions that is exploratory, where the goal is to develop pertinent hypotheses and propositions for further inquiry. The use of an exploratory case study applying 'what' questions should include the following steps (Dowlatshahi, 2010: 1369–1370):

(1)　review of existing academic and practitioner literature;
(2)　identification of critical cause-and-effect variables for the case study subject;
(3)　development of propositions and hypotheses; and
(4)　statement of the insights gained as a result of evaluating the propositions and developing and presenting the case study.

Another category of 'what' questions, similar to 'who' and 'where' questions (or their derivatives 'how many' and 'how much'), utilizes survey methods of analysis or the analysis of archival data. These survey methods are advantageous when the research goal is to describe the incidence or prevalence of a research phenomenon or when research outcomes are predictive (Yin, 2014: 10).

In case studies where the research subject might be one firm (single case study) or several firms studied, for example, in the course of an industry analysis (multiple case studies), the researcher explores crucial events, activities, or processes through in-depth analysis. Single firm case studies are developed to identify benchmarks within an industry (e.g., market size leader) or special and unique cases (e.g., technological innovators) or to figure out which firms are the worst performing in order to learn from their mistakes. Multiple cases are discrete experiments. Based on a replication logic, multiple case studies contrast and extend knowledge to develop the emerging theory, and this approach takes into account the real-world context in which the research phenomena occur (Eisenhardt, 1989: 534; Eisenhardt & Graebner, 2007: 25). While single case studies provide a description of an existing single phenomenon (Siggelkow, 2007: 20), multiple case studies naturally provide a stronger ground for theory building and thus yield more robust, sustainable, and reliable information. The larger the multiple case study sample, the better the prerequisites for finding common cause-and-effect relationships, which leads to a higher degree of generalizability of the research outcomes.

Case study research results are incrementally developed over a period of time. The methods for analysis progress through research phases (Atteslander, 2003: 84–85). When case study research is undertaken, the scientist uses complex reasoning that is multifaceted and iterative and considers various aspects simultaneously. Although the reasoning is largely inductive, both inductive and deductive processes are at work. The thinking process is also iterative, with a cycling back and forth from data collection and analysis to problem reformulation. Added to this are simultaneous activities of collecting and analyzing information and writing up the 'case story'. The research process should be flexible and open to new or even unexpected pragmatic information that reflects the observed reality (Creswell, 2009: 182–183).

The analyst emphasizes conducting detailed examinations of cases that arise in the natural flow of real life, trying to present authentic interpretations that are sensitive to specific social-historical contexts. The passage of time, which may involve years or decades, is integral to case studies. Analysts look at the sequence of events and pay attention to what happened first, second, third, and so on. Because qualitative researchers examine the same case or set of cases over time, they can see an issue evolve, a conflict or solution emerge, or a social relationship or network develop. The researcher can detect processes and causal relations (Neuman, 2006: 151). Actual information sources for developing a case study, whether available in hardcopy, electronic version, or transcript from interviews are listed below.

(1) **Academic literature**
   - books, journals, conference proceedings, etc.
(2) **Secondary company and industry sources**
   - company annual reports, balance sheets, press releases, etc.
   - official statistics, (e. g., International Monetary Fund (IMF), Eurostatistics, Organisation for Economic Co-operation and Development (OECD), United Nations (UN), etc.)
   - data provided by commercial market research institutions (e. g., DisplaySearch)
(3) **Primary study information sources**
   - face-to-face interviews or electronic or phone interviews (e. g., questionnaire results, minutes of meetings)

Researchers should be reflective in their use of the case study and more precisely specify the type of case study they are conducting: for example, whether their study targets a best case (e. g., industry benchmark) or worst case, whether a single case study or an interview-based multiple case study is utilized, and so on (Piekkari et al., 2009: 584). Welch et al. (2011: 744) propose a 'case study memo', which helps to systematically figure out the linguistic elements of a case study as well as provide explanations of the researcher's theorizing process and corresponding assumptions. Having the questions listed below in mind is very useful not only when reading and evaluating case study articles found in the academic literature but also when writing about one's own case study.

   - Does the case study article state the theoretical objectives and relevant research questions?
   - How are the theory and empirical data related and mutually integrated?
   - Is the research methodology properly explained and which information sources are used?
   - Are the case outcomes generalizable for theory development?
   - Do the case outcomes allow causal claims for the research phenomena (Welch, Piekkari, Plakoyiannaki, & Paavilainen-Mäntymäki, 2011: 744)?
   - Are there implications for management and business executives?
   - Are there proposals for future research in order to overcome current research gaps?

Like other research approaches, case study methods come along with drawbacks. First of all, no matter how large the sample is, researchers collect detailed information using a variety of data collection approaches and techniques; nevertheless, the outcomes still have the risk of being interpreted subjectively by the researcher (Creswell, 2009: 15). Reasons for subjective interpretation are, on the one hand, that the researcher, no matter how carefully the research is done, has an outsider perspective. Therefore, the researcher should have, on the other hand, some profound understanding of the subject of the case study, such as knowledge of the firm or the industry. The overwhelming advantage of case studies is that they provide authoritative, real-life business information. The specific case studies to be discussed in the following chapters of this book are used to combine and illuminate internationalization theories and market entry strategies and are designed to best serve the reader. The focus on Asian firms delivers interesting insights into modern high-technology industries and changing global business dynamics. Let us start with the first case study regarding Panasonic (Japan) in the following section.

Chapter review questions

1. What are the advantages and disadvantages of qualitative and quantitative research methods?
2. What research goals are served by *why, how,* and *what* questions?
3. Develop a draft of a single case study that aims to clarify a firm's international market entry strategies. (You can select the target firm.)

1.4 The Case Study of Panasonic: Do You Believe in its Future Business?

1.4.1 Company background

In 1918, Konosuke Matsushita established the company known as Matsushita Electric Housewares Manufacturing Works, which was changed to Matsushita Electric Manufacturing Works in 1929. The company has been using the name Matsushita Electric Industrial Co., Ltd., ever since its incorporation as a joint stock corporation in 1935. While it had used the National and Panasonic brand names over a long period, the Japanese management decided in 2003 to unify its global brand to Panasonic with the brand slogan 'Panasonic ideas for life'. Since October 1, 2008, the company has officially been named Panasonic Corporation (Panasonic, 2008).

Immediately after founding the company, Matsushita began production of an innovative attachment plug and a two-way socket, both of which he designed himself. These new products became very popular, earning the company a reputation for high quality at low prices. Matsushita Electric began printing English instructions for its products in 1931; and in April 1932, Konosuke Matsushita set up an export trading department to carry out research and marketing development in order to evaluate the company's international sales potential. This represented an innovative step in an industry where, in Japan, exports were traditionally left to large trading houses. With a unified policy for domestic and export markets, the company was able to actively expand its export business. With exports increasing, Konosuke Matsushita incorporated the export trading department as the Matsushita Electric Trading Company in August of 1935. In 1936, the founding owner sent three people to the US and Europe in order to learn about advanced industries there. They visited about twenty local factories, including Philips and Siemens (Matsushita, 2008).

In 1952, after intense negotiations, Matsushita Electric concluded a technical and capital cooperation agreement with Philips of the Netherlands, setting up Matsushita Electronics Corporation as an international joint venture. This was the result of Konosuke Matsushita's efforts to find an overseas business partner, convinced that the adoption of advanced Western technology was essential for Japan's post-war reconstruction. In 1954, Matsushita Electric allied with Victor Company of Japan (JVC), a record player producer that was established in 1927 by the Victor Talking Machine Co. of the United States. In 1959, ready to expand business activities abroad, Konosuke Matsushita founded Matsushita Electric Corporation of America in New York as its first overseas sales company. He urged his managers to adapt to their new host nation and to apply themselves to providing products that Americans would appreciate. The formation of an overseas sales network proceeded at a rapid pace.

The first European sales company established was National Panasonic GmbH in West Germany in 1962, which was used as a base to enter the European market. Since then, various sales companies have been established throughout the world. On March 22, 1974, Motorola Inc. of the US and Matsushita Electric of Japan signed a contract for the purchase of Motorola's television set operations in the US and Canada. The purpose of the acquisition was to start a television business in the US market. On May 22, 1987, Matsushita Electric and Beijing City in the People's Republic of China signed an agreement to establish an international joint venture to produce cathode ray tubes (CRTs) for color TVs. This was Matsushita Electric's first investment in China in the post-war period. The new company, Beijing Matsushita Color CRT Co., Ltd., started production in June 1989 with about 1,400 employees. The company first produced 21-inch color picture tubes and later added 14-inch and 18-inch tubes. The products were supplied to color television set plants in China (Matsushita, 2008).

MCA Inc. joined the Matsushita Group in November 1990. MCA was a multibillion dollar diversified international entertainment conglomerate engaged in the production and distribution of theatrical, television, and home video products, as well as the operation of two amusement parks in Hollywood, California, and Orlando, Florida. MCA brought a diversity of new capabilities into the Matsushita Group and also the promise of innovation in the field of electronic entertainment through the integration of hardware and software products. However, in June 1995, Matsushita Electric divested its engagement in business fields diversified from consumer electronics and transferred an 80 percent share of equities in MCA Inc. to the Seagram Company Ltd., a Canadian liquor manufacturer (Matsushita, 2008).

In the television set business, Matsushita concentrated its research and development resources during the 1990s on the development of the plasma technology. In 1996, Matsushita developed the world's first 26-inch plasma television set. In the field of plasma displays, the Japanese electronics firm was technologically ahead of its time. Would this be worthwhile in the future?

1.4.2 The market at the beginning of the 21st century

In 2001, as the market for plasma television set panels was expected to grow significantly and Matsushita Plasma Display Co., Ltd., began full-scale mass production of modules targeting high picture quality at an affordable price, Matsushita aimed to be the number one plasma display panel manufacturer in the industry by strengthening its manufacturing structure, including the commencement of production at its plant in China in December 2001 (Matsushita, 2002).

Also in 2001, Matsushita centralized its domestic manufacturing locations, having discontinued monitor tube production and implemented the joint global supply and purchase of television sets. As a pacesetter in the digital television set industry, Matsushita led the market in televisions with digital satellite tuners. In 2002, the company extended its line-up of flat-surface cathode ray tube television sets and augmented its plasma display panel product portfolio with new 36-inch and 42-inch models, followed by a new 50-inch television set model, all with the industry's highest levels of brightness and contrast to date and all equipped with digital satellite tuners. As a result of the upcoming flat-panel technologies, which resulted in a continued decline of the cathode ray tube television set business, Matsushita decided to reduce cathode ray tube production incrementally, which ended in the closure of all remaining cathode ray tube related operations worldwide beginning in 2006 (Matsushita, 2005).

In April 2002, Matsushita established eP Corporation, a common joint venture with Toshiba Corporation and Hitachi Ltd., which launched the world's first trial service integrating digital broadcasting and high-storage data casting. The introduction of this service enabled users in Japan to access multiple channels with advanced functions on demand as well as to participate in home shopping, home banking, and other interactive services (Matsushita, 2002). However, customers who have an affinity for using interactive services can use their Internet-linked computer and do not necessarily need a television set. Thus, the ambitious plans to create new markets for television sets with compatible terminals could not be realized as expected.

The decline of the conventional cathode ray tube business, which came along with an increasing cost pressure in flat-panel technologies, semiconductors, and other electronic components, caused a severe loss for Matsushita in 2002. Its efforts to reduce fixed costs and rationalize activities in parts and material purchasing were not enough to offset negative factors stemming from the price decline. Furthermore, the company incurred various restructuring charges, which included USD 1.23 billion related to employment reorganization programs, USD 1.35 billion for impairment losses associated with the closure or integration of several manufacturing locations, and a write-down of investment securities, resulting in a net loss of USD 3.24 billion (Matsushita, 2002). In terms of sales and net income, Matsushita recovered stepwise after 2002 and successfully managed a turnaround. The restructuring activities of 2002 resulted in an increasing profit.

The revised organization that Matsushita launched in 2002 as a result of its restructuring program was modified over the years. The organization was divided into five major business divisions. The first line of business is named AVC Networks Company and contains, for example, digital cameras, mobile communication, projectors, and data storage devices. Products such as air conditioners, laundry systems, vacuum cleaners, kitchen equipment, and home entertainment are housed in Appliances Company. Recently, new business fields, such as Eco Solutions (e. g., energy systems, lightning), Automotive & Industrial System Company (e. g., liquid crystal display, battery, automotive related systems), and Panasonic Healthcare were launched (compare Figure 2).

1.4.3 What comes next?

Mainly because of the initiative of Matsushita, which concentrated on plasma panel technology but aimed to manufacture and sell liquid crystal display (LCD) panels for flat-panel TVs, IPS Alpha Technology started operation in 2005 against an industry background of increasing international demand for LCD TVs. TV manufacturers faced a growing necessity to ensure a stable supply of high-quality panels at reasonable prices. Thus, Panasonic, Toshiba, and Hitachi decided to join forces to enable themselves to effectively respond to production price pressures and rising customer expectations for high-definition picture quality. Because the IPS Alpha joint venture incorporated Hitachi Displays' world-leading In-Plane-Switching (IPS) mode system technology, the three partner companies enjoyed favorable conditions for gaining highly competitive market positions based on standardization and high capital-efficient mass production of IPS mode LCD panels (Hitachi, 2008; HitachiDisplays, 2004). In June 2010, IPS Alpha Technology finally became a full-fledged wholly owned subsidiary of Panasonic Corporation. Beginning on October 1, 2010, the subsidiary company was named Panasonic Liquid Crystal Display Co., Ltd (Panasonic, 2010).

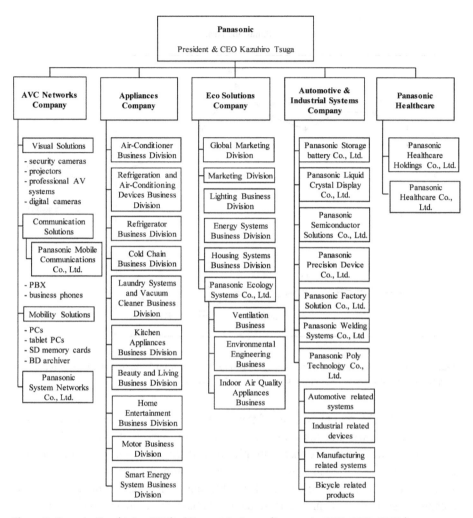

Figure 2. Organization (status 2015) of Panasonic Group (Panasonic, 2011, 2013, 2015a)

The incremental turnover of the joint venture majority by Panasonic was due to the fact that the global LCD business had developed greatly since 2006. This market attractiveness meant that existing and new competitors from Japan, South Korea, China, and Taiwan sharply increased their capacities during that time. In 2009, Panasonic reached a net income of USD 4.3 billion, which represented the highest profit ever during the period from 2006 to 2014 as the following figure illustrates (Panasonic, 2011, 2013, 2015a).

What happened in the ups and downs of the following years is rather similar to a roller coaster ride. In 2010, Panasonic profits turned into losses (USD 2.06 billion), while in 2011, the firm came back to USD 1.032 billion in profits. A year later, the largest Japanese electronics firm Panasonic reported a loss of USD 8.7 billion – the biggest in the company's ninety-five-year history. At the same time, net sales de-

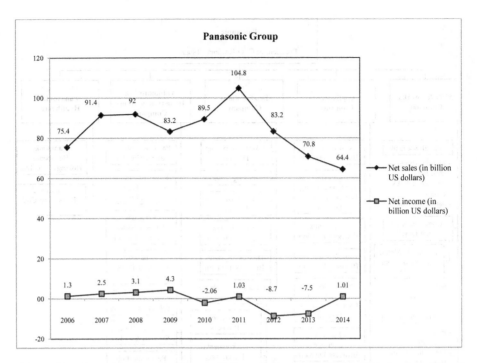

Figure 3. Net sales and net income of Panasonic Group for the period 2006 to 2014. Developed based on various firm related sources (Panasonic, 2011, 2013, 2015a)

clined as well. The primary causes of this were, according to Panasonic, the global economic slowdown and instability in the financial markets due to the European debt crisis as well as the extensive supply chain disruption caused by the flooding in Thailand that occurred in October 2011. Sales of flat-panel TVs and mobile phones plummeted in the period, although sales of PCs and some home appliances enjoyed a small boost. Panasonic moved to shake up its business following the purchase of Sanyo Electronics, including revamping its TV and chip operation and cutting jobs (Halliday, 2012).

For too long a time, the Japanese firm focussed its research and development efforts on plasma displays, which the management thought would become the leading display technology. However, liquid crystal display (LCD) panel technology assemblers like Sharp and Samsung improved their display performance significantly in terms of picture, brightness, sharpness, energy consumption, and viewing angle, which meant that it became increasingly difficult for Panasonic to be competitive. In 2013, Panasonic announced that production of new plasma units would end in December; and all related operations would be wrapped up by March 2014. Three of Panasonic's factories stopped building new units. In the press release, Panasonic said that due to rapid, drastic changes in the business environment that led to increasing supply, which caused price pressure from more affordable LCD TVs, the 'unhappy decision had to be made'. As for the future, Panasonic communicated that plasma research and development efforts would likely be diverted to OLED. The company sees televisions using the OLED technology as one of the key future products, and it is working to insure that it can make affordable OLED TVs that still leave room for profit before putting any up for sale. If and when that day comes, sticklers for the picture quality offered by plasmas should be more than happy with OLEDs (Savov, 2013).

At the all-time height of its losses in 2012, electric car manufacturer Tesla Motors and Panasonic announced that together they would develop nickel-based lithium-ion battery cells for electric vehicles. Panasonic had been rumored for months to be a battery cell supplier (Garthwaite, 2010). And three years later, Panasonic's chairman and CEO, Joe Taylor, said at the 2015 Consumer Electronics Show that he expects Tesla to produce 500,000 electric vehicles by 2020, with the help of the so-called Gigafactory, a USD 5 billion production facility. The Giga Factory is a massive production plant Tesla and Panasonic are building together in the state of Nevada. It will primarily serve to produce lithium-ion batteries for Tesla's cars at a lower cost. Panasonic jointly builds the battery cells used in the Model S and has promised to invest 'tens of billions of yen' (hundreds of millions of dollars) in the plant. The cost of batteries has often been cited as the biggest hurdle Tesla faces in growing its footprint. With the new Gigafactory, Tesla expects to lower the cost of battery production by nearly 30 percent. The Gigafactory, scheduled to open in 2017, is planning to hire more than 6,500 people and will cover 10 million square feet (Kim, 2015).

Panasonic is also expanding its Automotive & Industrial Systems Company, which is an in-house company of Panasonic Corporation that operates a B2B solutions business on a global scale. The business covers in-car infotainment-related equipment, in-car electronics, batteries, electronic devices, semiconductors, manufacturing-related systems, and so on. With a focus on the automotive and industrial fields, Panasonic intends to work to enhance customer value through the provision of solutions in a wide range of fields, from devices to systems.

'We also strive to leverage our collective capabilities to achieve the Panasonic vision: A Better Life, A Better World' (Panasonic, 2015b).

Chapter review questions

1. Before reading the case study, which products did you mainly link with the Panasonic brand? Did you change your opinion after reading the case study?
2. Suppose you are in the shoes of Panasonic's management. Which businesses would you further develop for the future? Please provide reasonable arguments to explain your answer.

Bibliography

Aaboen, L., Dubios, A., & Lind, F. (2012) Capturing processes in longitudinal multiple case studies. *Industrial Marketing Management*, 41: 235–246.

Anderson, N., Herriot, P., & Hodgkinson, G. P. (2001) The practitioner-researcher divide in industrial, work and organizational (IWO) psychology: Where are we now, and where do we go from here? *Journal of Occupational and Organizational Psychology*, 74(4): 391–411.

Atteslander, P. (2003) *Methoden der empirischen Sozialforschung*. Berlin: Walter de Gruyter.

Baker, R., Thompson, C., & Mannion, R. (2006) Q methodology in health economics. *Journal of Health Services Research & Policy*, 11(1): 38–45.

Birkinshaw, J., Brannen, M. Y., & Tung, R. L. (2011) From a distance and generalizable to up close and grounded: Reclaiming a place for qualitative methods in international business research. *Journal of International Business Studies*, 42: 573–581.

Breslin, M., & Buchanan, R. (2008) On the case study method of research and teaching in design. *Design Issues*, 24(1): 36–40.

Brosius, F. (2013) *SPSS 21*. Heidelberg: Huethig Jehle Rehm GmbH.

Creswell, J. W. (2009) *Research design, qualitative, quantitative, and mixed methods approaches*. London: Sage Publications.

Dobrovolny, J. L., & Fuentes, S. C. G. (2008) Quantitative versus qualitative evaluation: A tool to decide which to use. *Performance Improvement*, 47(4): 7–14.

Dowlatshahi, S. (2010) A cost-benefit analysis for the design and implementation of reverse logistics systems: Case studies approach. *International Journal of Production Research*, 48(5): 1361–1380.

Eisenhardt, K. M. (1989) Building theories from case study research. *Academy of Management Review*, 14(4): 532–550.

Eisenhardt, K. M., & Graebner, M. E. (2007) Theory building from cases: Opportunities and challenges. *Academy of Management Journal*, 50(1): 25–32.

Garthwaite, J. (2010) Tesla and Panasonic make it official: buddy up for batteries. Retrieved June 1, 2015 from http://gigaom.com/2010/01/07/tesla-panasonic-make-it-official-buddy-up-for-batteries/

Gerring, J., & McDermott, R. (2007) An experimental template for case study research. *American Journal of Political Science*, 51(3): 688–701.

Halliday, J. (2012) Panasonic and Sony mired in Japanese electronics slump. Retrieved May 28, 2015 from http://www.theguardian.com/business/2012/feb/03/panasonic-sony-japanese-electronics-slump.

Hitachi (2008) IPS Alpha Technology to build a state-of-the-art IPS LCD panel plant in Himeji City, Hyogo Prefecture. Retrieved 20.07.2011 from http://www.hitachi.com/New/cnews/080215c.html

HitachiDisplays (2004) Hitachi, Toshiba and Matsushita agree to establish a TV LCD panel joint venture. Retrieved July 21, 2011 from http://www.hitachi-displays.com/en/news/2012476_18571.html

Holmström, J., Ketokivi, M., & Hameri, A.-P. (2009) Bridging practice and theory: A design science approach. *Decision Sciences*, 40(1): 65–87.

Kim, E. (2015) Tesla will be making 500,000 cars a year by 2020. Retrieved June 1, 2015 from http://uk.businessinsider.com/panasonic-ceo-tesla-will-be-making-500000-cars-a-year-by-2010–2015–1?r=US.

Kleining, G., & Witt, H. (2001) Discovery as basic methodology of qualitative and quantitative research. *Qualitative Social Research*, 2(1).

Lewin, K. (1952) *Field theory in social science: Selected theoretical papers by Kurt Lewin*. London: Tavistock.

Mahoney, J., & Goertz, G. (2006) A tale of two cultures: contrasting qualitative and quantitative research. *Political Analysis*, 14: 227–229.

Matsushita. (2002) National/Panasonic Matsushita Electric Annual Report 2002. For the year ended March 31, 2002.

Matsushita (2005) Matsushita to close cathode ray tube operations in North America and Europe. Retrieved February 19, 2008 from http://panasonic.co.jp/corp/news/official.data/data.dir/en051130–3/en051130–3.html

Matsushita (2008) Corporate history. Retrieved February 10, 2008 from http://www.panasonic.net/history/corporate/h_pre.html

Neuman, L. W. (2006) *Social research methods, qualitative and quantitative approaches* (6th ed. ed.). Boston: Pearson Education Inc.

Obermann, K., Scheppe, J., & Glazinski, B. (2013) More than figures? Qualitative research in health economics. *Health Economics*, 22(3): 253–257.

Orum, A. M., Feagin, J. R., & Sjoberg, G. (1991) The nature of the case study. In A. M. Orum, & G. Sjoberg (Eds.), *A Case for the case study*. Chapel Hill: University of North Carolina Press.

Panasonic (2008) Matsushita shareholders approve name change to 'Panasonic Corporation'. Retrieved August 23, 2015 from http://news.panasonic.com/press/news/official.data/data.dir/en080626–3/en080626–3.html

Panasonic (2010) Transfer of management rights relating to IPS Alpha Technology. Retrieved July 20, 2011 from http://panasonic.co.jp/corp/news/official.data/data.dir/en100630–5/en100630–5–1.pdf

Panasonic (2011) Annual report 2010. Retrieved May 4, 2015 from http://www.panasonic.com/global/corporate/ir/annual.html

Panasonic (2013) Annual report 2012. Retrieved May 4, 2015 from http://www.panasonic.com/global/corporate/ir/annual.html

Panasonic (2015a) Annual report 2014. Retrieved May 4, 2015 from http://www.panasonic.com/global/corporate/ir/annual.html

Panasonic (2015b) Automotive & Industrial Systems Company. Retrieved June 1, 2015 from http://www.panasonic.com/global/corporate/ais/company.html

Piekkari, R., Welch, C., & Paavilainen, E. (2009) The case study as disciplinary convention: Evidence from international business journals. *Organizational Research Methods*, 12(3): 567–589.

Poole, M. S., & Van de Ven, A. H. (1989) Using paradox to build management and organisational theories. *Academy of Management Review*, 14(4): 562–578.

Savov, V. (2013) Panasonic concedes plasma TV defeat, ends production. Retrieved August 24, 2015 from http://www.theverge.com/2013/10/31/5050038/panasonic-plasma-tv-production-end

Schendra, C., F.G. (2008) *Regressionsanalyse mit SPSS*. Munich: Oldenbourg Wissenschaftsverlag.

Siggelkow, N. (2007) Persuasion with case studies. *Academy of Management Journal*, 50(1): 20–24.

Slack, N., Lewis, M., & Bates, H. (2004) The two worlds of operations management research and practice: Can they meet, should they meet? *International Journal of Operations & Production Management*, 24(4): 372–387.

Tranfield, D., & Starkey, K. (1998) The nature, social organization and promotion of management research: Towards policy. *British Journal of Management*, 9(4): 341–353.

Van De Ven, A. (2011) Engaged scholarship: Stepping out. *Business Strategy Review*, 22(2): 43–45.

Van de Ven, A. H., & Engleman, R. M. (2004) Event- and outcome-driven explanations of entrepreneurship. *Journal of Business Venturing*, 19: 343–358.

Van de Ven, A. H., & Johnson, P. E. (2006) Knowledge for theory and practice. *Academy of Management Review*, 31(4): 802–821.

Vansteenkiste, M., & Sheldon, K. M. (2006) There's nothing more practical than a good theory: Integrating motivational interviewing and self-determination theory. *British Journal of Clinical Psychology*, 45: 63–82.

Wacker, J. G. (2008) A conceptual understanding of requirements for theory-building research: Guidelines for scientific theory building. *Journal of Supply Chain Management*, 44(3): 5–15.

Wahyuni, D. (2012) The research design maze: Understanding paradigms, cases, methods and methodologies. *Journal of Applied Management Accounting Research*, 10(1): 69–80.

Welch, C., Piekkari, R., Plakoyiannaki, E., & Paavilainen-Mäntymäki, E. (2011) Theorising from case studies: Towards a pluralist future for international business research. *Journal of International Business Studies*, 42(5): 740–762.

Yin, R. K. (2014) *Case study research. Design and methods.* London: Sage Publications Ltd.

2 Internationalization Theories

2.1 The International Product Life-Cycle Theory

2.1.1 Market entry according to the product life-cycle phase

The international product life-cycle theory developed by Vernon was introduced in 1966 (Vernon, 1966). Based on panel research of enterprises from the United States of America, Vernon's product life-cycle explanations further developed the existing trade theories introduced by Heckscher-Ohlin and Leontief (Vernon, 1972: 4–6). Vernon assumed that the flow of information across national borders would be restricted and that products undergo predictable changes that have an impact on the firm's internationalization strategies. The product life-cycle model was developed on these assumptions: the production process is characterized by economies of scale, the cycle changes over time, and tastes differ in diverse countries (i.e., each product does not account for a fixed proportion of expenditure for buyers at different income levels). Because information does not flow freely across national boundaries, three important conclusions follow.

1. Innovation of new products and processes is more likely to occur near a market where there is a strong demand for them than in a country with little demand.
2. An entrepreneur is more likely to supply risk capital for the production of a new product if demand is likely to exist in his home market than if he has to turn to a foreign market.
3. A producer located close to a market has a lower cost in transferring market knowledge into product design changes than one located far from the market (Vernon, 1972: 6).

The international product life-cycle theory claims that the market entry of a product is carried out in a foreign market depending on the position of the product in its country-specific product life-cycle curve. In the 1950s and 1960s, United States products led in the worldwide markets in many industries, while Europe and Japan required time to build up their own industries and infrastructures after World War II. Consequently, Vernon assumed that the United States served as a truly innovative market with customers with high purchasing power compared to other countries.

As illustrated in Figure 4, Vernon claimed that, for a certain time period, producers based in the U.S. are likely to have a virtual monopoly on the manufacturing of new products introduced in the U.S. An innovative product at its growth phase is produced inland and sold at relatively high prices. The output volume increases in the course of the market penetration inland, and experience curve effects appear. Due to the product's attractive market growth forecasts, the number of enterprises that produce this product increases in the home country. As a result, standardization and product cost aspects become important in connection with the necessity for

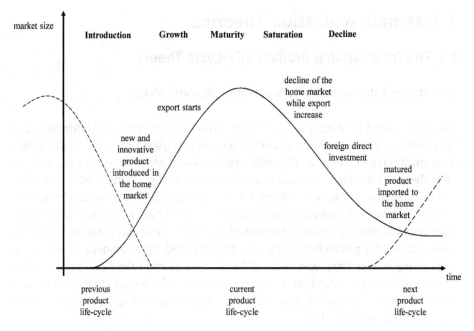

Figure 4. Changing market entry strategies according to the product's life-cycle position

mass production outputs. At later stages in the growth phase of the product life-cycle, some foreigners start to demand the new and innovative product; and U.S. exports begin (Vernon, 1972: 12).

While the growth rates decline during the maturity stage of the product life-cycle in the U.S. home market, export activities to other countries increase. As foreigners' incomes grow and lower income consumers abroad begin to buy the mature product, prices begin to fall, while, in parallel, U.S. exports further increase. As the product sales continue and market volumes increase in foreign markets, it becomes economically desirable for U.S. firms to establish foreign production. The time it takes until foreign production begins is dependent on the economies of scale, tariffs, transportation costs, income elasticity of demand, and the income level and size of the foreign market. At the end of the product life-cycle, manufacturing and sales in the U.S. market become more and more unimportant. As a result, local manufacturing runs out due to the relatively high production costs in comparison to foreign countries. The remaining market volume during the decline phase of the product life-cycle is completely imported from abroad, while, at the same time, U.S. firms introduce new and highly innovative products that launch the next product life-cycle (Vernon, 1972: 13).

2.1.2 Review of Vernon's model

To sum up, a firm's market entry activities depend on the product's position in the corresponding life-cycle. At first, the new innovative product is developed, produced, and sold in the U.S. home market. In the second phase, product exports start; and while this product becomes mature, direct investments abroad begin. Finally, import from abroad increases, production is discontinued in the home market, and the demand is completely supplied by foreign countries. At this stage, the product has reached the decline phase of its life-cycle.

Vernon's approach has made an essential contribution to the internationalization concept disciplines. The product life-cycle model provides a useful framework for explaining the post-World War II expansion of U.S. manufacturing and investment activities. However, its explanatory power has waned with changes in the international environment (Robock & Simmonds, 1989: 47). Holding an innovative market leadership position does not necessarily last. For example, Japanese consumer electronics firms such as Sony started to replace previously leading consumer electronics firms in the U.S. during the 1960s. At the beginning of the 21st century, Japanese consumer electronics firms suffer from competition from South Korean, Chinese, and Taiwanese firms, which took market share from the Japanese in various fields.

The model can be criticized in general because it assumes an ideal product life-cycle with coherent foreign activities. The theory is limited by the assumption that there is an attractive U.S. home market from which U.S. firms start their global activities. This model assumption is, from the 1960s perspective, substantiated for many industries where the U.S. was ahead of Europe and Japan. It is true that large home markets provide the best prerequisites for experience curve effects and economies of scale. However, the *general model validity* is hard to test empirically due to the complexity of the product life-cycle. Industry-specific factors, such as tariff and non-tariff trade barriers, behavior preferences of the management, and investment incentives that significantly influence manufacturing costs, as well as cross-border trade and capital flows are not considered by the model (Luostarinen, 1980: 77). Vernon's model is focused on manufacturing industries rather than on services industries.

Today, due to globalized trade patterns and intensified competition, technology and product life-cycles are shorter, while, in parallel, investments in R&D, operations and marketing, and so forth are increasing. Consequently, firms are often under pressure to sell their products globally – right from the beginning of the product life-cycle – in order to realize early economies of scale effects. Moreover, multinational firms often maintain different market entry concepts, such as export and foreign direct investment, in parallel. Nowadays, the customers' purchasing power does not differ significantly in many industrially developed countries. (Vernon correctly assumed a U.S. consumer's higher purchasing power relative to the rest of the world in the 1950s and 1960s.) Moreover, customers' expectations concerning the technical and quality performance of a product and service have become similar in many countries worldwide. As a result, the segmentation of the product life-cycle phases and corresponding conclusions for local sales, export, foreign direct investment, and import, according to the model, is rather arbitrary (Tesch, 1980: 164–167).

As a result of increased global business dynamics in recent years, there are cases of innovative firms that were unknown a couple of years ago. Meanwhile, some of these firms are playing a significant role in the international market (e.g., Lenovo from China). Interestingly, taking the case of the online-based business concept of the Chinese Alibaba.com, we can deduce some minor similarities with Vernon's approach. Alibaba's global success at the beginning of the 21st century is based, among other reasons, on its quasi-monopoly positioning in its huge Chinese home market. Alibaba.com currently takes advantage of economies of scale and experience curve effects in China similar to those Vernon indicated as an advantage for U.S. manufacturing industries in the post-war period.

Around a decade after its first publication in 1979, Vernon retracted the life-cycle model and agreed that there were fewer differences among countries in factor costs and market conditions (Barkema, Bell, & Pennings, 1996: 152). From today's view, after decades of major economic and political progress in world trade, the international product life-cycle theory has lost much of its validity. Consequently, further internationalization models have been developed, which are described in the following sections of this chapter.

Chapter review questions

1. Following Vernon's model assumptions, describe reasons for differentiated international market entry modes based on a product's life-cycle position.
2. Compare today's global business environment framework with the 1950s and 60s, and describe why the international product life-cycle theory lost much of its validity. Summarize the conceptual weaknesses of Vernon's product life-cycle theory.

2.2 Location Concepts

2.2.1 Historical foundations

The location discussion in connection with international trade theories has a long history. The mercantile doctrine, the major economic theory from the 16th to the 18th century, claims that the prosperity of a country (accumulated in gold or other precious metals) should be increased by high exports and low imports. The more one country wins from bilateral trade through the trade surplus accumulated in the national treasury, the more the other country loses (Robock & Simmonds, 1989: 140). The mercantile doctrine was replaced by Adam Smith's 'theory of absolute advantage' published in *The Wealth of Nations* in 1776. Smith, who was ahead of his time when he supported liberalized trade systems, argued that countries differ in their manufacturing performance (*absolute cost advantage*). If one country specializing in a particular product exports the product to a country from which it imports another product the trade partner specializes in, all participating countries will benefit from international trade. Import restrictions such as customs duties reduce the gains from specialization and cause a nation to lose wealth (Hill, 2005: 147– 151; Parkin, Powell, & Matthews, 2000: 914).

David Ricardo further developed Smith's idea regarding *comparative cost advantage* as discussed in *On the Principles of Economy and Taxation*, published in 1817. He claimed that countries should focus on items they can manufacture most efficiently in comparison to other nations. Consequently, countries should export those goods where they have a comparative advantage and import other products where the trade partner country has an advantage. Thus, differences in productivity among countries initiate trade ambitions and result in a higher standard of living for the participating states (Hill, 2005: 150 – 151; Mankiw, 2007: 223).

During the post-World War II period, location concepts with regards to firms' internationalization strategies attracted attention. Issues such as where it is most profitable to locate a firm's production with regards to local market imperfections (compare transaction cost theory), transportation, plant size, advantages of monopolistic competition, and incorporation of technology became the center of interest (Churchill, 1967: 86– 87). Swedish economists Heckscher and Ohlin claimed that countries differ in their factor endowments, such as ground, labor, and financial capital. These differences cause divergent competitive advantages among nations. In addition, countries have comparative advantages in those goods for which the necessary factors of manufacture are comparatively abundant locally, which causes the price of goods to be lower because their corresponding input costs are lower. Thus, a country should manufacture and export those products that use factors that are abundant at home. At the same time, nations that have a comparative disadvantage tend to import those goods whose production requires the factors that are relatively scarce in their country (Brakman, Garretsen, Van Marrewijk, & Van Witteloostuijn, 2006: 119; Robock & Simmonds, 1989: 36).

Location Models

Location concepts focus on the access and optimal allocation of the input variables needed for efficient and innovative manufacturing and service output (Rasmussen, Jensen, & Servais, 2008: 72). In general, it is claimed that country- and industry-specific factor endowments influence a firm's innovation, business orientation, and performance: for example, whether firms rather focus on home markets or international markets. For foreign firms, as a consequence, the strategic decision for market entry primarily depends on the location factors of the target country (Pan & Tse, 2000: 540; Tesch, 1980: 132–138).

Two central categories of location factors can be distinguished: the category of the *macro environment* and, taking a more narrow perspective, the category of the *firm's industry environment*. These categories will be introduced and discussed in the following sections.

2.2.2 Location factors

2.2.2.1 The macro environment

The discussion about a firm's resources, structures, and strategies, as well as its interface with its market environment is also found in the literature within the category of 'institutional theories of organizations'. The institutional theory serves as a framework for identifying and analyzing the factors that support the viability and legitimacy of organizations. In general, these factors include societal, economic, and political-legal regulations, as well as an organization's tradition and history (Bruton, Ahlstrom, & Li, 2010: 422; Glover et al., 2014: 104). These factors have a direct impact on the strategies and organizational decisions of firms (North, 1990: 6–10). With the aim of improving their position and legitimacy, firms should adhere to rules such as regulatory structures and practices (Glover et al., 2014: 104).

Contextual risks are a result of the external uncertainties embodied in the macro environment of the firm's international target market. For example, political-legal uncertainties arise from instability in the political system or from policies of the local government, such as those concerning private ownership (e. g., expropriation and intervention), operational risk (e. g., price control and local content requirements), and transfer risk (currency inconvertibility and remittance) (Pan & Tse, 2000: 540).

Aspects of the institutional environment can have a direct effect on a firm's market entry strategy in a foreign target market. For example, legal restrictions on foreign ownership of domestic enterprises, as for example seen in India, establish definite limits on foreign equity holdings. Country uncertainties regarding the protection of intellectual property rights further contribute to environmental risks and can result in a firm's reduced investment activity (Delios & Beamish, 1999: 917). Demographic characteristics can result not only in lower demand for a technology but also in modification and adaptation of existing technologies (Davidson & McFertidge, 1985: 9).

A well-known tool for scanning macro-environmental factors for a firm is PEST (political, economic, social, technology) analysis. In some sources, PEST is supplemented by ecological and legal factors, thus the acronym becomes PESTEL or PESTLE (Koumparoulis, 2013: 33–34). Drawbacks of PEST analysis are that originally less attention was paid to ecological issues. However, *ecology* has become an increasing challenge related to the global pollution of water and air as well as exploitation of natural resources. Current global business behavior should be viewed in light of, hopefully, an increasing public awareness regarding ecological challenges. S.E.E.L.E. (society, ecology, economy, law, expertise) emphasizes societal (not narrowly 'social' according to PESTEL) and ecological issues and better considers modern service-industry driven societies. Important elements of the macro-environmental scan when applying S. E.E.L.E. are the following:

Society	– overall acceptance of equal human rights; – freedom and diversity of religion; – family life attitudes; – marriage and divorce rates; – attitudes towards handicapped people; – embedding of children and pensioners; – age distribution of the population; – birth and death rates; – quality of health care and the pension system; – integration of immigrants; – education and research; – attitudes towards technology; – materialistic vs. non-materialistic priorities in life; – rate of saving vs. consumption; – preferences in leisure time;
Ecology	– climate conditions and natural events; – availability of raw materials and natural resources; – attitudes regarding exhausting/protecting the environment; – quality of life and health; – quality of air and water; – level of noise disturbance; – industry emission standards; – environmental standards for traffic; – acceptance/refusal of chemical or genetically manipulated animals and plants; – attitudes towards renewable energies and nuclear power;
Economy	– liberalized market economy vs. planned economy; – gross domestic product trends; – stability of the banking and finance system; – availability and cost of capital; – currency policy and exchange system; – national state surplus/ deficit rates; – unemployment rates; – inflation and deflation rates; – national trade balances (export vs. import); – average wage and salary level;
Law	– overall protection of human rights; – free election and multi-political party system; – private property rights; – demonstration rights; – freedom of opinion; – free or censored mass media; – freedom for authors, writers, and correspondents;

Expertise	– specific knowledge utilized in industries;
	– plant utilization and industry efficiency;
	– quality consciousness;
	– innovation potential;
	– technological affinity of the population;
	– willingness to make use of new and complex techniques; and
	– national infrastructure including access to World Wide Web and logistics.

Figure 5. Elements of the S.E.E.L.E. analysis

The study of market entry abroad necessarily assumes the recognition and understanding of the respective environmental macro structures. A firm that plans business activities in a foreign country needs to collect and evaluate necessary information based on the S.E.E.L.E. elements and their interconnections. In general, the educational system (as a fragment of 'society') established by the national government should attempt to provide qualified and ethically responsible people for the firms and organizations. At the same time, firms should be aware of their social responsibility. A 'hire and fire' policy that aims to exploit the employees for short-term objectives or, alternatively, internally developing and improving the qualifications of the firm's personnel reveal different behavioral and ethical aspects of a firm's culture. These examples of diverse firm policies necessarily suggest positive or negative consequences for its national environments.

When local governments in a foreign market set new legal standards in order to reduce environmental damage (e.g., product labels that show the electricity consumption of an apparatus), the new standards hopefully cause a change in customer needs and preferences (e.g., product purchases with reduced power utilization). Consequently, such standards influence the destiny of a manufacturing firm and the sales potential of the products. If the firm has reliable, sophisticated market research and forecasting, it is better able to forecast new political and technological trends and appropriately focus the corresponding R&D activities. Suppose an enterprise performs well; its business will result in a higher number of employees. If not, employees need to be released; and the firm may face bankruptcy, which contributes to an economy's higher unemployment rate (negative impact on its macro-environment).

A firm that targets foreign direct investment and compares different potential target markets may raise, among others, questions such as the following: How will costs and earnings develop in the respective regions in the future? Are the factor costs in countries with relatively low wage levels associated with lower educational levels that result in lower productivity and employees that are less conscious of quality? How much training is necessary for the work force? Do the work ethics and the loyalty of the staff differ culturally from the atmosphere at home? (Meyer, 2006: 37). Because factors of the macro environment vary from country to country, they provide the basis of diversified opportunities and threats for the international business activity of the firm. An opportunity is a condition in the macro environment that, if properly utilized, helps a firm achieve a competitive advantage, while a threat may hinder a company's efforts to attain strategic competitiveness in global business (Hitt, Ireland, & Hoskisson, 2015: 40 – 41).

As is clear from the arguments and examples mentioned above, there are various linkages between the macro and the industry environments. These elements continuously evolve. Changes lead to modifications in the cost and revenue structure, which may be favorable or unfavorable to the firm (Rasmussen et al., 2008: 73). Thus, a continuous and permanent scan of the firm's macro-environment, usually carried out by the firm's marketing department, is of vital importance to the company.

2.2.2.2 The industry environment

Industry groups consist of firms with similar missions, organizational structures, value added activities, and strategies related to their products and services (Wheelen & Hunger, 2010: 162– 163). The industry or task environment is a set of industry-specific location factors that directly influence a firm in its competitive position relative to local rivals and, logically speaking, its market entry and penetration strategy abroad. The best-known representative of *industry analysis* ('five forces model'), which is thematically similar to the *market-based view*, is M. E. Porter (compare: Porter, 1980; 2003; Porter & Fuller, 1986; Porter & van der Linde, 1995). In contrast to the resource-based view (competitive advantages depend on the firm's resources), the market-based view claims that sustainable competitive advantage and superior returns depend on the management's recognition and utilization of the market and the influencing industry forces (Peters et al., 2011: 877).

According to Porter (1990: 34), two central concerns underlie the choice of a competitive strategy. The first is the industry structure in which the firm competes. Industries differ widely in the nature of competition, and not all industries offer equal opportunities for sustained profitability. The average profitability in pharmaceuticals is high, for example, while this is not the case in consumer electronics. The second central concern in a competitive strategy is positioning within an industry.

In each industry, the nature of competition depends on five competitive forces:
(1)   the threat of new market entrants,
(2)   the threat of substitute products or services,
(3)   the bargaining power of suppliers,
(4)   the bargaining power of buyers, and
(5)   the rivalry among the existing competitors.

A firm's performance is limited by these specific industry properties. The appearance and the strength of the five forces vary from industry to industry and determine long-term industry profitability. These factors influence the attractiveness of the industry and the corresponding profits of the engaged firms (Porter, 1990: 35). According to the market-based view, the sources of value for the firm are embedded in the competitive situation characterizing its external product markets. Interaction among competitive industry forces, such as the bargaining power of suppliers and buyers, influences a firm's profitability in the foreign target market (Hitt et al., 2015: 39; Müller-Stewens & Lechner, 2011: 173; Wheelen & Hunger, 2010: 158–159). For example, a higher bargaining power for a firm in comparison to the bargaining power of the suppliers suggests that a firm might achieve higher performance because the existing suppliers have fewer alternatives within the industry.

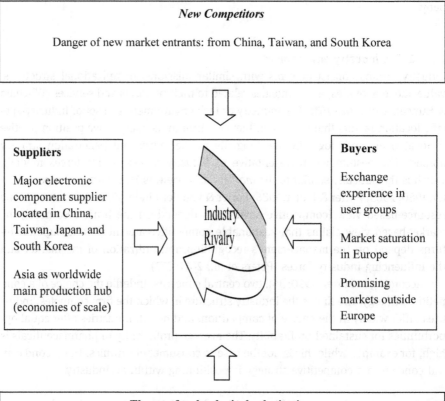

New Competitors

Danger of new market entrants: from China, Taiwan, and South Korea

Suppliers

Major electronic component supplier located in China, Taiwan, Japan, and South Korea

Asia as worldwide main production hub (economies of scale)

Industry Rivalry

Buyers

Exchange experience in user groups

Market saturation in Europe

Promising markets outside Europe

Threat of technological substitution

Electronics device interconnectedness (e.g., washing machine, smart phone, and home energy management)

Figure 6. Industry environment of the Slovenian household appliance manufacturer 'Gorenje' (Gorenje, 2015) concerning its European Union markets (2015), Source: Five forces adopted from Porter (1999), p. 34

Competitive dynamics are also influenced by barriers to entry resulting from the structure of the market (Grant, 1991b: 117–118; Makhija, 2003: 437). An industry environment that has high entry barriers is attractive to enter and provides, at least temporarily, higher returns for the existing companies, which take advantage of limited (foreign) competition (Peters, Siller, & Matzler, 2011: 878–879). Transactional risks related to market entry in foreign target markets arise as a result of the behavior of local firms, which may take action to maintain or increase entry barriers through offensive price strategies or lobbying their local governments (Pan & Tse, 2000: 540).

In the course of the development of industry analysis, the importance of the regional industry cluster (e.g., supplier-customer inter-firm relations; supporting service providers such as logistics, information technology, etc.) gained increased attention in location theories (McCann & Sheppard, 2003: 650–651). For example, for a firm considering a market entry through foreign direct investment, it tends to be more efficient to locate its production site close to existing local industry networks with access to an existing supplier instead of operating from a distance.

Firms considering international market entry activities can evaluate and compare different industry clusters according to the following questions, among others: Are there any component supplier clusters available or under development in this region? Is the location an attractive one for competitors to initiate foreign direct investment activities? What infrastructure is available? How far away from the industry cluster are the major markets? How will the freight rates develop, which depends on the number of logistics firms that offer services in that region? (Meyer, 2006: 37). The rationale of the 'incubator' hypothesis is that a newly established industrialized area (industry cluster) offers firms attractive conditions for investment. In addition, enterprises usually benefit, at least temporarily, from tax incentives and reasonable prices for real estate. Through concentration in a cluster, firms create economies of scope by sharing storage facilities as well as transportation, which facilitates exports and imports. Especially with regard to technology-oriented complexes, for example science parks or economic development zones, the 'incubator hypothesis' has been useful (Rasmussen et al., 2008: 73).

2.2.2.3 The case study of Sharp (Japan): Leader in liquid crystal display technology – and then?

2.2.2.3.1 Company origins

Many Japanese firms that began exporting to Western markets in the 1960s and 1970s were faced with established Western competitors that had broader product lines and were solidly established in their home markets. The only feasible alternatives were either to locate market niches for which there were no products or to concentrate all their resources on the products that had the greatest market demand and provided the easiest access to customers (Abegglen & Stalk, 1985: 169). By adopting either of these two alternatives, Japanese companies could achieve competitive costs relative to those of their Western competitors, resulting in the ability to undercut the prices while maintaining high quality (Chen, 2004: 169). The Japanese firm Sharp serves as a typical industry case exemplifying this strategic concept.

In 1912, Sharp's founder, Tokuji Hayakawa, invented the 'Tokubijo' snap buckle and established a metalworking shop in Tokyo to manufacture and market 'Tokubijo' snap buckles. In 1951, Sharp succeeded in developing the first television set prototype. One year later, the Japanese firm signed a cooperative license agreement with RCA of the USA, which allowed Sharp to use patented technology for television set technology. In 1953, Sharp began the mass production of television sets for the first time in the history of Japan. In 1960, Sharp launched the first color television set on the market. Fifteen years later (1975), the Japanese firm started its first foreign direct investment activities and established a television unit in 1973, Sharp has for more than thirty years pursued liquid crystal display development, which has resulted in numerous pioneering products, such as the 'AQUOS' line of LCD televisions (Fujitsu, 2005; Sharp, 2007b).

2.2.2.3.2 Technological pioneer in LCD technology

A milestone in the history of Sharp was its ambitious strategic decision to start developing alternative display concepts for television set production that might replace the conventional cathode ray tube technology. In 1986, the Japanese firm established liquid crystal display laboratories within the corporate research and development group of the firm. Two years later, in 1988, Sharp developed the world's first 14-inch color thin film transistor (TFT) LCD. In 1991, Sharp completed its construction of a TFT LCD plant in Tenri, Nara (Japan), and successfully launched the world's first HDTV LCD projector and the world's first wall-mounted LCD TV. At that time, the European market had reached a sales volume of around 30 million units of cathode ray tube television sets, which was the dominating technology. Despite the mainstream competitors, Sharp concentrated its major financial and research and development resources on LCD technology. At the beginning of the 1990s, it was neither clear when CRT technology might be replaced nor whether the competing flat panel plasma technology might succeed in competing with LCD (Sharp, 2007b). In 1994, Sharp announced the construction of the world's largest TFT LCD plant in Taki, Mie Prefecture in Japan. Just one year later Sharp established Wuxi Sharp Electronic Components Co., Ltd. (WSEC), a joint company in China for the manufacture and sale of LCDs.

Why is the consistent and unflustered concentration on LCD technology by the management of Sharp, in fact, impressive? The investment decision was proactive but also very risky due to the nebulous market forecasts for flat panel market development. For instance, in Europe, a mass market for LCD TVs did not exist during the 1990s. Nevertheless, Sharp continued its R&D and manufacturing efforts. In 1999, Sharp launched the world's first 20-inch LCD TV (Sharp, 2007b). At this time, European manufacturers – such as Thomson and Philips, for example – continued to manufacture television sets based on the obsolete cathode ray tube technology. Thanks to the entrepreneurial capacities of Sharp's management, tightly linked with excellent research and development resources in LCD technology – which were at that time much advanced relative to the competitors – Sharp secured a favorable market position for the coming years. The financial data of Sharp demonstrate that the consequent positioning in the innovative LCD segment was strategically well done. The Japanese firm calmly maintained its focus strategy on the long term. While the firm's turnover stagnated between 1999 and 2002, Sharp profited from the upcoming LCD technologies and their mass market penetration from 2003 until 2008 (compare Figure 9).

Instead of serving the consumer electronics mass markets with a broad range of products, Sharp preferred to concentrate on markets based on advanced display technology expertise, energy saving, and electric and electronic components. Accordingly, the Japanese firm divided its organization into strategic business units called, for example, LCDs, digital information equipment, electronic devices, energy solutions, health environment equipment, and others (Sharp, 2014a, b). Most of the products have familiar technology platforms. In comparison with its Japanese competitor Sony, Sharp focuses on related business segments instead of pursuing a conglomerate diversification. The strategic concept of Sharp significantly differs from its Korean rival Samsung, which pursues market penetration strategies offering a wide product portfolio operating in conglomerate business segments. The organization chart (Figure 7) illustrates Sharp's main business segments.

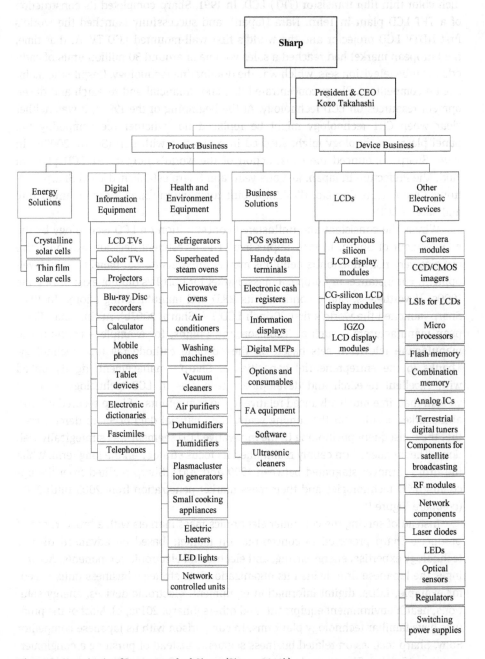

Figure 7. Organization [Status 2014] of Sharp (Sharp, 2014b)

At the beginning of the 21st century, Sharp continued efforts to expand its research and development as well as its manufacturing capacities of technologically advanced displays. In order to strengthen its competitive position in selected business segments, Sharp created network relations through bilateral relationships with other firms that usually had their origin in Japan. For example, in 2000, Sharp and Pioneer entered into a technological collaboration for next-generation digital products. In 2001, Sharp established ELDis Inc., a joint company with Tohoku Pioneer Corporation and Semiconductor Energy Laboratory Co., Ltd., to manufacture and market substrates for organic displays. In the same year, Sanyo Electric Co., Ltd., and Sharp agreed on a global collaboration for the development of home appliances. In 2002, Sharp started the construction of a 776,000 square meter Kameyama Plant in Japan, which was designed for state-of-the-art integrated production of LCD TVs, ranging from manufacture of LCD panels to final assembly of finished LCD TV sets (Sharp, 2007a, 2008b).

At that time, Sharp's factory was the world's first vertically integrated production facility, carrying out the complete range, from manufacture of LCD panels to final assembly of television sets. The fusion of liquid crystal technologies and television audio-visual technologies resulted in high-quality LCD television sets and accelerated the transition from cathode ray tubes to LCDs in the global markets. The Kameyama Plant was not far from other previously established Sharp LCD plants, such as the Tenri Plant. Numerous companies in the flat-panel-display industry moved to the area, enabling Sharp to deepen its networks with related companies, which supported Sharp's continued LCD component and product developments (Sharp, 2008b).

In February 2005, Sharp Corporation and Fujitsu Limited announced they had entered into an agreement regarding the transfer of Fujitsu's LCD operations to Sharp. Fujitsu had been producing high-resolution, high-image-quality LCD displays primarily for use in computer monitors. In particular, Fujitsu's original technology for large-screen LCDs, requiring superior image quality, became the industry standard; and the company had leveraged that technological leadership in developing its LCD business. Fujitsu determined that the best way to realize the full potential of this business was by transferring it to the leading company in the LCD business, Sharp (Fujitsu, 2005).

The agreement called for Fujitsu to transfer to Sharp the LCD research and development, manufacturing, and sales operations of its consolidated subsidiary, Fujitsu Display Technologies Corporation (FDTC), along with the related Fujitsu Laboratories Ltd. research center. As a result of the transfer, Sharp took over FDTC's personnel at the Yonago plant as well as 'Fujitsu Laboratories' personnel involved in FDTC-related research and corresponding intellectual property rights held by the Fujitsu Group (Fujitsu, 2005). The transfer expanded Sharp's development and production capabilities in the small and mid-size LCD segment. In addition, by enhancing its ties with Fujitsu as a supplier of key components, Sharp further reinforced its LCD business foundation (Fujitsu, 2005).

In December 2007, Sharp Corporation and Toshiba Corporation announced that the two companies had agreed to collaborate closely in the LCD business, a move that was expected to enhance the companies' corporate value, profitability, and global competitiveness. The alliance allowed each company to make full and effective use of its resource strength, particularly Sharp's capabilities in LCDs and Toshiba's expertise in advanced semiconductors. Sharp and Toshiba initiated the collaborative partnership in 2008, starting with an expansion of reciprocal procurement – Sharp's procurement of system components for LCDs from Toshiba and Toshiba's procurement of Sharp's LCD modules for television sets of 32 inches and larger. Through the alliance agreement, Sharp aimed to satisfy about 50 percent of its total demand for LCD system components for its television sets in 2010, while Toshiba targeted meeting 40 percent of its demand for LCD modules in the same year (Sharp, 2008c).

Around 2005, the global market for LCD TVs was growing; and this trend was expected to continue in the coming years. While various types of displays were brought to market, Sharp was channelling its resources into developing LCD TVs characterized by thin lines, light weight, high resolution images, and a long lifetime and also into achieving progressive advances in reducing power consumption. Large-scale integrated circuit (LSI) systems for TVs were increasingly required to support advanced functions and higher levels of performance alongside their core role of image processing. As television sets shifted to higher levels of resolution, Toshiba's system LSIs for TVs supplied Sharp with advanced expertise and achievements in image processing in products that met the most exacting requirements of major television set manufacturers. By bringing together such technologies, Sharp and Toshiba promoted business advances through development of differentiated products. Each company aimed to secure a leading position in the LCD TV market and reinforce its capabilities in LCDs and semiconductors by overcoming increasingly intense global competition (Sharp, 2008c).

In February 2008, Sony and Sharp announced they would establish a joint venture to build a generation 10 TFT LCD plant targeting large-size LCD TV panels of 40 inches and larger. Sony and Sharp invested USD around 3.56 billion respectively. Sony held a 34 percent share of the new company, and Sharp held 66 percent. (DisplaySearch, 2008a). The joint venture for the development and manufacture of LCD panels was seen as a symbol of continuation of a long-term relationship between the two Japanese firms because already, by 1996, Sharp and Sony had agreed on the joint development of large-screen flat display panels.

For Sharp, because the firm could not rely on its own brand strength to sell its huge panel manufacturing capacities in the markets, the partnership with Sony also served as a means of targeting higher price segments traditionally hold by Sony. It was anticipated that Sharp would be able to sell a considerable part of its panel manufacturing output capacities through Sony TV products and Sony's worldwide distribution channels. Sharp adjusted its policy to retain more than 30 percent of its panel output for its own LCD TV assembly; thus far, the ratio had been only 10 to 15 percent, with other LCD TV makers procuring the rest. Sharp shipped 8 million LCD television sets in 2007, less than Sony's 9.5 million and Samsung's 13.4 million units. The continued necessity of feeding the production lines emerged at a time when Sharp was facing competitive pressure from other less-known brands. With 'everybody buying panels and components from everybody', the Sony and Sharp joint venture serves as an illustrative example of the industry relationships and mutual procurement policies of Japanese firms (DisplaySearch, 2008a).

Sharp aimed to become an innovative pioneer instead of following the mass market trend as the case of solar cells used for alternative energy generation illustrates. (Solar cell manufacturing has similarities to LCD display manufacturing.) However, despite all its efforts, Sharp continued to face drawbacks in creating the reputable and powerful image abroad that it had in its home country. Obviously, the marketing and communication policy outside Japan needed to be better adjusted to the behavioral attitudes of Western customers such as those in Europe. Investment in the traditional, premium brand company 'Loewe AG' was apparently an opportunity for Sharp to gain access to exclusive European distribution channels.

2.2.2.3.3 The development of Sharp's operations in Europe
In 2007, Sharp started the manufacture of LCD modules in a newly established facility near the city of Torun. Torun is located in the Pomeranian 'special economic zone' (WarsawVoice, 2006: 2). The Polish government established various so-called economic zones, of which each has various sub-zones. Tax exemptions and other incentives available to investors are among the main advantages of the zone. A multinational firm such as Sharp benefits from corporate tax reductions on income from its activities in the Pomeranian special economic zone, which reaches up to 50 percent of Sharp's invested capital there (PolandBusiness, 2007a, b).

According to Hans Kleis, CEO of Sharp Electronics Europe, the LCD TV market, from a 2006 perspective, was supposed to grow continuously in Europe. Hans Kleis further forecasted that countries such as Poland, the Czech Republic, Hungary, and Slovakia would become increasingly important for LCD TV sales. Investments in regional manufacturing capacities seemed the logical conclusion. For Sharp, the location of Torun offered an excellent connection to already booming LCD television markets in Western Europe, particularly Germany. Therefore, Sharp planned an expansion of production capacities in order to be able to manufacture complete LCD TVs in Torun (bfai, 2007; Moschek, 2007: 1).

Japanese companies such as Sharp differentiate strategic suppliers (kankei kaisha) that belong to the keiretsu conglomerate from independent suppliers (dokuritsu kaisha) that do not belong directly to the keiretsu. In utilizing both types of supply sources, Japanese companies are able to achieve economies of scale and gain access to their suppliers' capabilities for strategic inputs by using strategic partnerships. It is this unique combination of the firms' and suppliers' know-how in producing differentiated components for a product that can provide an organization with sustainable competitive advantage (Kotabe & Murray, 2004: 10). As a part of Sharp's keiretsu network, the Polish factory in Torun holds the position of a European strategic component manufacturer (kankei kaisha) that supplies its modules for the final assembly of television sets at Sharp Electronica Spain S.A. (an example of Sharp's vertical integration) (Moschek, 2007: 1).

Sharp attracted further investors to Poland, such as the Japanese TV set assembler Orion TV, which chose Lysomice as a future location for its LCD TV assembly. Orion used Sharp's display panels in its LCD television sets. Besides Orion TV, several Japanese subcontractors and component suppliers that do not belong directly to Sharp's keiretsu network decided to establish their plants near the Sharp facilities in Poland. Among them were enterprises such as Tensho, a producer of plastic elements; Nitto Denko Corporation (polarizing films); Sumika Electronic Materials (polarizing films and light diffusion panels); Toland Tokai Okaya Manufacturing (metal frames); Kimoto Co. Crystal Logistics, which will invest in warehouse buildings; and NYK Logistics, which will lease magazine surface for Sharp and its subcontractors (Olsson, 2007: 1). Some of Sharp's main suppliers and logistic firms 'followed its customer Sharp to Poland. The narrowly knit market entry network around Sharp and the position of the firms in the vertically integrated industry chain in Europe is illustrated in the figure below.

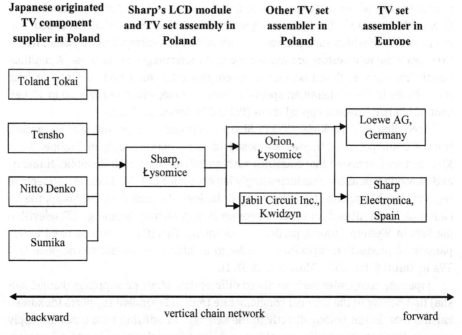

Figure 8. Vertical procurement, manufacturing, and sales network for LCD television sets of Sharp in Europe [status 2007]. Source: designed base on various company related documents (Olsson, 2007; Sharp, 2007a)

Sharp's local partner, the US-based firm Jabil Circuit, Inc., invested Euro 13 million in a new factory in Kwidzyn, which is located in the economic zone as well. The factory was established in 1994 by Philips, which sold it to Jabil at a price of Euro 12 million in December 2004 (Philips, 2004: 28, 107). A major part of the LCD flat panel display production was reserved for the German-based Loewe AG (Moschek, 2007: 1). Why Loewe?

While Sharp was well known for innovative and quality products in Japan, the firm was confronted with rather weak brand recognition in Europe. Therefore, in 2002, Sharp's management decided, in order to overcome the brand weakness within a relatively short time, to invest in the reputable Loewe AG. Loewe's television set products were located in the premium price segments and were known for their superior design and quality. The agreement stipulated that Sharp would supply LCD modules to Loewe. Sharp agreed to subscribe up to 2.3 million shares in 2002. Two years later, Loewe had slipped into financial difficulties due to upcoming flat panel television technologies. The risk of technological substitution from conventional to flat screen had been ignored for too long by the German premium assembler. This development caused severe consequences because Loewe had positioned its marketing focus on providing leading technology linked with premium prices but kept running its set manufacturing based on bulky cathode ray tube technologies. In 2004, Sharp increased its stake in Loewe from the previous 8.9 percent to up to 28.8 percent (Sharp, 2004). Sharp's additional investment equalled EUR 15 million, made the Japanese firm Loewe's most important strategic shareholder, and helped the traditional German manufacturer survive. In the same year, another traditional well-known German consumer electronics assembler Grundig went bankrupt.

From January 2005 onwards, Sharp and Loewe launched a so-called Joint European Development Center in Kronach (Germany) in order to develop a completely digital electronics platform for LCD TVs and peripheral devices. The research and development concentrated on the European broadcasting standard for digital television (DVB). Toshishige Hamano, corporate senior executive director with responsibility for the international business of the Sharp Corporation, commented as follows:

> As an established manufacturer of high-quality televisions, Loewe is the ideal partner for us in Europe. We are convinced that our strategic cooperation will strengthen both corporations, especially in the rapid development of the dynamically expanding LCD TV market *(Sharp, 2004)*.

According to Chang (1995: 384), Japanese companies make rather frequent small initial investments in their core business and expand their operations if this investment performs well. Later, they diversify into new business areas through foreign market entry. This process takes a comparatively longer period of time than in the case of Western companies, which tend to prefer large investments linked with an expectation of early return on investments. Sharp's financial engagement at Loewe AG and its incremental increase of shares from 8.9 to 28.8 percent during the period from 2002 to 2004 underlines Sharp's careful and long-term oriented investment policy.

There is nothing wrong with it except for the risk that, meanwhile, product and technology life cycles become much shorter in high-technology industries, where Sharp was competing against aggressive market penetrating Chinese and Korean companies.

Sharp maintained its European research activities at Sharp Laboratories of Europe, Ltd., located in Oxford, the United Kingdom. As per 2008, Sharp kept running manufacturing capacities for consumer electronics products at Sharp Electronica España S.A., Barcelona, and Sharp Electronics Ltd., Middlesex, the United Kingdom. Further manufacturing locations outside Europe and Japan were in China, Taiwan, Malaysia, Indonesia, the Philippines, and the USA, where Sharp also established local research and development activities at Sharp Laboratories of America, Inc., in Washington (Sharp, 2008a).

In 2007, the London-based investment firm EQMC acquired 10.13 percent of Loewe shares and became the second largest investor after Sharp. Obviously, the management of Sharp hesitated to greatly increase its financial engagement at Loewe. History has proved that the management of Sharp was right. In 2014, Loewe AG declared bankruptcy and was taken over by a German-based investor called Stargate. The reasons for Loewe's failure were its limited product portfolio, concentrating on television sets of larger scale at a price level of Euro 3000 and more per TV unit. At that time, the competition in the global LCD markets had become intense and economies of scale effects reached increasing importance. Loewe was comparatively too small and less known outside European countries such as Austria; Switzerland; and its own base, Germany. Due to the bankruptcy of Loewe and its re-establishment with a modified shareholder structure, Sharp's capital participation at Loewe has been reduced to 4.19 percent since July 31, 2014, which has caused a worsening market position for Sharp (Loewe_AG, 2014).

However, the problems of Sharp were not limited to the Loewe case. For a long time, Sharp followed a concentration strategy based on its LCD technology expertise, which was applied in television sets and solar photovoltaic models. In order to further expand its LCD business, which developed well until 2007, Sharp mainly concentrated on other Japanese partners targeting similar expertise—for example, Fujitsu, Sanyo, and Sony. Simultaneously, Samsung and LG Electronics from South Korea as well as Foxconn (Taiwan) developed more progressively than most of the Japanese firms. In 2012 and 2013, Sharp accumulated losses of more than 9 billion US dollars (Sharp, 2015a, b).

Sharp vertically integrated its value added activities within the industry chain of component supply, manufacture, and sales of LCD television sets, along with a network of external supporting firms. This caused an increased dependency on LCD display technology and limited its flexibility. Price competition, particularly in the field of LCD television sets, which is the core of Sharp's business, had increased over the years. In 2012, the LCD display manufacturing joint venture with Sony – which, meanwhile, also slipped into severe financial difficulties – was terminated (Sony, 2012b).

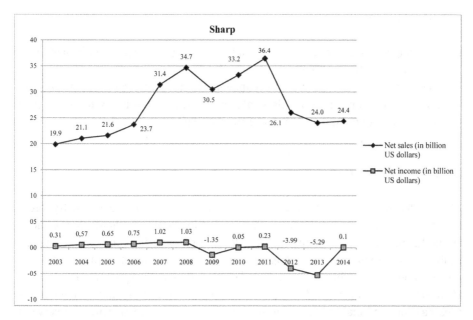

Figure 9. Net sales and net income of Sharp for the period 2003 to 2014 (Sharp, 2005, 2010, 2011, 2012, 2013, 2014a, 2015a)

In parallel, Sharp failed to successfully enter new upcoming business fields, such as smartphones, tablets, and navigation systems, where the Japanese firm could use its own LCD technology, thus combining its product portfolio (Tabuchi, 2012b). At the same time, global competition in the solar module segment became intense, which caused solar photovoltaic manufacturers to reduce their orders to Sharp or even to enter bankruptcy (Bilby, 2013; Chaffin, 2013; SolarOne, 2010). All in all, the solar photovoltaic business developed far below expectations for Sharp.

In 2014, due to the accumulating losses of Sharp Group, which was searching for cash revenues, Sharp withdrew its activities from Poland and sold its LCD factory (including its AQUOS brand) to the Slovakian-based company Universal Media Corporation (UMC) (Sharp, 2015b). In August 2015, Sharp started negotiating with Hon Hai Precision Industry (Foxconn), seeking to transfer its LCD display panel business to an international joint venture. Under the proposed plan, Hon Hai and possibly other parties, including Japan's state-controlled Innovation Network Corporation, would make investments in the newly independent LCD firm. In July 2015, Sharp's CEO, Kozo Takahashi, said he would be open to restructuring both the display and consumer product sides of the company in light of declining revenues. Sharp and Foxconn currently operate a large-scale LCD plant in Osaka as a joint venture. Both firms are key suppliers to Apple (Roger, 2015).

The question is what Sharp's management is going to do in the future if its core business, LCD, is outsourced to a joint venture with Foxconn, one of the fastest learners and most aggressive firms in the electronics business.

Chapter review questions

1. Applying a macro and an industry analysis, what factors led to the severe losses of Sharp in 2012 and 2013?
2. Taking the perspective of Sharp's management, describe the firm's current situation and develop a sustainable strategic concept for the firm's future. Provide reasonable arguments in support of the strategy.

2.2.3 The Diamond Model

About a decade after categorizing the factors that affect competitive industry forces, Porter expanded the 'competitiveness discussion' to country levels in what is known as the 'diamond model'. At the national level, location effects are what Porter describes as the *competitive advantage of nations*. The domestic environment provides the best prerequisites for firms to initiate foreign business engagements (Porter, 1990: 14; Rasmussen et al., 2008: 75–76). According to Porter, competition in many industries has internationalized not only in manufacturing but increasingly in services. Firms compete with truly global strategies involving selling worldwide, sourcing components and materials worldwide, and locating activities in many nations to take advantage of national divergent resource endowments. Porter's diamond approach of internationalization is based on his empirical observation, which concludes that enterprises that are successful worldwide ('global champions') frequently originate in one country. His observation leads to the thesis that those enterprises, due to their industry environment, enjoy particularly favorable conditions, which make it possible for them to become internationally active and to attain a competitive advantage in other countries relative to the resident enterprises. Porter distinguishes four central factors and two supplementary factors that influence gaining a competitive advantage in foreign markets (Porter, 1990: 14, 73–99).

Central factor 1: production factor conditions

Human resources refer to the quantity, skill, and cost of personnel and management, taking into account standard working hours and the work ethic. In connection with this, the so-called progressive factors attain special importance. Progressive factors are, for instance, the education and qualifications of the population, the potential for generating high innovation, efficient use and combination of human resources, and continuous adaptation to the requirements of (foreign) markets.

Physical resources refer to the availability and cost of a nation's land, natural resources, infrastructure, country location, and geographic size.

Knowledge resources refer to the nation's stock of scientific, technical, and market knowledge concerning goods and services. Knowledge resources reside in universities, government research institutes, private research facilities, government statistical agencies, business and scientific literature, market research and databases, trade associations, and other sources.

Capital resources are the amount and cost of capital available to finance industry. Capital is not homogeneous, but comes in various forms, such as secured and unsecured debt. The total stock of capital resources in a country and the forms in which it is deployed are influenced by the national rate of savings and by the structure of national capital markets, both of which vary widely among nations.

Infrastructure is the type, quality, and user cost of infrastructure available that affects competition, including road systems, logistics, communications systems, payments, or funds transfer. Infrastructure also includes health care, housing stock, and cultural institutions, which affect the quality of life and the attractiveness of a nation as a place to live and work.

The quality of the production factors is more important to Porter than the quantity. Unlike the classical trade theories of Ricardo or Heckscher-Ohlin, Porter claims that it is advantageous for a country if physical resources (e. g., natural raw materials) are rare since the waste of resources is avoided through alternative innovative technologies that finally help to spare the environment (Porter, 1990: 75–76). The case of Russia, a country rich in natural resources but comparatively weak in modern and technologically driven industries such as electronics, automotive, chemical, and others, supports Porter's thesis. Finally, physical resources over a period of time lose importance and become increasingly substitutable since an artificial way of producing them can be found or alternative production methods can be developed (Welge & Holtbrügge, 2015: 67).

Central factor 2: home demand conditions

All factors that have an influence on the level of purchase demand are part of the category 'home demand conditions'. Nations gain competitive advantage in industries where the home demand gives local firms a clearer or earlier picture of buyer needs than foreign competitors can have (Porter, 1990: 86). The size of the home market can be a criterion for competitive advantage (economies of scale). This efficiency could also lead to a domination of the industry in other countries (Hitt et al., 2015: 250).

Quality and customer-tailored service becomes more important than just quantity recorded in sales volumes or units. Particular characteristics of domestic demand, such as design, technology, and product functions, require specific attention by the industry (Welge & Holtbrügge, 2015: 67). As a result, firms are forced to be innovative, which positively influences the development of the whole industry. The expectations and wishes of customers at home can often result in innovative technological trends for worldwide sales in the future (Kutschker & Schmid, 2011: 449–450). The rate of growth of home demand can be as important to competitive advantage as its absolute market size. Rapid domestic growth forces a nation's firm to adopt new technologies faster and, consequently, allows first mover advantages and valuable experience curve effects (Porter, 1990: 94).

Central factor 3: supporting industries

Porter describes the supplying and supporting industries in a country as, for instance, logistics, the educational system, and research and development capacities. Sophisticated, developed supply networks form the basis for stable production of technologically innovative standards with reasonable sourcing prices because supplying enterprises are confronted with high competitive pressure. Qualified suppliers are able to provide considerable input for further technological development (Welge & Holtbrügge, 2015: 67). Competitive advantage emerges from close working relationships between vendors and the industry. Suppliers help firms perceive new methods and opportunities for applying new technology. Firms gain quick access to information and innovation potentials. The exchange of R&D know-how and the joint problem of solving technical issues lead to faster and more efficient solutions. Through this process, the pace of innovation within the entire national industry is accelerated (Porter, 1990: 103).

Central factor 4: firm strategy, structure, and rivalry

Porter claims that the goals, strategies, and ways of organizing firms in industries vary among nations (Porter, 1990: 108). National advantage results from a good match among these choices. The pattern of rivalry at home also has a profound role to play in the process of innovation and in the ultimate prospects for international business. The higher the competitive pressure at home, the more enterprises are forced to internationalize. Nations will tend to succeed in industries where the management practices and modes of organization favored by the national environment are well suited to the industries' sources of competitive advantage. Important national differences in management approaches occur in such areas as the way of motivating employees, the hierarchical structure of the enterprise, the strength of individual initiative, the ability to coordinate across functions, and management's influence on customer relations (Hitt et al., 2015: 250–251; Porter, 1990: 108–109; Welge & Holtbrügge, 2015: 68).

Two additional factors: government and the role of chance

The government positively or negatively influences the four central determinants mentioned above. Therefore, the role government and the role of chance should not be seen as separate independent factors. Factor conditions are affected by policies toward capital markets, legal property rights, a nation's infrastructure, and the educational system. Governmental institutions establish technical standards for products (e.g., specification of safety and hygiene standards and emission standards), which influence the behavior of the market actors. Furthermore, the government is often a major buyer of specific goods, among them defense products or aircraft for the national airline (Porter, 1990: 126–128).

Chance events are often beyond the influence of firms such as emerging new technologies (e.g., electric cars, 3-D printers). Such events often change the structure of the entire industry and provide opportunities for innovative firms. Advanced knowledge-driven industries, such as differentiated, innovative products, services, and technologies, are the most significant industries for a nation's welfare. They are necessary in order to achieve competitive advantage and, therefore, should be fostered by the national government. Advanced technologies are more scarce because their development demands large and often sustained investment in both human and physical capital (Porter, 1990: 77).

2.2.4 Review of the location concepts

The external environment of firms involved in international trade provides many opportunities but, simultaneously, is becoming increasingly complex and competitive. The liberalized global trade and capital flow framework and advanced logistics and communication systems provide many attractive chances and allow easier entry of firms into the international markets than was possible decades ago. In parallel, environmental uncertainty increases as a result of the amount of complexity plus the degree of change existing in a firm's external environment. Considering these developments, Dai et al. (2013: 555) emphasize that 'location' is decomposed into two separate factors: 'place' and 'space'. Place refers to the conventional location-specific attributes, while space emphasizes geographic distance and network characteristics. Thus, traditional locational 'place' concepts should be amplified by the issue of 'space' in order to better understand multinational enterprise activities in the global markets. Similarly, Beugelsdijk et al. (2013: 414) argue that the term space should refer to characteristics among places combining within-country variations (e.g. investment behavior of firms with regards to a regional industry cluster within one country) and integrate these with between-country variations (e.g. comparison of the firms' investment behavior concerning industry cluster between countries).

According to the location theory, before firms decide their market entry strategy, they have to scan the external macro and industry environment in order to identify possible opportunities and threats in light of internal resources that reflect the strengths and weaknesses of the company. The more the firm is involved in global business and the higher the number of potential competitors, the greater the market research complexity. Internationalization in today's context and complexity is less about just entering foreign markets than it is about increasing the firm's exposure and response to permanently changing international business dynamics (Jones, 2001: 193).

The location theory assumes that the decision to make a direct investment in a particular country is certainly determined by its location factors. However, empirical studies of the relative influence of these individual factors, because of their enormous complexity, are rather difficult. The location factor approach does not supply a reliable contribution regarding the relative meaning of each of the individual factors (Welge & Holtbrügge, 2015: 69). Multinational firms make use of diversified globally distributed operational networks, which even broadens the complexity of the location approaches.

Porter claims in his diamond model that the competitiveness of enterprises is influenced by country-specific conditions. Some enterprises, therefore, have better prerequisites for successful international business activities because of favorable home market surroundings than others. Criticism arises because it is empirically hard to measure the meaning of competitive advantage, and some assumptions are rather speculative. The theoretical assumptions and the influence of each of the location factors as well as their relations are empirically hard to test. The model lacks the ability to provide behavioral patterns or precise recommendations for how to achieve competitive advantage for the firm, which could be of interest to national governments that seek to foster their economies (Grant, 1991a: 542)

The diamond model does not answer the question that asks under which circumstances it is desirable to enter the market through export or alternatively through foreign direct investment (Kutschker & Schmid, 2011: 452). Furthermore, the approach focuses on the home market conditions, which ignores the fact that multinational enterprises make use of cross-border value-added activities depending on the costs at home and abroad. The model neglects other countries and their impact on the competitiveness of firms in the home country and vice versa. This has led other authors to introduce the 'double diamond'. While the 'single diamond' model by Porter focuses on the 'home country' conditions, the 'double diamond' simultaneously takes into consideration the elements of the 'home country' and the 'elements of the foreign markets' with regards to their mutual influence on the performance of the competing firms originating in the home and the foreign markets (Rugman & D'Cruz, 1993: 17; Rugman & Verbeke, 1993: 76–77).

Esterhuizen (2006: 73–74) stresses the importance of human resources for the firm and, consequently, a nation's competitiveness and amplifies the diamond to the 'nine factor model' by adding human resources, divided into categories such as 'workers, politicians and bureaucrats, entrepreneurs, managers, and engineers', which are crucial to gaining a nation's competitive advantage.

Despite all its weaknesses, location concepts and the diamond model have become widely known. The diamond model's strength is its simplicity and pragmatic approach. The model emphasizes that a firm cannot develop independently from each nation's environment and rather depends on various factors, such as infrastructure, the educational system, resource availability, and the political-legal system. The diamond model is one of the best known models within the category of location models. It expands traditional internationalization trade theories, connecting strategic management issues of firms with macro and industry-specific elements of nations and their industries (Grant, 1991a: 540–548).

2.2.5 Case study: Market entry of Asian high-technology firms in Europe

2.2.5.1 Location-specific macro analysis

In recent years, international business research has delivered valuable knowledge concerning the market entry strategies of firms conducting business in the Far East, especially in China (Belderbos & Zou, 2006: 1096; Child & Yan, 1999: 3). On the other hand, research on the market entry concepts of Asian high-technology firms conducting business in Europe seems to be comparatively underrepresented. This case study expands the understanding of Asian firms doing business abroad. We are witnessing an emerging market domination of Asian-based firms in the global markets, particularly in advanced, knowledge-driven industries, such as high-technology businesses (Fu & Zhang, 2011: 330; Wu & Mathews, 2012: 524).

In this study, high-technology firms are categorized as being a part of the 'electronics industry' when their core value added activities are positioned in the area of computer hardware components, audio, electronic displays, micro-electric components, and electronic household devices. Electronics can be seen as a sub-segment of high-technology industries, which are characterized by relatively short-lived product and technology life cycles, among other characteristics. Shortened technology and product life cycles in high-tech industries mean that firms that are technologically leading today may disappear from the market tomorrow if upcoming technologies are ignored by the firm's management.

Additionally, there is a relatively intense and permanent cost pressure in electronics industries. Electronic products, such as smart phones, television sets, and laptops, are highly standardized and, therefore, usually provide the best prerequisites for intense price competition (Kita, 2001: 1). Manufacturing and processing knowledge plays a superior role in gaining a competitive advantage through realizing economies of scale. Firms that underestimate the link between ever-changing technologies and efficient manufacturing definitely risk quickly falling from the market (McIvor, Humphreys, & Cadden, 2006: 374).

Mainly as a result of emerging firms from South Korea, China, and Taiwan, worldwide competition in electronics has greatly intensified in recent decades; and market entry activities did not stop at the European borders. As a result, traditional Western electronics firms, such as Thomson, Grundig, Philips, and Loewe, but also Japanese firms (e.g., Sanyo, Pioneer, and JVC) lost competitive power against their Asian rivals or even declared bankruptcy.

On the macro-level, this case study discusses, among other things, whether country-specific electronics industry clusters developed and how they evolved over time in Europe. On the micro level, the market entry activities of Asian-based high-technology firms doing business in Europe are described. This study allows descriptions of the changing local industry configurations of high-technology firms.

In general, countries located in western Europe, such as the United Kingdom, Spain, and Germany, served as major European investment target regions for Asian-based firms during the 1980s and 1990s but significantly lost importance thereafter. Asian-based high-tech firms, during the last decade, mainly concentrated on the new European Union (EU) member states located in the east, such as Poland, Hungary, the Czech Republic, and Slovakia (LG.PhilipsLCD, 2006; UNCTAD, 2010; World_Bank, 2013). Consequently, the analysis of location-specific macro-economic indicators, such as GDP, inflation rates, and so forth, concentrates on those countries: Poland, the Czech Republic, Slovakia, and Hungary. Interestingly, Bulgaria and Romania, which have also been members of the EU since 2007, could not attract Asian investors to any significant extent and, for that reason, are not considered in the following case study discussion (European_Union, 2013).

In general, firms prefer to invest in regions that belong to countries that are connected through trade and capital flows and/or memberships in free trade zones, with the EU serving as an excellent example (Easton & Araujo, 1994: 81). This location-specific pattern influences the multinational firm's choice for its foreign direct investments (Bandelk, 2002: 411; Dong, Zou, & Taylor, 2008: 82). The political and economic challenges related to the transition from centrally planned economies to market economies in the central and eastern European (CEE) countries have been tremendous and, in most cases, have been successfully met (Svejnar, 2002: 4). As a result of EU membership, firms that have invested in the CEE area, such as Poland, the Czech Republic, Slovakia, and Hungary, have taken advantage of borderless, liberalized trade and capital flow patterns. Additionally, these countries have relatively stable political-legal environments. These markets are often more promising and indicate higher sales growth volumes for electronic products (locality-specific advantages) when compared to saturated western European markets (DisplaySearch, 2010; Dunning, 2001: 174).

An analysis of the country-specific macro-economic data delivers evidence that Poland is the largest national economy based on its gross domestic product (GDP) volume followed by the Czech Republic. Both countries reached an impressive GDP growth over the period from 2002 until 2013 (compare Table 1). This is not the case for Hungary, which recorded its highest GDP levels between 2006 and 2008 but, significantly, was falling behind in performance between 2009 and 2012. Hungary also suffers from the highest inflation rates when compared to Poland, the Czech Republic, and Slovakia. The Czech Republic indicates the lowest unemployment rate and, as a logical consequence, the highest average wage levels. Poland is also attractive when the average wage level is considered and compared with other new EU member countries (IMF, 2013; OECD, 2013; WTO, 2013). Table 1 provides a summary of GDP, average wages, inflation, and unemployment rate for the Czech Republic, Poland, Hungary, and Slovakia for the period from 2003 until 2013.

2.2.5.2 Business activities of high-tech firms from the Far East: A country perspective

Next the manufacturing breadths and depths of Asian-based electronics firms in the Czech Republic, Hungary, Poland, and Slovakia are analyzed. The multiple-case study method aims to describe the evolution of country-specific electronics industry clusters in these target countries.

Czech Republic
Panasonic (Japan) has been operating a liquid crystal display (LCD) panel plant in the town of Zatec, Czech Republic, since 2007. However, against the background of worsening business performance for the Panasonic group, the Japanese firm initiated a restructuring program. As one outcome, Panasonic closed its Zatec LCD panel factory for televisions at the end of 2012. The firm maintains operations in its second Czech plant in Plzen, where Panasonic does the final assembly of LCD television sets (Reuters, 2013).

In 2005, the Chinese firm Changhong established its first European subsidiary in the Czech Republic. The LCD television set assembly factory is located in the industrial zone of the city of Nymburk, from which Changhong serves its European markets. LCD panels are imported from China (Changhong, 2013).

In 2000, the Taiwanese Hon Hai Precision Industry Co. (Foxconn) invested around 45 million Euro in existing manufacturing facilities previously owned by the national Czech firm HTT Tesla in the town of Pardubice in the eastern part of the country. In 2008, Foxconn opened a second facility in Kutna Hora. Based on original equipment manufacturing (OEM) contractual relationships, Foxconn manufactures electronic devices for HP, Cisco, and others, thus making Foxconn the second largest exporter in the Czech Republic by 2011 (Czechinvest, 2012).

Hungary
Samsung Electronics established a television set assembly factory in 1989. To realize the firm's vertical integration strategy, Samsung Electronics procures a major part of its needed displays from Samsung SDI's factory, which is also located in Hungary (established in 2002). In addition, Samsung SDI, Hungary, has delivered components (e. g., plasma display panels) not only to Samsung Electronics but also to Philips, Hungary (Naver, 2004). In 2013, due to worsening operating performance, Samsung SDI closed its operations in Goed, Hungary (Samsung, 2014). Samsung SDI was not alone. In the same year, within the framework of a joint venture agreement with the Taiwanese TPV Technology Limited, Philips closed its Hungarian television set plant operations. Manufacturing capacities were transferred to TPV's Poland factory, locat-

Table 1. GDP, average annual wages, inflation, and unemployment rate for the Czech Republic, Hungary, Poland, and Slovakia for the period from 2002 until 2013.
Sources: GDP, inflation and unemployment (IMF, 2013), average annual wages (OECD, 2013)

GDP (in billion EUR; constant prices)	2003	2004	2005	2006	2007	2008	2009	2010	2011	2012	2013
Czech Republic	96.921	108.007	120.575	128.866	148.567	151.944	146.134	157.316	157.261	159.068	144.809
Hungary	78.081	87.175	88.209	91.704	91.706	88.040	80.952	79.374	71.328	76.278	76.086
Poland	223.459	269.729	295.746	314.303	360.070	323.623	336.043	361.998	335.252	375.342	375.091
Slovakia	47.782	50.286	53.574	57.999	64.194	67.690	64.109	67.204	69.022	70.127	71.126

Average annual wages (in EUR; current prices)	2003	2004	2005	2006	2007	2008	2009	2010	2011	2012	2013
Czech Republic	6,696	7,726	8,280	9,290	10,406	10,629	10,975	11,911	11,891	12,459	11,021
Hungary	7,630	8,485	9,062	9,594	10,120	10,767	10,819	11,213	8,723	9,027	10,140
Poland	6,322	7,417	7,948	8,170	9,096	8,673	9,015	9,737	9,136	10,371	10,487
Slovakia	7,048	7,806	8,757	9,491	10,282	10,762	11,007	11,552	11,692	11,905	11,629

Inflation (in percent)	2003	2004	2005	2006	2007	2008	2009	2010	2011	2012	2013
Czech Republic	0.11	2.78	1.84	2.54	2.86	6.34	1.03	1.46	1.93	3.29	1.42
Hungary	4.65	6.78	3.55	3.88	7.94	6.07	4.21	4.88	3.96	5.71	1.73
Poland	0.80	3.53	2.20	1.19	2.49	4.42	3.50	2.60	4.30	3.70	0.90
Slovakia	8.43	7.45	2.79	4.26	1.90	3.95	0.93	0.70	4.08	3.74	1.46

Unemployment (in percent)	2003	2004	2005	2006	2007	2008	2009	2010	2011	2012	2013
Czech Republic	7.81	8.32	7.92	7.15	5.32	4.39	6.66	7.28	6.73	6.98	6.95
Hungary	5.50	6.30	7.30	7.50	7.70	8.00	10.50	10.90	10.94	11.07	10.24
Poland	19.64	18.97	17.75	13.84	9.60	7.12	8.17	9.64	9.63	10.09	10.33
Slovakia	19.64	18.36	16.38	13.47	11.23	9.58	12.12	14.49	13.683	13.98	14.26

ed in Gorzow, which was opened in 2008 (Philips, 2011). Samsung Chemicals, a subsidiary of Samsung Cheil Industries Inc., continues operations in Hungary (Samsung, 2015).

Poland

In 2009, Samsung Electronics acquired the Polish household manufacturer (e. g., washing machines) 'Amica' (Economic_Review, 2013). In addition, Samsung runs a research and development center in Krakow. Samsung has also operated a television set assembly plant in Poland since 2009. As a result, Samsung's television set lead time, from production to sales, is just five days within its European markets. The delivery time takes just one day from its television set factory in Poland to Germany.

Toshiba (Japan) established its Polish television set plant near Wroclaw in 2007. Toshiba's Poland factory has procured most of its liquid crystal display panels for its TV assembly from LG Display (a former joint venture called LG.Philips LCD), which is located in the Wroclaw area as well. Toshiba invested 19.9 percent interest in the LG Display plant in Poland (Finanznachrichten.de, 2007: 1).

From 2007 until 2011, Toshiba's business performed at a reasonable level mainly due to increasing LCD sales volumes in Europe and worldwide. However, since 2008, due to the relative strength of the Japanese Yen, intensified competition in the LCD business, and upcoming fast developing competitors from China and Taiwan, Toshiba, like other Japanese firms, was confronted with shrinking sales. During the course of a worldwide restructuring program, Toshiba sold its Polish operations, called 'Toshiba Television Central Europe', to Taiwan-based 'Compal Electronics' in 2013. After the transfer of ownership to Compal, Toshiba continues to sell electronic devices manufactured at the plant, through an original design manufacturer (ODM) partnership with Compal (Toshiba, 2013).

Sharp started its LCD module production in Łysomice near Torun (Poland) in 2007. The city of Torun is located in the 'Pomeranian special economic zone' (WarsawVoice, 2006: 2). Sharp has invested 44 million Euro in its Polish subsidiary, which became an important component supplier in Europe. However, in 2014, due to the accumulating losses of the Sharp Group, the Japanese company withdrew its activities from Poland and sold its LCD factory (including its AQUOS brand) to the Slovakian-based company Universal Media Corporation (UMC) (Sharp, 2015b). Beginning in 2004, Sharp held 29 percent of Loewe AG (Kronach, Germany) capital and delivered electronics components and displays to Loewe AG (Bastian, 2006). However, in 2013, the German premium brand Loewe filed for bankruptcy, suffering from heavy losses for years as it has struggled for survival in a market dominated by Asian-based rivals (Loewe, 2013). As a consequence of the bankruptcy of Loewe, Sharp's strategic positioning has worsened in its European markets.

One of Sharp's former OEM partners, the US-originated 'Jabil Circuit Inc.', invested 13 million Euro in a manufacturing factory in Kwidzyn, which is located in the same economic zone where Sharp operated. Jabil manufactures electronic components for various consumer electronics products. The factory was established in

1994 by Philips, which sold it to Jabil at a price of 12 million Euro in December 2004 (Philips, 2004). Today, Jabil's customers include Philips, Sharp, and Orion. Firms like Jabil benefit from the public assistance offered to businesses within the zone, including tax incentives for their investments (WarsawVoice, 2006: 1).

In 1999, South Korean LG Electronics initiated its TV assembly operations in Mława. LG Display began producing LCD modules from 2007 onwards in Wroclaw. Displays manufactured in Wroclaw are delivered and assembled into television sets at LG's Mława factory. In Wroclaw, LG Electronics also manufactures washing machines and refrigerators (LG_Electronics, 2008).

In 2004, the French Thomson and the Chinese TCL agreed to establish a joint venture in the television set assembly business. As a part of the agreement, Thomson transferred its Polish television set factory to the joint venture with TCL (TCL, 2004). However, TCL experienced severe financial difficulties during the venture operations. As a result, TCL China downsized its European business and closed its television set assembly operations in Poland (Zyrardow) in 2007 (TCL, 2007a). The joint venture was finally liquidated in the same year (TCL, 2007b).

Slovakia

Samsung Electronics is the largest electronics company in Slovakia. In 2010, revenues reached 3.24 billion Euro and 3.16 billion Euro in 2011. Samsung's television set plant in Galanta was established in 2002. Samsung planned to sell its factory in early 2012 but decided to remain as the Slovakian government agreed to further support the Galanta factory for a total of 28 million Euro. Samsung runs a second company in Voderady, where LCD modules are being completed after being imported from South Korea and then finally assembled into complete TVs in Galanta (Slovak_Investment, 2012).

Sony opened its first CEE production facility in Trnava in 1996. In 2007, Sony opened a new LCD TV manufacturing plant in Nitra, one of the largest and most modern plants worldwide (Sony, 2007b, 2013a). However, for the past couple of years, Sony has operated with losses because of the firm's poorly performing consumer electronics business division, among other reasons (Sony, 2008d). As a result, Sony's management decided to reduce its stake in the television set business and started to look for investors, including investors for its Slovakian operations. Finally, the Taiwanese Hon Hai Precision acquired 90 percent interest in the Nitra plant from Sony. In this plant, Hon Hai manufactures its own television sets but also television sets for Sony, based on an original equipment manufacturing (OEM) contract relationship. Sony Supply Chain Solutions Europe (a subsidiary company of Sony) has rented a part of the facilities and continues the operation of the logistics centre, which has been located next to the Nitra production plant. Nitra remains the most important production location of LCD televisions for Sony in the European region based on its OEM relationship with Hon Hai (Hon_Hai, 2013).

The Japanese Panasonic operates two manufacturing subsidiaries in Slovakia. Panasonic AVC Networks Slovakia in the city of Krompachy manufactures DVD and Blu-ray/3D Blu-ray devices. Panasonic Electronic Devices Slovakia is split between two manufacturing sites, one in Trstená and the other in Stará Ľubovňa, where Panasonic manufactures tuners, chargers, remote controls, iPod adapters, elements for steering wheels, and speakers for cars (Slovak_Investment, 2012).

Figure 10 illustrates the bilateral relationships of the consumer electronics firms discussed above and the corresponding country-specific industry clusters for the year 2007.

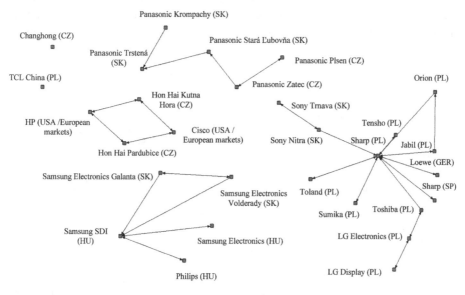

Figure 10. Electronics industry clusters in the CEE (status 2007); CZ = Czech Republic, SK = Slovakia, HU = Hungary, PL = Poland, (SP = Spain, and GER = Germany do not belong to CEE region) [UCINET network analysis]

As illustrated in Figure 10, in 2007, Samsung concentrated on Hungary and Slovakia, where the South Korean Chaebol installed a cross-border, vertically integrated value chain from display to final device assembly (ownership and internalization advantage). LG Electronics and a cluster of Japanese firms, such as Toshiba, Sharp, Toland, Sumika, and others, selected Poland. Changhong (China) and the Taiwanese Hon Hai Precision as well as the Japanese firms Sony and Panasonic selected the Czech Republic and Slovakia for their display, electronics component, television set, and audio manufacturing activities.

Since 2007, the electronics industry has experienced changes in firms' competitive power on a global scale, which also has affected Europe. As a result, Sony significantly reduced its own television set business operations and sold the majority of property to the Taiwanese Hon Hai Precision, which has become significantly stronger not only in the European markets but worldwide. TCL China withdrew its activities in Poland and concentrates on its Chinese home markets. Sharp sold its

Polish operations. Panasonic focused on the Czech Republic and Slovakia but due to financial difficulties of the Panasonic Group, had to close its display factory in the Czech Republic in 2012.

The comparison of Figure 11 (status 2014) and Figure 10 (status 2007) illustrates the shift of competitive power from Japanese to South Korean and Taiwanese electronics firms in recent years in Eastern Europe. Poland and Slovakia could further develop their country-specific electronics industry cluster. This is not the case for the Czech Republic and Hungary, where production capacities were shut down (e.g., Philips, Panasonic). Changhong is attempting to remain an independent final assembly location for television sets (displays are procured from Changhong, China).

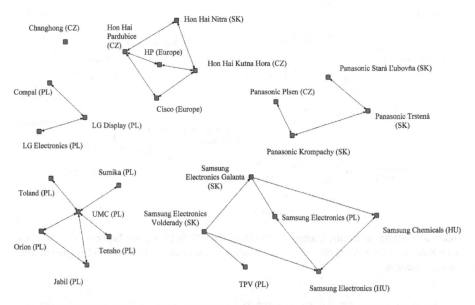

Figure 11. Electronics industry cluster in the CEE (status 2014), CZ = Czech Republic, SK = Slovakia, HU = Hungary, PL = Poland [UCINET network analysis]

Overall, Samsung has developed successfully and become the strongest electronics firm, with major production hubs in Poland, Hungary, and Slovakia. As per the end of 2012, the South Korean Chaebol reached around 35 percent market share and was leading in the LCD television set markets in the CEE (ownership advantages through economies of scale effects). In the 3D and large-size television set segment (e.g., 42 inch and more), Samsung even reached more than 40 percent market share in CEE countries such as Poland, Rumania, and Hungary (news1.Korea, 2012). Such market shares provide the best prerequisites for economies of scale (ownership advantages) (Dunning, 1980b: 9) and for realizing Samsung's cost advantages. The Korean Chaebol successfully established cross-border value chains ranging from display assembly (Slovakia) up to final device assembly (Poland and Hungary). Samsung's narrowly knit logistics and branches network allows it to reach each European sales destination faster than its competitors, which provides fundamental advantages for its customer response and order handling flexibility (internalization advantages) (Dunning, 2000: 164; Economic_Review, 2013).

Among the new EU member states, Poland has become the major production hub for the consumer electronics components, display, and television set business (e. g., Sharp, LG, Samsung, and TPV) followed by Slovakia (e. g., Samsung, Panasonic, and Hon Hai Precision) and the Czech Republic (e. g., Panasonic, Changhong). Hungary was relatively strong in the 1990s. However, since 2004, Hungary has not kept pace with the other new EU member states. Hungary's worsening position in the field of electronics production correlates with the development of the country's macro-economic indicators—for example, its negative GDP development, combined with relatively high inflation rates during recent years when compared with other new EU member states.

Poland, on the other hand, has been able to successfully develop its electronics industry cluster, which goes hand in hand with positive macro-economic indicators, such as a stable GDP growth and relatively low average wages and inflation rates (location-specific advantages) (Dunning, 2000: 164; 2001: 177). Simultaneously, Poland serves as the largest market (market volume) for electronics products among the new EU member countries in the east (location-specific advantage). The first investors, such as LG Electronics (1999) and Sharp (2007), brought further electronics component and service suppliers to Poland.

Taking a more micro perspective, Japanese firms like Sony and Sharp lost their favorable competitive position in recent times, while South Korean companies (above all Samsung) and Taiwanese firms (particularly Hon Hai Precisions) became significantly stronger in Europe. Samsung, through its high degree of vertical manufacturing (internalization advantage) of various products in Poland, Slovakia, and Hungary, has increased its local presence tremendously. Hon Hai Precision, through its acquisitions of some Sony factories in Europe, gained access to Sony's specific ownership advantages, such as its state-of-the-art research and manufacturing assets and Sony's well-established distribution channels in Europe. The shift of competitive power from Japanese to South Korean and Taiwanese firms, as witnessed in Europe, follows a global trend. As seen for the last years, increasing investments of South Korean and Taiwanese companies come along with factory shut downs of Japanese firms.

Political decision makers may take into consideration the fact that local electronics industry clusters, especially in Poland and Slovakia, have been successfully established. However, the vast majority of investors located their production facilities in areas where subsidies and tax benefits are granted (compare, for example, the so called 'customs free zones' in Poland) (PAIZ, 2009; PolandBusiness, 2007b). The case of Samsung in Slovakia, where the South Korean firm threatened to shut down its Galanta factory if the government did not provide further financial support, illustrates 'the price' for attracting investors (Slovak_Investment, 2012). Therefore, politicians, not only in Europe but in general, should always raise a question mark when they consider granting subsidies: Do firms like Samsung really target regional sustainable investment initiatives or rather prefer to create a kind of 'subsidy competition' among regions and countries?

Instead of single foreign country markets, the challenge of overcoming entry barriers in worldwide industry networks has moved to the center of consideration. Without access to these organizational grids, a firm is unable to compete and survive in international business. To become an accepted member of an industry is the first issue for a firm that has international business intentions. Therefore, it is of vital importance that a firm proves to be a reliable actor in the areas of quality, service, delivery punctuality, competence, and innovative potential regarding future technologies. A poor performance in one market of the world easily has a negative impact on the firm's general reputation and on the related global business and corresponding customer relations in other regions.

Chapter review questions

1. Explain the major reasons that Poland has become a leading investment hub for high-technology firms that originated in the Far East.
2. Describe the investment policy of Chinese and Taiwanese electronics firms in Europe.
3. What are the potential advantages and risks for Samsung in terms of its investments (behaviors) in several east European countries?
4. Comparing 2007 and 2014, how did firms' position in the high-tech industry cluster evolve over time in Eastern Europe? How did Japanese firms develop relative to Chinese, Taiwanese, and South Korean competitors?

2.3 The Internalization Theory

2.3.1 The issue of transaction costs

The internalization theory of Buckley and Casson (1998) is based on the transaction cost approach of Coase (1937) and the market-hierarchy paradigm of Williamson (1975). Firms have two fundamental possibilities when dealing with transactions: externally in the market (e. g., contracts) or in-house through hierarchy (e. g., production). The transaction costs in the market need to be compared with the internal coordination costs that arise when operations are carried out in-house. Contractual transactions do not perform as expected by the contracting parties or even fail because of the actors' bounded rationality phenomena (e. g. individual preferences) and the issue of market imperfections (e. g. limited information) (Zhao, Luo, & Suh, 2004: 525).

Market imperfections

- First, market transactions are not free of costs for the firm because of limited information and a lack of reliable future market forecasts and because of time lags between initiation and completion of the international business activity.
- Second, there is a monopoly (or monopsony) incentive in terms of 'internalization of the market' (forward or backward integration) in order to implement the desired price.
- Third, the bilateral concentration of market power (bilateral monopoly) leads to an indeterminate or unstable bargaining situation.
- Fourth, there are market imperfections caused by an inequality between buyer and seller with respect to knowledge of the nature or value of the product.
- Finally, market imperfections arise from government interventions in international markets through tariffs or restrictions on capital movements and from discrepancies among countries in rates of income and profit taxation (Buckley & Casson, 1976: 37–38).

The extent and degree of being confronted by market imperfections mainly depends on three transaction dimensions: *asset specificity, uncertainty,* and *frequency.* These dimensions are introduced below (compare: Williamson 1975; 1985).

Asset Specificity

Asset specificity refers to the degree to which an asset can be redeployed to alternative uses and by alternative users (Williamson, 1991: 281–282).

There are six types of asset specificity:

(1) site specificity (causing an influence of operational efficiency of the business actor),
(2) physical asset specificity (e.g., specialized equipment, tools, and technologies),
(3) learning and experience curve assets of human resources,
(4) brand name,
(5) dedicated assets (investments caused by a particular customer), and
(6) temporal specificity (non-separability of applied technologies).

Bilateral dependence between market actors (e.g., supplier and customer) rises with increasing asset specificity (as a result of explicit investments causing 'actor-specific sunk costs') and, therefore, increases the financial risk. The probability of internalization of value added activities (e.g., vertical forward integration by the supplier or vertical backward integration by the client firm) increases with an enhanced investment specificity (Williamson, 1991: 281–282).

Uncertainty

Actors' uncertainty related to market transactions is the result of imperfect information (e. g., understanding of performance and quality of the product or service) combined with the bounded rationality phenomena of the actors. Uncertainty as a result of market imperfections necessarily requires market research activities and the initiation, negotiation, and conclusion of contracts (which cause ex-ante costs). Contract supervision and putting through agreed conditions after the contract is signed cause ex-post costs. Because market actors can never rely on perfect and complete information, contracts naturally are imperfect as well because it is impossible to consider all potential eventualities in the course of the market transaction process in concrete contractual terms. The higher the uncertainty, the more difficult it is to include the entire complexity of possible future developments in contracts and, as a consequence, the higher the risk that the market transaction will fail (Williamson, 1975: 9 – 10; Zajac & Olsen, 1993: 136).

The danger of opportunistic behavior from the transaction partner rises in accordance with the perceived degree of uncertainty. Opportunism refers to the incomplete or distorted disclosure of information, especially calculated efforts to mislead, distort, disguise, obfuscate, or otherwise confuse (Williamson, 1985: 47). The costs of negotiating, monitoring, and enforcing contract conditions in order to ban opportunistic behavior have a tremendous impact on the amount of transaction costs (Hill, 1990: 501). Because contracts can help to mitigate the risk of opportunism in a relationship, they are frequently classified as contractual governance mechanisms (Hoetker & Mellewigt, 2009: 1027– 1028).

In addition to (formal visible) contracts, which help to clarify the relationship expectations between the actors, invisible influencing factors such as trust and commitment also have a significant impact on the development of mutually shared expectations related to contractual relationships. The development of trust and commitment can be supported by the contracting actors' efforts, such as timely communication, smooth exchange of correct information, and coordination of activities (Walter, Müller, Helfert, & Ritter, 2003: 361). However, all these efforts aiming to develop and maintain a trusting contractual relationship cause administrative costs.

Frequency

The more frequently equal transactions are carried out in the market, the lower the average costs of a transaction due to the actors' learning and experience curve effects. In addition, mutual trust between the transaction partners may rise, which minimizes the contractual negotiation costs of the transaction partners. With an increasing frequency of transactions and mutual trust, the desire to internalize market transactions (hierarchy) decreases (Williamson, 1999: 1089).

Market transactions are recommended as an efficient business form
- the more standardized the product and service that is the subject of the transaction;
- the higher the actors' degree of information, which results in transactional transparency;
- when product offer and demand are sufficient, such as in polypol market forms; and
- the more frequently transactions are carried out by the actors.

Backward integration out of manufacturing into the supplier's value added activities would be implied by hierarchy.

The *hybrid* mode of business is located between market and hierarchy with respect to control mechanisms, legal responsibility, and costs and corresponding financial risks. An international joint venture and franchising serve as examples of hybrid business modes (Williamson, 1991: 283, 293). Hybrid business models are chosen by actors attempting to balance their market uncertainty risk with the financial risk of internalizing market transactions.

2.3.2 Emergence of multinational enterprises

Buckley and Casson transferred the contents of the transaction cost concept to the idea of the multinational enterprise (MNE). Market imperfections (as previously defined in the transaction costs theory) for intermediate products require coordination efforts for global business activities. The desire to increase coordination efficiency has led to the phenomena of emerging MNEs. MNEs internalize the markets across national boundaries whenever the costs of internal organization of market activities are lower than market transactions. Decision determinants for favoring or disfavoring internalization depend on (Buckley & Casson, 1976: 33 – 34) the following:
(1) industry-specific factors, such as the nature of the product and the structure of the market;
(2) region-specific factors, which relate to the geographical and societal characteristics of the markets;
(3) nation-specific factors, such as political and fiscal relations between the nation concerned; and
(4) firm-specific factors, which reflect the ability of the management to internalize the market.

As illustrated in Figure 12, MNEs appear whenever it is cheaper to allocate international resources and value added activities internally than by making transactions in the markets (Brown, 1976: 39; Buckley & Casson, 1976: 33). Because MNEs own and control resources and activities in different countries, they become able to maximize their profits in a world of imperfect markets. The higher the internal efficiency of in-house procurement and operations, the more desirable is the internalization of international market transactions (Caves, 1982: 36).

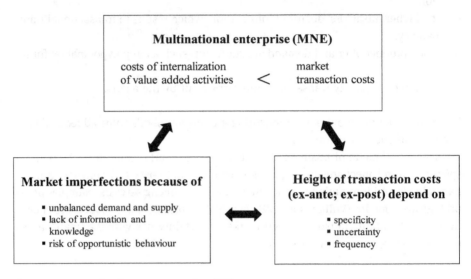

Figure 12. Reasons for the emergence of an MNE

Buckley and Casson emphasize the role of an MNE as a cross-boundary developer and transferor of various kinds of knowledge and skills. In an imperfect market system, foreign investment has allowed MNEs to bypass imperfect external conditions through internalization (Buckley & Casson, 1976: 109 – 110).

2.3.3 Review of the internalization theory

The internalization theory extends the market imperfections approach as claimed in the transaction cost theory by focusing on failings in intermediate-product markets rather than on final products. The internalization model identifies transaction costs as a main impulse for internationalization (Buckley & Casson, 1976: 33; Robock & Simmonds, 1989: 45). Buckley and Casson (1976: 33) identified different factors determining the internationalization decision, which does not depend only on market imperfections but also on organizational capabilities, particularly in terms of internal market organization and coordination. As a result of their study, they were the first to describe and explain the emerging MNE phenomena, which has been increasingly seen since the 1970s. They also considered the role of knowledge (disparities) in driving foreign investment decisions as opposed to market transactions (Zuchella & Scabini, 2007: 35). MNEs appear when it is cheaper to allocate international knowledge resources internally than via the market mechanism (Brown, 1976: 39).

Buckley and Casson (1976) focus on industry-specific factors related to internalizing markets for intermediate products in multistage production processes, for example through vertical integration. A vertically integrated firm is determined mainly by the interplay of comparative advantage, tariff and non-tariff trade barriers, and regional incentives to internalize. The firm will become an MNE whenever the combination of these factors makes it optimal to locate different operational stages of value added activities in different countries (Buckley & Casson, 1976: 34–35).

However, there are other motives for enterprises to internationalize, such as for example the necessity of a supplier 'to follow its customer' to foreign markets. Moreover, the actual amount of transaction costs can hardly be quantified. Uncertainty is perceived differently by the operating management, and costs usually change in the course of time. Due to the influence of the transaction cost theory (Williamson, 1975; Williamson, 1985) the internalization model is based on 'rationality' but pays very limited attention to behavioral-sociological aspects, such as the ethics, culture and norms, or personal preferences of the management (McIvor et al., 2006: 392). Buckley and Casson (2009: 1568) moderate the critics by claiming that rationality does not imply the necessity of complete information. Instead, a rational decision maker collects only enough information to reduce uncertainty.

The latest research considers the behavioral aspects of trust-building and learning as drivers for the success of MNEs in international markets (Vahlne & Ivarsson, 2014: 244). Internalization may be rather disadvantageous in countries where the protection of invested private capital is not secure (consider, for example, the proceeding cases of expropriation of MNEs that originated in the oil industry in Venezuela).

The internalization concept of Buckley and Casson (1976) explains the growth of MNEs domestically and internationally. The approach focuses on a firm's motives to internationalize but does not consider appropriately the potential of national governments and their political-legal influence on MNE investment decisions. For example, in countries such as China or India, it is advisable to establish a joint venture with local firms in order to enter the foreign market successfully. The need to found a joint venture with a local partner influences the firm's decision alternatives and may hinder realizing the concept of a complete internalization (e.g., through foreign direct investment) of foreign country activities into the firm's hierarchy (Robock & Simmonds, 1989: 47).

Chapter review questions

1. Describe the 'uncertainty' phenomenon and propose alternatives for how to handle it in international business.
2. Explain the core message of the internalization theory of Buckley and Casson and deduce conceptual drawbacks.
3. Grounded in the internalization theory, explain why multinational enterprises (MNEs) have developed successfully in recent decades.
4. What do you think about the future of MNEs considering the current political, societal, and international business developments around the globe?

2.4 The Eclectic Paradigm

2.4.1 Advantage categories

The 'eclectic theory of international production' was developed by Dunning, who claims that the choice of the international market entry strategy depends on the availability and combination of so-called *advantage categories* for a multinational enterprise (MNE). Dunning distinguishes three types of advantage categories: ownership-specific, internalization, and location advantages (Dunning, 1979: 269–272; 1980a: 1980; Dunning, Cantwell, & Corley, 1986: 38).

Ownership-specific advantages
The more ownership-specific advantages are possessed by an enterprise, the greater the inducement to internationalize them; and the wider the attractions of a foreign rather than a home country production base, the greater the likelihood that an enterprise will engage in international production. Such ownership-specific advantages may take the form of legally protected rights, patents, brand names, trademarks, or even a commercial monopoly in the market. Furthermore, if access to resources such as raw materials becomes essential for the production of a product, exclusive control over particular distribution channels seems desirable. Ownership-specific advantages may arise from the size or technical characteristics of firms, the economies of scale in production, and qualified entrepreneurial capacity.

The eclectic approach of international production in an enterprise can be described like this: a national firm supplying its own market has various avenues for growth. It can diversify horizontally or laterally into new product lines or vertically into new value chain activities. Alternatively, the firm can acquire other enterprises; or it can enter and exploit foreign markets. When it makes economic sense to choose the last route, the firm becomes an international enterprise (defined as a firm that services foreign markets). However, in order to be able to produce alongside indigenous firms domiciled in these markets, it must possess additional ownership advantages sufficient enough to outweigh the costs of servicing an unfamiliar or distant environment. The function of an enterprise is to transform, by the process of production, valuable inputs into more valuable outputs (Dunning, 1980a: 9–13). Ownership advantages secure multinational enterprises' competitive superiority over other firms supplying particular foreign markets (Rasmussen et al., 2008: 71).

Internalization advantages

Market imperfections arise wherever information about the product or service being marketed is not readily available or is costly to acquire and, as a result, wherever transaction costs are high. The risk of market failure causes enterprises to internalize market transactions in intangible assets (e. g., knowledge) or tangible assets (e. g., manufacturing facilities) (Dunning, 1979: 288; 1995a: 476). In-house value chain activities help the enterprise reduce the cost of information search in the market, expenses for negotiation and contracting with outside suppliers, and protection of intellectual property rights. Internalization advantages develop certain enterprise-specific capabilities concerning experience curve, operational scale effects, and organizational skills. The issue of 'internalization' deals with the question as to *why* firms choose to engage in foreign direct investment rather than buy or sell intermediate products, in other words performing market transactions (Dunning, 2000: 179).

Besides the phenomena of market imperfections, local governments' intervention in the allocation of resources may also encourage firms to internalize their ownership advantages. This arises particularly with respect to government legislation toward the production and, where there are differential tax and exchange rate policies, which multinational enterprises may wish either to avoid or exploit them (Dunning, 1980a: 11).

Location-specific advantages

The ability of an MNE to acquire ownership-specific advantages is clearly related to the endowments that are specific to the countries in which they operate and particularly those endowments that are specific to their country of origin. Location-specific advantages answer the question 'where?' firms choose to locate their value adding activities or the question 'why do firms produce in one country rather than in another?' (Dunning, 2002: 386). Location advantages evaluate the alternative that it is more profitable for the MNE to use its ownership advantages together with factor inputs outside the home country (Rasmussen et al., 2008: 71). Examples of location-specific advantages are government policy (with respect to tariff and non-tariff import barriers, investment incentives, etc.), access and costs of raw material and labor, market volume and attractiveness, and transportation and communication infrastructure (Dunning, 1980: 9–30).

2.4.2 Market entry strategy according to advantage categories

Dunning derives the following recommendations for international business engagements from the ownership-location-internalization (OLI) advantage categories. The OLI-paradigm suggests that MNEs that have merely ownership-specific advantages and neither internalization nor location-specific advantages should deal with their foreign business in the form of international contracts (e.g., licenses). However, the greater the ownership and internalization advantages possessed by firms and the more the location advantages of creating, acquiring (or augmenting), and exploiting these advantages from a location outside its home country, the higher the probability that foreign direct investment activities will be undertaken (Dunning, 1994: 23–25). Where firms possess substantial ownership and internalization advantages but location advantages favor the home country, then domestic investment will be preferred to foreign direct investment; and foreign markets will be supplied by exports (Dunning & Dilyard, 1999: 13). The advantage category connections and corresponding market entry strategies are illustrated in Figure 13.

Figure 13. A firm's international market entry modes are deduced depending on the advantage categories

Initially addressed as a *static* model, Dunning further developed the eclectic paradigm several times over a period of more than twenty years, paying more attention over time to dynamic competitiveness and the strategic aspects of the firm (compare: Dunning, 1973, 1983, 1993, 2001). Changes in the global markets witnessed since the 1990s, the deepening integration of global capital and logistics, the liberalization of cross-border markets, and the emergence of several new countries as important players in the global economic arena caused Dunning to modify and enlarge each of the OLI categories with *dynamic* components (Dunning, 2001: 187).

Resources and capabilities, such as the ability to internally produce and organize proprietary assets, that match existing market needs at any given moment of time (static ownership advantages) were enlarged by context-specific issues to increase income generating assets over time (dynamic ownership advantages). Dynamic means, for example, that the trade-off of resources that can be internally developed with those externally acquired (e. g., through bilateral relationships with other market actors) becomes more crucial than the resources themselves (Dunning, 1995b: 198; 2001: 174).

Location-specific advantages have been traditionally expressed by the availability of a country's unique immobile natural resources, which the MNE may make use of. This category was enlarged by distinctive and non-imitable, location-bound created assets, such as the presence of firms that have specific local market knowledge (e. g., access to local customers because of suitable and efficient marketing communication). MNEs might form relationships to complement their own core competences (e. g., advanced production technology) with the specific knowledge (e. g., marketing) of those local firms (Dunning, 2001: 178). Geographic locations that used to be regarded as targets for the supply of raw materials (e. g., static location advantages) are also becoming recognized as possible sources of learning and innovative capabilities (e. g., dynamic location advantages). The need for the firm's efficiency improvement through rationalization highlights the importance of management's strategic capabilities through holding a dynamic perspective (Dunning, Pak, & Beldona, 2007: 534).

2.4.3 Review of the Eclectic Paradigm

The achievement of Dunning's paradigm is that multiple reasons are considered that influence an MNE's choice of market entry strategy. The appearance and combination of advantage categories serves as the basis for management decision making as to whether to proceed with exports, contractual entry modes such as licensing or franchising, or foreign direct investments.

The creation of the eclectic paradigm is based on different models, such as the internalization theory, the resource-based view, and the location theory. In a parallel manner, criticism of the paradigm is related to its grounding in other theories. Hohenthal (2001: 80) criticizes the paradigm for mixing three different and sometimes overlapping sets of explanations from location concepts (location-specific advantages), resource-based theory (ownership advantages), and transaction cost theory (internalization advantages). This conglomerate of theories makes the eclectic paradigm very complex, limits validity testing of the model, and makes it difficult to use. The three advantage categories are formulated too generally, which makes it impossible to develop a concrete recommendation for an MNE's internationalization strategy.

The eclectic paradigm presupposes that different firms have broadly similar objectives and respond to economic signals both consistently and following the same strategic direction. The model ignores the fact that a firm can also utilize different market entry modes (e. g. export and license) depending on its diversified businesses in the same foreign target country (Robock and Simmonds, 1989: 48).

The eclectic paradigm rather is suitable when considering circumstances in manufacturing industries instead of in internet-based service businesses. Due to the influence of the transaction cost theory, the eclectic paradigm assumes a rationally thinking actor who makes decisions mainly based on cost calculations. On the one hand, transaction costs are difficult to specify and quantify. On the other hand, the assumption of rational thinking is hard to accept fully when it comes to behavioral aspects, such as preferences or aversions of the management, which also influence market entry decisions. The strategic concept concerning foreign market entry is not mandatory based on the pure rational trade-off of logical circumstances but usually influenced by the founding entrepreneur and/or the operating management and their individual experiences in terms of a particular target market.

Chapter review questions

1. Considering the eclectic paradigm, describe when a firm's management should arrange its foreign market entry through exports.
2. Summarize what kind of 'market imperfections' are discussed in the transaction cost theory. Identity linkages between the 'phenomena of market imperfections' and the 'internalization advantage category' as defined in the eclectic paradigm.
3. Summarize in your own words why foreign direct investments are recommended according to the eclectic paradigm when ownership, location, and internalization advantages are available?

2.5 The Uppsala Model of Internationalization

2.5.1 Incremental market entry through accumulated knowledge

During the mid-1960s, Carlson, one of the pioneers of internationalization process theories, argued that firms pass cultural barriers when entering foreign markets. With increasing experience in foreign operations, the enterprise is willing to enter one market after another (Carlson, 1966: 15). Firms handle the risk problem through an incremental decision-making process, where information acquired in one phase is used in the next phase to take further steps. Through this incremental behavior, the organization can maintain control over its foreign activities and gradually build up its knowledge of how to conduct business in diversified foreign markets (Carlson, 1966: 15; Forsgren, 2002: 258).

Based on the empirical observations of Swedish pharmaceutical, car, steel, pulp, and paper firms, Johanson and Vahlne (1977, 1990) further developed the ideas of Carlson and introduced the gradual internationalization theory. Their research results, in connection with articles from other scholars at the University of Uppsala concerning the internationalization processes of firms (compare: Carlson, 1975; Forsgren & Johanson, 1975; Johanson & Wiedersheim, 1975), later became known as the 'Uppsala internationalization model' (Björkman & Forsgren, 2000: 11). The Uppsala approach assumes that enterprises, due to a lack of foreign market knowledge, which is connected to corresponding market uncertainty, follow an incremental internationalization chain pattern.

Incremental internationalization pattern

At the start, there is no regular export. Business is concentrated in the home market. Then export begins via independent representatives (agents), later through sales subsidiary, and eventually foreign manufacturing may follow at the end (Johanson & Vahlne, 1977: 24)

Lack of knowledge, due to differences between countries with regard to language and culture, is an important obstacle when making decisions connected with the development of international business activities. As a consequence, another pattern can be derived: firms prefer entering new markets with lower psychic distance. Psychic distance is defined in terms of factors such as differences in language, culture, political systems, and others that disturb the flow of information between the firm and the market. Thus, firms start internationalization by going to those markets with somewhat lower geographical distance, which they can better understand and where the perceived market uncertainty is relatively low (Johanson & Vahlne, 1977: 23–26; 1990: 13).

In their incremental internationalization model, Johanson and Vahlne (1977: 30) distinguish between the *state aspects* (market commitment and market knowledge) and the *change aspects* (current activities and commitment decisions).

(1) *State aspect/market commitment:* the degree of commitment is higher the more the resources are integrated and the more their value is derived from these activities. Vertical integration means a higher degree of commitment than a conglomerate foreign investment. An example of resources that cannot easily be directed to another market is a marketing and sales organization with country-specific product modifications and service with highly integrated customer relations. The more specialized the resources are to the specific market, the greater is the degree of commitment.

(2) *State aspect/market knowledge:* structure of competition, supplier and customer characteristics, and cultural aspects belong to market-specific knowledge, which can be gained only through experience during operation in the foreign market. Experiential knowledge, which is associated with particular conditions in the market in question, cannot be transferred to other individuals or markets. It

can be considered a unique resource. The more valuable the resource for the firm, the stronger is the commitment to the market.

(3) *Change aspect/current business activities:* for instance, marketing and sales activities belong to running firm operations. The higher the investments in advertising in a foreign market, the more technologically sophisticated and differentiated the product, the larger the total commitment as a consequence of current activities.

(4) *Change aspect/commitment decisions:* enterprise decisions to commit resources (i.e., financial, human workforce, and advertisement) to foreign markets depend on a firm's general business experience as well as market-specific experience. Additional commitments are made in small steps unless the firms have very large resources and/or market conditions are stable and homogeneous or the firm has more of its experience from other markets with similar conditions. Further market experience leads to a stepwise increase of the operations and of the integration with the foreign market environment, thus resulting in higher market commitment (Johanson & Vahlne, 1977: 29).

The internationalization process of a firm was similarly described by Luostarinen (1980) as a stepwise and orderly utilization of outward-going international business operations (compare Figure 14). The incremental and orderly geographical expansion from countries with close business distance to more distant markets causes an increasing dependence on marketing, purchasing, production, finance, the human resources department, and other functions of the company in international markets. Physical distance represents a restricting force to the flow of information and disfavors countries located farther away as a target market (Luostarinen, 1980: 129, 200 – 201).

Market uncertainty in international business is related to knowledge. Learning is a process of accumulating knowledge either through access to information or business experience. The introduction of the concept of organizational learning represents a dynamic process where firms seek experiential knowledge about individual clients and markets, as well as about institutional factors, such as how to deal with local laws, governments, and cultures. Information is accumulated through activities and presence in foreign markets, which increases costs. These costs arise in the process of collecting, encoding, transferring, and decoding knowledge, as well as changing the resource structures, processes, and routines in the organization. Thus, knowledge plays a crucial role in strategic international business decision-making (Eriksson, Johanson, Maikgard, & Sharma, 1997: 352; Luostarinen, 1980: 48–49).

Internationalization is a process that is difficult to plan well in advance. Organizational structures and routines are built gradually as a consequence of learning: first, a firm's internal capabilities and competence (e.g., language qualifications of employees) and second, foreign market requirements (e.g., process quality consciousness and service expectations). In this process, understanding the history of the firm is important. Sporadic interaction with actors in foreign markets provides little experience. The more the firm pursues durable and repetitive linkage with ex-

Assumptions

Psychic distance
Disturbance in flow of information because of

- language
- culture, attitudes, religion
- geographical locations
- political systems

Results in

Lack of foreign market knowledge

Recommendation

Experiential self-learning

Two paths to market entry

Incremental internationalization process

- no export

  ↓

- indirect export

  ↓

- export

  ↓

- sales subsidiary

  ↓

- foreign direct investment

- start business in markets with lower geographical distance

  ↓

- expand business towards markets with higher geographical distance

Figure 14. Two major internationalization process paths according to the Uppsala model

ternal participants abroad, the better the basis for the improvement of internal organizational routines and procedures (Eriksson et al., 1997: 354).

2.5.2 Review of the Uppsala model

According to the Uppsala approach, firms internationalize incrementally from physically and culturally close foreign business markets to more distant countries. During the internationalization process, the firm gains experience that forms the basis for further foreign activities in countries that are located even farther away from the home market. The organizational learning process through accumulated experiential knowledge and through ongoing activities is very important for the firm and its successful international business expansion. How the organizations learn and how their learning affects their organizational behavior are the crucial elements of the Uppsala concept. The more market knowledge the firm acquires through its own experience, the less is the perceived risk and the higher is the propensity for foreign market entry.

During the last decades, the Uppsala model became one of the most cited, discussed, and criticized models in the international business literature (Barkema & Drogendijk, 2007: 1132; Hadjikhani, 1997: 47). It is claimed that the model is too deterministic because it considers Swedish firms only, and research is grounded on a relatively small number of firm cases. In modern international business, firms are less inclined to repeat the value chain in each country, reconfiguring it instead globally in terms of where revenues are high or costs are low. The model tends to ignore the fact that a firm also faces a risk by not entering a foreign market – the risk of not participating in an up-coming industry cluster of supplier and customer networks where the firm's competitors are looking for their chance for business (Forsgren, 2002: 258, 260).

The Uppsala model narrowly focuses on 'knowledge' and 'learning' as major influencing factors for market entry decisions and business performance in the course of the internationalization process (Dunning, 2000: 184). There is a tendency toward shorter product life-cycles and faster knowledge transfer due to improved communication and information technologies. The contents and information value of the model are largely restricted to the initial stages of internationalization processes and have a rather reactive character, leaving little room for entrepreneurial strategic choice (Autio, Sapienza, & Almeida, 2000: 909).

Recent research findings concerning the phenomenon of new venture firms indicate that firms show a more rapid pace of internationalization; and, contrary to Johanson and Vahlne's panel of Swedish enterprises, smaller rather than larger firms make large internationalization steps in a shorter period of time (Hashai & Almor, 2004: 479). International new venture firms from their firm inception tend to disregard domestic markets in favor of the international marketplace, which seems to be more attractive (Young, Dimitratos, & Dana, 2003: 34). These firms make use of existing business relations in globally knit networks. Instead of focusing on 'self-learning', knowledge about foreign markets can be acquired through relationships and interaction with other market actors. The prediction of the Uppsala concepts that internationalization is always a one-directional process cannot be confirmed. Firms have the opportunity to recall their foreign engagement if the performance in particular markets is below their expectations (Forsgren, 2002: 264). Technological and product life-cycles have shortened compared to the past. Thus, an incremental and rather slow international market entry involves the risk that investments are not amortized because technologically advanced products are just around the corner.

Furthermore, psychic distance is perceived differently by operating managers in international business. People develop subjective mental maps of space (e. g., foreign geographical location) and distance (e. g., culture and language) that need not necessarily correspond to reality. Therefore, it is hard to assume that international business performance naturally correlates with the degree (which is difficult to measure) of psychic distance (Stöttinger & Schlegelmilch, 2000: 170–172).

Accumulated internationalization knowledge that affects both business knowledge and institutional knowledge is not limited to specific country markets. Organization-specific experience in foreign business can be used in all markets (Eriksson et al., 1997: 353). Therefore, Björkman and Forsgren (2000: 12) argue that the model is less valid for very large multinational enterprises and firms with extensive international experience in high-technology industries. The Uppsala approach focuses on manufacturing products where production takes place in the domestic market, and the goods are sold at arm's length in overseas markets. Therefore, the business activities of many small firms in the service industry, where manufacture and delivery are inseparable, do not fit into the export-based Uppsala model for the process of internationalization (Jones, 2001: 192).

The Uppsala internationalization theory has been further criticized for its tendency to ignore or de-emphasize strategy as the evolutionary development of an existing state rather than the result of explicit economic analysis and decision making (Jones & Coviello, 2002: 8). The concept concentrates on experiential learning through commitment decisions and business activities abroad. However, the model is not able to accept the possibility of imitative learning, i.e., monitoring other firms acting in a similar way and assimilating from them. Firms are occasionally forced to follow the client when they enter foreign markets. An organization can also look for radically new alternatives alongside current business modes and decide market entry according to the forecasted market opportunities and not according to its current level of foreign business experience. Thus, the possible internationalization routes are more multifaceted than anticipated in the Uppsala model (Forsgren, 2002: 260, 274).

Several decades after publishing the Uppsala concept in the academic literature, Johanson and Vahlne concluded that firm behaviors and economic and regulatory environments have changed considerably or did not exist when the Uppsala model was published (Johanson & Vahlne, 2003: 92). Markets and industries have become increasingly integrated worldwide. Internationalization processes are characterized by networks of relationships in which firms are linked to each other in various complex patterns. Instead of focusing on a single firm's progress in 'self-learning' and 'knowledge accumulation' as recommended in Uppsala, internationalization processes should be seen from a business network perspective of the environment faced by an internationalizing firm (Johanson & Vahlne, 2009: 1411). The network theory of internationalization is introduced and explained in the next section of this book.

Chapter review questions

1. Describe the meaning of the terms 'knowledge' and 'learning' and relate them to the internationalization process paths of the Uppsala concept.
2. What makes the Uppsala concept different from other internationalization concepts?
3. List conceptual weaknesses of the Uppsala model.

2.6 Network Theory of Internationalization

2.6.1 Inter-organizational relationships

In general, a network is a model or metaphor that describes a number of entities that are connected (Axelsson & Easton, 1992: XIV). In the case of international industrial networks, the entities are actors involved in the economic process that converts resources into finished goods and services. The network model is based on the assumption that a firm's changing internationalization situation is a result of its positioning in a network of firms and their connections to each other (Zuchella & Scabini, 2007: 48). The market is depicted as systems of social and industrial relationships among various parties. The network concept encompasses a firm's set of relationships, both horizontal and vertical, with other entities, such as system and component suppliers, manufacturers, merchandisers, customers, and competitors, and includes relationships across industries and countries (Gulati, Nohria, & Zaheer, 2000: 203; Windeler, 2005: 215). By entering global networks, firms gain international knowledge through learning from other network actors, which assumes the establishment, development, and protection of international business relations (Håkansson & Johanson, 2001: 9; Mathews, 2002: 208; Samiee, 2008: 4).

Learning through relationships

Internationalization is a process of increasing involvement in international operations, which results in an accumulation of knowledge about markets and institutions abroad (Ellis, 2000: 443; Welch & Luostarinen, 1988: 36). Modern internationalization processes are particularly characterized as a course of learning through network relationships (Sharma & Blomstermo, 2003: 739–740, 750).

The network perspective draws attention to long-term business activities that exist among firms such as suppliers and customers in industrial markets. While the traditional Uppsala approach focuses on the circumstances and internationalization process of the individual firm, the network theory pays attention to the firm's interconnections with local and foreign units (Björkman & Forsgren, 2000: 13; Zuchella & Scabini, 2007: 48). Through its 'combinative capability', a firm exploits knowledge (collected in industry networks) for expansion into new markets. Thus, the efficient organization of knowledge transfer among the firm units is of vital importance for business performance (Kogut & Zander, 1993: 636; Zuchella & Scabini, 2007: 52).

Networks among buyers and sellers, which form the basis of effective communication, have to be established, thus providing firms with the opportunity and motivation to internationalize. Relevant information disseminates via social interaction (Ellis, 2000: 447). The nature of relationships influences the strategic decisions of the participating firms (Coviello & Munro, 1997: 365). Relationship-based strategies for market entry range from long-term oriented licensing agreements and contract manufacturing to international joint ventures with two or more partners (Mathews, 2002: 207–208).

2.6.1.1 The impact of the resource-based view

The resource-based view (RBV) holds that a firm acquires competitive characteristics not simply as a function of its market location, such as its position in the value chain within a certain industry (compare: Penrose, 1959). Competitive advantages are particularly derived from a firm's 'inner resources' (e. g., managerial, organizational, technological resources, etc.) as well as from the firm's capacity to absorb and integrate 'external resources' through relationships (Fahy, 2002: 62; Mathews, 2002: 222; Wernerfelt, 1984: 171).

According to Barney (1991: 105–106), a firm's resources should have the following attributes to gain sustained competitive advantage.

How to gain competitive advantage according to the resource-based view

-   The first attribute is resource value. Resources are valuable when they enable a firm to conceive of or implement strategies that improve efficiency and effectiveness.
-   Second, resources need to be rare, which means that current and potential competitors cannot rely simultaneously on them. A firm enjoys a competitive advantage when it is implementing a value-creating strategy that cannot be implemented by a large number of competitors that have limited access to the necessary resources (e. g., technological knowledge).
-   Third, sustained competitive advantage can be reached if valuable resources can only be imperfectly imitated by competitors.
-   Finally, rare and valuable resources cannot be substituted by competitors who are able to implement strategically equivalent resources (Barney, 1991: 105–106).

Consequently, the assumption that more knowledge would be likely to improve the efficiency and profitability of the firm acts as an incentive to acquire new knowledge and shape the scope and direction in the firm's search for knowledge inside and outside its own organization (Penrose, 1995: 77). Based on the foundations of the RBV, Grant (2000: 117) argues that the fundamental prerequisite for market power is the presence of market entry barriers based upon a firm's resources in the market, as for example scale economies, patents, international experience advantages, and brand reputation. The ability to establish a cost advantage requires possession of scale-efficient plants, superior process technology, ownership of low-cost sources of raw materials, or access to low-wage labor. Differentiation advantage is conferred by superior quality and innovative products linked with proprietary technology or an extensive sales and service network.

The RBV perceives the firm as a unique bundle of idiosyncratic resources and capabilities where the primary task of management is to maximize value through the optimal deployment of existing resources and capabilities. In line with RBV, particular fostering of the knowledge resource is of vital importance in order for the firm to gain competitive advantage. Grant (1996: 111) describes 'knowing how' as 'tacit knowledge' and 'knowing about facts and theories' as 'explicit knowledge'. The critical distinction between the two lies in transferability and the mechanisms for transfer across individuals, space, and time. Explicit knowledge is revealed by its communication and tacit knowledge through application. Communication efficiency is a fundamental resource property, thus an important strength of the firm. At both individual and organizational levels, knowledge absorption depends upon a recipient's ability to add new knowledge to existing knowledge (Grant, 1996: 111).

Knowledge transferability is important, not only between firms such as suppliers and customers, but even more critically, within the firm. Consequently, the creation of tacit knowledge and the ability to transfer it effectively within the organization, which includes its foreign operations, should move into the focus of management. Transmission capacity is defined as the ability of a firm (or the relevant business unit within it) to articulate uses of its own knowledge, assess the needs and capabilities of the potential recipient thereof, and transmit knowledge in a way that allows it to be used in another location of the firm's organization at home or abroad (Martin & Salomon, 2003: 363). The resource interaction in the coupling and matching of internal and external network processes affects knowledge transfer efficiency and, finally, has a vital impact on the firm's overall business performance (Gadde, Hjelmgren, & Skarp, 2012: 215).

A firm's industry network engagements, initiated in order to better manage resource assets, come along with advantages and also with potential risks. Knowledge and experience serve as the most valuable firm resources. Protection of these resources from imitation by securing intellectual property rights (e.g., patents, copyrights, and trademarks) is of interest but, naturally, has limits. The choice of market entry mode affects the protection of strategic knowledge. For example, a wholly owned subsidiary provides better prerequisites for knowledge safekeeping than an international joint venture (Martin & Salomon, 2003: 368). Why? In a joint venture, knowledge is shared with the partner firms (e.g., manufacturing process know-how). Consequently, through the process of learning and imitating, the joint venture partner firm may eventually become a competitor. Protection of intellectual property is always a challenge, and the key is to be faster than the competition if a leading technology firm wants to keep its competitors at bay. Innovators with advanced technological and managerial knowledge resources have to adapt their market entry concepts carefully and intelligently and should think twice when deciding with whom in the market to form a long-term partnership, such as an international joint venture (Teece, 2000: 96).

Mathews (2002: 8) analyzed international activities, examining the cases of incumbents (firms that are already established in the worldwide market) and international latecomers (those with delayed global market entry) as examples based on the RBV. Latecomers are firms that delay their global market entry relative to the majority of their competitors. They use the benefits of their network relationships, which are a valuable resource and help them overcome market entry barriers such as limited knowledge about international markets, suppliers, and customers (Mathews, Hu, & Wu, 2011: 186). Learning from network partners allows a rapid substitution for less developed inner resources and experience; thus, international latecomers or small- and medium-sized firms can leverage advantages from the incumbents, for example through long-term partnerships. Within the global economy, international latecomers can more readily build their global operations by linking up with existing players than was possible in the past (Mathews, 2002: 8, 222).

2.6.1.2 Resources and dynamic capabilities

Innovative firms that successfully act in the global arena usually exhibit so-called dynamic capabilities to gain, reconfigure, and integrate external and internal resources in order to match current market expectations and also to create market changes for the future (Liao, Kickul, & Ma, 2009: 264). Dynamic capabilities reflect a firm's capacity to deploy resources through developing, carrying, and exchanging information, which leads to specific and identifiable processes concerning product development, international market entry, and relationship building (Lin, McDonough III, Lin, & Lin, 2012: 264). Particularly in web-based service industries, imperfectly imitable capabilities (e.g,. innovative ideas) become more important as a source of competitive advantage than conventional asset resources, such as real estate, land, and others (Erramilli, Agarwal, & Dev, 2002: 237). In stable markets where changes are predictable, dynamic capabilities rely on existing knowledge; and the learning process is limited to organizing and assembling resources as a consequence of market changes. However, because of liberalized global trade patterns, international markets have become more complex and, as a consequence, less predictable. Based on the RBV grounding, Teece et al. (1997: 515) highlights a firm's ability to achieve new forms of competitive advantage, necessary in turbulent and uncertain markets, as dynamic capabilities and mentions two key aspects related to this.

– *First,* the term 'dynamic' refers to the capacity to renew competencies so as to achieve congruence with the changing business environment. Certain innovative responses are required when time-to-market decisions are crucial, the rate of technological change is rapid, and the nature of future competition and markets is difficult to determine. All these elements are valid in order to characterize the high-technology industries and their competitive market environments.

- *Second,* the term 'capabilities' emphasizes the key role of strategic management in appropriately adapting, integrating, and reconfiguring internal and external organizational skills, resources, and functional competencies to match the requirements of a changing environment. Capability is a special type of an organizationally embedded nontransferable firm-specific resource, whose purpose is to improve the productivity of the other resources possessed by the firm (Makadok, 2001: 389; Teece et al., 1997: 515).

Successful players in the global marketplace are firms that can demonstrate timely responsiveness and rapid and flexible product innovation coupled with the management capability to effectively coordinate and redeploy internal and external competencies. Management activity cannot lead to the immediate replication of unique organizational skills through simply entering a market and piecing the parts together overnight. Replication takes time, and the replication of best practices always may be illusive. The potentials for firm capabilities are understood in terms of organization structures and managerial processes that support productive activity (Teece et al., 1997: 515, 517). Dynamic markets force firms to react, within the shortest possible time period, to changing business situations and so to renew competencies in order to respond innovatively in the market (Eisenhardt & Martin, 2000: 1107; Zuchella & Scabini, 2007: 87– 88).

2.6.1.3 The case study of Sony: Resources reshuffled – dynamic capabilities disappeared?

2.6.1.3.1 Company origins (the period from 1945 until the 1980s)

In September 1945, a thirty-eight-year-old engineer named Masaru Ibuka, with about twenty employees and USD 1,600 of his personal savings, established a telecommunication engineering firm, Tokyo Tsushin Kogyo K.K. Another engineer by the name of Akio Morita soon joined the team. At the beginning, the company considered producing everything from electric rice steamers to miniature golf equipment. However, the company was never able to make a steamer that worked properly, so Ibuka and Morita decided to manufacture sound-recording devices instead (Frisch, 2004: 4–6).

Tape recorders had been developed in Germany in the 1930s by Grundig and Telefunken. In the United States after 1945, Ampex led the market in developing and manufacturing tape recorders. At that time, Matsushita, Hitachi, and Toshiba, the largest Japanese electronics manufacturers, were developing their first semiconductors under the technical license of Radio Corporation of America (RCA). In 1952, the business focus of Ibuka shifted from magnetic tape recorders to transistors. He learned that Western Electric, the parent company of Bell Laboratories, where semiconductors had been discovered in 1948, was offering a technical license for manufacturing transistors in return for a royalty. The agreement stipulated a USD 25,000 advance payment against royalties (Nathan, 1999: 27–31).

The company began using the Sony trademark on its products beginning with the TR-55 transistor radio in 1955. In the late 1950s, Sony expanded its consumer use manufacturing portfolio to microphones, cassette-tape players, and television apparatuses. In 1957, the company introduced the world's smallest transistor radio with built-in speakers. By January 1958, the firm had grown to 500 employees and was worth more than USD 100 million and officially changed its name to Sony Corporation (Frisch, 2004: 10–11; Nathan, 1999: 53). In 1960, Sony's engineering team introduced the world's first transistor television.

Japanese firms are well known for their complex network of interlinked companies (keiretsu). A classic keiretsu consists of a bank, a trading company (sogo shosha), and various manufacturing companies. Besides this horizontal network of associated business groups, there are vertically connected manufacturing firms at the core and suppliers at the periphery. These networks of companies represent a 'network of knowledge', which aims to make the core company independent from outsiders such as banks and invulnerable to competition (Chang, 1995: 391; Imai, 1987: 32–35). Following the philosophy of 'keiretsu organization', Sony began to expand its business fields in the 1960s. For example, Sony founded Sony Enterprise Co. Ltd. in 1961 to manage the Sony Building in Ginza. Over the next years, Sony Enterprise added Sony Plaza, a retail chain, to market imported goods; a French restaurant named Maxim's de Paris; Sony Travel Service, an insurance agency; and other services such as financing. Building on the theme 'not hardware but heartware for everyday life' to unite a diverse range of businesses, Sony Enterprise continued to move in new directions. Similar to a trading house, it put together a plan to import fine foreign goods and, in the mid-1970s, started to import sports equipment and fashionable luxury items. Sony was at the same time successfully exporting its consumer electronics products and expanding its overseas operations (Sony, 2008b).

Sony opened its first overseas branches in Hong Kong in 1958, in the US in 1959, and in Zurich, Switzerland, in 1960. Most of Sony's entrances into new areas of business were through international joint ventures with foreign companies. One of the first international joint venture operations involved products connected to Sony's core electronics business. In March 1965, Sony and Tektronix, Inc., of the US formed Sony-Tektronix Corporation in Japan with equal start-up capital from each company. At the time, it was highly unusual for a foreign company to have more than a 49 percent share in a joint venture with a Japanese company. Tektronix was a well-known instrumentation and measuring equipment manufacturer, commanding over 80 percent of the global market for oscilloscopes. The international joint venture expanded its operations into new fields, including the further development of electronic measuring instruments, graphic displays, broadcast equipment, and optical devices. With such a variety of products, Sony-Tektronix was able to meet the needs of a wide range of customers. Interestingly, in 1966, Sony signed a contract with IBM aimed at cooperation on production of magnetic computer tapes, which, however, turned out to be rather unsuccessful (Sony, 2008b).

Until the 1970s, Sony mainly relied on domestic battery suppliers for its transistor radios, transistor televisions, and tape recorders. But the demand for batteries was growing as Sony focused manufacturing on portable consumer electronics. If Sony had its own battery manufacturing facility, the company could not only meet its own requirements but also tap into the rapidly growing market for small batteries used in cameras, watches, and calculators. Therefore, Ibuka and Morita wanted to have their own battery manufacturing facilities. In February 1975, Sony and the Union Carbide Corporation (UCC) of the US established a battery manufacturing and marketing joint venture called Sony-Eveready Inc. UCC manufactured and marketed batteries under the Eveready brand name, was the largest producer of batteries in the world, and wanted to do business in Japan. An equal amount of the initial capital was provided by both parties, and Morita was appointed president. The international joint venture began importing dry cell batteries from the United States and marketing them under the Sony-Eveready name in Japan (Sony, 2008c). From today's perspective, using products such as smart phones and electric cars as examples, Sony was ahead of its time when the company entered the battery manufacturing business within its consumer electronics core business in the 1970s. Unfortunately, Sony did not focus very much on the further development of the battery business and, instead, searched for other businesses in order to achieve additional diversification.

2.6.1.3.2 Diversification towards movie and entertainment

In the late 1980s, Sony diversified away from its core competencies in consumer electronics and entered the movie, music, and entertainment industry. In January 1988, it bought CBS Records. In November 1989, Sony purchased Colombia Pictures Entertainment, one of the biggest motion-picture companies in the world, and integrated it into the company in new business units called Sony Music Entertainment and Sony Pictures Entertainment. These two major acquisitions generated mixed media coverage throughout the United States and Japan (Sony, 2008b). In 1995, a new Sony division called Sony Computer Entertainment launched a home video game system and the play station (Frisch, 2004: 19, 25, 31).

Entering these fields reflected Morita's ambitions for the entertainment business and his naturally close relations with the US market, which had been developed over decades ever since Sony's foundation. Moreover, Morita intended to serve the entire value chain by combining the making of and watching of movies with Sony's hardware (e.g., camera, studio equipment, audio, video, and televisions sets). However, resource allocations toward unfamiliar segments such as the movie and music business caused a weakening position in electronics, the core business of the Japanese firm. In order to develop its new diversified business fields, Sony started to reroute its financial, research and development, and human resources away from the firm's technological and innovative resource competencies in electronics.

Over the years, Sony became involved in diversified business fields such as electronics; game pictures; financial service; music; movies; banking; life insurance; and, recently, medical/healthcare. The current organizational structure reflecting the diversified business of Sony (status 2015) is illustrated in Figure 15 below.

2.6.1.3.3 Loss of core competencies in electronics

Recall that in 1968, Sony introduced the Trinitron television technology, with superior color and brightness performance relative to its competitors (Frisch, 2004: 12–13). The transistor radio and the Trinitron television technology were state-of-the-art and led the worldwide markets and, thus, supported the successful growth of Sony until the 1980s. During this time, Sony continuously increased its in-house supply network up to about seventy-five manufacturing plants. The firm's 'optimization sharing plan' enhanced supply chain innovation. This helped Sony achieve an efficient supply chain management system within and across its units, which incorporated upstream suppliers and downstream distributors and retailers within the organization (Samiee, 2008: 4). The introduction of the Walkman in 1979 further boosted the reputation of Sony as the driving pioneer in the consumer electronics industry, which contributed at the same time to the overall vitality and strength of the firm.

Sony kept major know-how and expertise with respect to its electronics technology inside the company. Sony neither agreed to further joint ventures with other firms – for example, those operating in the television set industry – nor purchased major components such as displays from suppliers outside Sony's group periphery. This firm culture gave Sony an invulnerable, independent, 'going alone' reputation in the electronics industry but, simultaneously, created the risk of making the firm blind to emerging technological innovation outside its organization. And soon Sony would need to pay the bill.

In the 1990s, Sony's management failed to recognize new, upcoming trends in consumer electronics, such as flat panel technologies. This went along with unsuccessful developments in other business operations when, for example, Sony failed

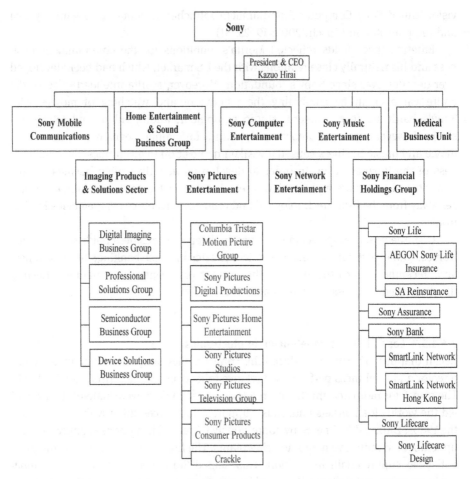

Figure 15. Organization [status 2015] of Sony Group. Source: Author based on annual reports and company information (Sony, 2012c, 2015; Sony_Financial_Holdings, 2014; Sony_Pictures, 2014)

against competitors at setting the technological industry standards for several electronic systems, such as the Betamax-Video, the Multimedia-Compact-Disc, and the Atrac MP-3 format. Further joint research and development activities concerning the multimedia disc with Philips started in 1979 and were renewed in 1992 (joint development towards the introduction of a DVD industry standard). Unfortunately, the Sony and Philips partnership failed against the high-definition DVD of the rival alliance of Toshiba; Hitachi; Pioneer; JVC; Thomson; Mitsubishi Electric; and, later, Panasonic, which had supported Sony at the beginning of the technological battle (Sony, 2008b; WeltOnline, 2008).

In 2008, there were some bright spots when Sony, with its Blu-ray Disc™ technology, succeeded in the competition against its Japanese rival Toshiba, which was the leading firm in developing the high definition DVD standard (Sony,

2008b; WeltOnline, 2008). However, the hardware-based Blu-ray disc business performed below expectations. At the initial stage of its market launch, customers hesitated to switch their movie collection from DVD to Blu-ray. A couple of years later, emerging Internet-based movie streaming technologies invited new players such as Amazon, Netflix, and others and limited the Blu-ray disc sales to a considerable extent. Technology and product life cycles in consumer electronics became significantly shorter compared to the 1970s and 1980s, as Sony's management realized to their regret.

In recent years, Sony has tried to regain competitive strength as a technological leader in the electronics industry by concentrating on the next flat panel generation technology, called *organic light emitting diode* (OLED) technology. OLED displays have been supposed to replace LCD/LED soon, thus driving the flat-panel TV business in the future. In 2008, Sony was the first company to launch commercially available OLED TVs (11-inch, 960x540-pixel, model XEL-1), which were selling in limited quantities for about USD 1700 in Japan and USD 2500 in the US. Sony developed the OLED technology mainly by itself (DisplaySearch, 2008b). However, Sony's main competitors, such as Samsung, LG Electronics, Panasonic, and others, were not sleeping and further improved the LCD/LED technologies utilized in their television sets. As result, the so-called 4 K technology was launched for LCD/LED television sets, which caused Sony to announce in 2015 (seven years after the XEL-1 was introduced) that the company would further delay sales plans for serial production of large quantities of its OLED TVs. Instead, Sony would concentrate as well on the 4 K technology for the time being (Cox, 2015). Another drawback for Sony's Blu-ray business is the fact that 4 K technology indicates an advanced 4096x2160 pixel display solution, while Blu-ray only reaches 1920 x 1080 pixels.

One of Sony's biggest mistakes was that it was delayed too much, relative to its competitors such as Sharp and Samsung, in the building of its own LCD module assembly lines. The LCD module contributes around 70 percent to the television set value-added activities. Thus, naturally, the question arises, how will Sony manage to reset in the television set (LCD) industry?

2.6.1.3.4 Access to LCD technology through inter-organizational relationships

The lack of LCD manufacturing capacities led Sony to establish a joint venture called S-LCD Corporation with its South Korean rival Samsung (Ihlwan, 2006). In 2004, the final contract was signed to establish a seventh generation LCD panel joint production line at Tangjeong, Chung Cheong Nam-Do, South Korea (Sony, 2006c). Through the international joint venture with the well-branded television set manufacturer Sony, Samsung, for its part, could increase its marketing, sales, and distribution assets and balance the investment risk in LCD module manufacturing. The international joint venture formed the common supply basis to provide LCD modules to Sony Corporation and Samsung Electronics, which, at the same time, are competitors in the final industry stage of LCD television sets. A dilemma?

At the beginning of the joint venture operations with Samsung, Sony had concerns about quality. The company not only dispatched its own engineers to the joint venture to vet LCD displays it also insisted that every panel it used should be shipped through its LCD-TV factory in Inazawa, near Nagoya, Japan. There the panels went through another rigorous quality check before electronics components, such as digital tuners, power units, and other parts, were added. At the end of that quality check procedure, approved displays were assembled into television sets or shipped off as modules to Sony's assembly plants in Spain and Mexico (Ihlwan, 2006). After the initial period of joint venture operations, manufactured panels were shipped directly from S-LCD to the assembly plants of Sony without a double inspection.

Sony confirmed that the joint venture has been instrumental in the company's introduction of the successful Bravia LCD TV line up. At the same time, Samsung's own LCD television set business has made considerable progress. The South Korean Cheabol has emerged as a trend-setter in the LCD panel industry, aided by Sony expertise that has helped ensure high-quality display performance. 'The Sony-Samsung alliance is certainly a win-win', declared Lee Sang Wan, president of Samsung's LCD unit. Sony's executive deputy-president, Katsumi Ihara, who had led Sony's television set division and then was appointed to oversee key consumer-electronics product lines, also credited the alliance with helping to revive the company's LCD television set business fortunes (Ihlwan, 2006). In July 2006, Sony and Samsung announced they would expand their cooperation towards an eighth generation amorphous LCD panel production line (Sony, 2006b, c).

Surprisingly, only two years later, Sony reviewed its ambitious relationship with Samsung and announced plans for a new alliance partner, Sharp Corporation of Japan. 'This is a major step toward attaining our goal of becoming the top TV manufacturer worldwide', proclaimed Ryoji Chubachi, president of Sony Corporation of Japan, at the start of the press conference in April 2008. Through the joint manufacturing facilities at Sharp's Sakai factory, the first tenth-generation plant in the world, Sony thought it would be able to take advantage of higher assembly efficiency and achieve price superiority over its main competitors, such as Samsung Electronics (Otani, 2008). Sony's new joint venture ambitions with Sharp not only influenced Samsung, Sony's previous panel investment partner, but also Taiwanese panel makers such as AU Optronics, which also has supplied large numbers of LCD panels to Sony (DisplaySearch, 2008a).

What is the truth behind the sudden joint venture termination with Samsung? Over the years, Sony became engaged in severe competition in LCD TVs with Samsung Electronics in the leading worldwide markets, utilizing their common supply of LCD displays created through the joint venture. Outside the European and North American markets, Samsung Electronics often holds a larger share than Sony, such as in promising markets in the newly emerging economies of Brazil, Russia, India, and China. According to Torii Hisakazu, vice president of Display Search market research institute, 'No matter what market Sony might decide to go after, Samsung Electronics is always its biggest competitor' (Otani, 2008).

Additionally, Sony has lacked any real way to differentiate its products from those of Samsung Electronics. One of the main reasons has been the common LCD panel. Sony and Samsung use LCD panels of the same dimension, produced with the same efficiency, and manufactured by the joint venture S- LCD Corporation, located in South Korea. Thus, both firms use panels with similar cost structures. Naturally, Sony injects its own technology in the form of backlights and other components when it comes to building the panels into modules, thus creating Sony panels. Even so, as long as Sony and Samsung Electronics use the same basic panels, it is difficult to end up with any real difference in price, according to Chubachi, Sony Corporation's president (Otani, 2008).

2.6.1.3.5 Market entry strategies for Europe as part of a global value chain

In Europe, Sony operated two wholly owned production facilities for the manufacture of LCD television sets, which were located in Barcelona, Spain, and in Trnava, Slovakia (Sony, 2006c). The Spanish subsidiary was established in 1973 (EU_Japan, 2010). In order to meet the rapidly increasing demand for LCD TVs in Europe since 2005/2006, Sony decided to construct a new factory in Nitra, Slovakia, located 40 kilometers east of Trnava. Sony has been producing TV sets there since February 2006. At that time, Sony developed ambitious plans to regain competitive strengths in the television set business, among other business segments, through expanding their European market presence. Sony opened a new LCD TV manufacturing plant in Nitra (Slovakia) in 2007, one of the largest state-of-the art plants worldwide (Sony, 2007b, 2013a).

In August 2007, the Nitra site began producing a limited number of Bravia LCD TVs, followed by successful serial production starting in October 2007. Sony invested EUR 73 million in the brand new factory, which serves as a typical example of a greenfield investment. Production lines that had operated in the Trnava factory were scheduled to be relocated to the Nitra factory in 2008. By the end of 2008, the Nitra plant had a production capacity of three million LCD TVs per year and around 3,000 employees. Following the relocation of the LCD TV production lines to Nitra, the Trnava factory continued producing tuners for Bravia LCD TVs and providing technical support for Playstation computer game devices. After the transfer from Trnava to Nitra, Sony continued to run its LCD TV assembly in Barcelona, Spain, along with Nitra, Slovakia (Sony, 2007, Sony, 2008d).

The Barcelona factory was supposed to serve as a nearby manufacturing base for western European markets, while Nitra, due to its geographical location, could focus on central and eastern European markets. The Barcelona site also operated as the European technology center for Sony's LCD TV assembly. The Nitra factory would make use of its state-of-the-art equipment to concentrate mainly on large-size, high-end Bravia LCD sets for the common European market (Sony, 2006c). As Katsumi Ihara, corporate executive officer of Sony Corporation, commented, 'Following our ten-year experience producing television sets in Trnava, Slovakia, we are very pleased to officially announce the foundation of a brand new factory in Nitra. This will allow us to expand our LCD television set business in Europe. We are convinced that the new plant will have an outstanding importance with regards to market penetration of Sony's superior technology and design performance. We seek to develop Sony's Bravia brand to become the leading LCD television set brand in Europe' (Sony, 2006c).

With regards to procurement flexibility and transportation cost economics for component supply in Europe, Sony's joint venture with Sharp made sense. At that time, the major LCD panel assembly lines of Sony's previous partner, Samsung, were located in Asia (Sony, 2006b). Thus, these transportation-sensitive electronic LCD modules needed to be shipped and imported to Europe, which causes time delays and costs. Sony's new LCD manufacturing partner, Sharp, was able to deliver its LCDs from Torun, Poland (Sharp, 2008a). The modules produced at Sharp in Poland could be delivered in less than one day to Nitra, Slovakia. Both Japanese firms make use of the expanded common European market, which profits from the cessation of country border controls. The future was supposed to be bright, but something went wrong.

The LCD market in Europe became saturated in 2008; and, within a very short time, Sony's management realized that its LCD television set business performed far less well than expected (Sony, 2008f). In parallel, the entertainment business (movies and music) did not develop as successfully as planned, which further weakened the firm's overall business performance. Net sales stagnated and went down. The analysis of net income (loss) presented in the figure below underlines Sony's worsening situation. The data indicate, for example, for 2009 (loss of USD 1.1 billion), 2010 (loss of USD 0.492), 2011 (loss of USD 3.13 billion), and 2012 (loss of USD 4.85 billion) (Sony, 2014; Sony_Financial_Holdings, 2014).

Concerning the highest loss in the firm's history, in 2012, Sony announced various reasons for the loss, such as the unfavorable impact of foreign exchange rates, the impact of the Great East Japan Earthquake, the floods in Thailand, and the deterioration in market conditions in developed countries (Jordan, 2012). The main reason for the loss, however, was the performance of Sony products in its major markets. As a former executive of Sony, Mr. Yoshiaki Sakito, commented, 'Sony makes too many models; and for none of them can the company say, this contains our best, most cutting-edge technology. Apple, on the other hand, makes one amazing phone in just two colors and says, this is the best' (Tabuchi, 2012a).

Considering the fact that Sony was accumulating further losses, the management decided to reorganize its business, which came along with plans to reduce its stake in the television set business. Thus, the management started looking for investors. Finally, the Taiwanese Hon Hai Precision acquired 90 percent equity in the Nitra plant from Sony in 2010. Today, most of the television sets in the European markets are assembled by Hon Hai, based on an original equipment manufacturing (OEM) contract relationship with Sony. Nitra remains the most important production loca-

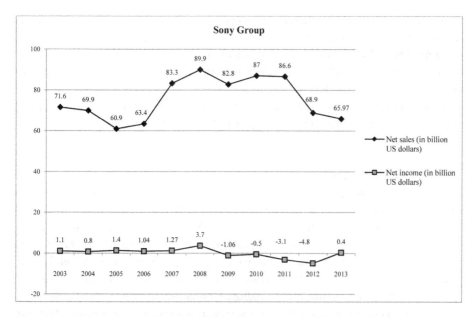

Figure 16. Net sales and net income of Sony Group for 2003 to 2013. Source: Author based on annual reports (Sony, 2004, 2005, 2006a, 2007a, 2008a, 2009, 2010, 2011, 2012a, 2013b, 2014)

tion of LCD televisions for Sony in the European region, based on its OEM relationship with Hon Hai (Hon_Hai, 2013).

In 2010, Sony Barcelona Tec was sold to a joint venture between the Spanish companies Ficosa International SA and Comsa Emte SL (EU_Japan, 2010). Finally, at the end of June 2012, Sharp and Sony announced that their joint venture relationship to produce and sell large-sized LCD panels and modules would terminate and that Sony would sell its shares (representing 7.04 percent of the issued shares) in Sharp Display Products Corporation (SDP) to SDP (Sony, 2012b).

Businesses other than LCD panel and television sets – for example, personal computers (PC) – also performed below forecasts and caused the management to try to sell them out. Consequently, in 2014, Sony officially gave up on laptops and desktops, announcing plans to sell its Vaio PC business to a Japanese investment group. The company sold 7.5 million units in 2013, and its products have been available all around the world. Sony positioned itself as a manufacturer of high-end laptops but maneuvered its products too far into high-price markets, where PC buyers are usually reluctant to go. At the same time, the Chinese Lenovo, which meanwhile has become the world's largest PC maker, has seen further growth for its PC revenues (Newman, 2014).

For decades, Sony ranked as one of the most reputable and best-known brands in the global and European consumer electronics markets. Sony was known for its unique ability to develop and manufacture all of the major components used in television sets. However, Sony missed upcoming flat panel technologies in the television set industry and also mobile handheld business because, among other reasons, it had routed too much of its resources to the movie, entertainment, and gaming business since the 1990s. As per today, it seems difficult for Sony to gain back its technological leadership position in television set manufacturing. As the Sony management experienced to their regret, product and technology life cycles have become shorter. Continued adaptation to the fast-changing technological environment has become a pivotal strategic issue for organizations' management (Wu & Wu, 2014: 543).

2.6.1.3.6 How about the future?

Entrepreneurial models in the academic literature stress the importance of a firm's founders and their influence on the strategic orientation of the enterprise and its internationalization paths (Zahra, Korri, & Yu, 2005: 21). Sony's entry into the entertainment business was to a great extent caused by the ambitions of Akio Morita, one of the firm's cofounders. Morita's affinity for the US contributed to Sony's early commitments in the American market and, despite its traditional Japanese roots, the firm's open mind set towards a multinational management philosophy. Sony's company culture and global reputation still serves as a valuable competitive advantage because it represents one of the most internationalized enterprises among Asian-based electronics firms involved in the high-technology business.

Despite Sony's difficulties against the background of increased competition worldwide, Sony has tried for a long time to maintain traditional Japanese firm values, reflected in its employee treatment philosophy, such as long-term employee relationships. In return, the firm expects unconditional loyalty from its company staff (Chen, 2004: 157–163; Frisch, 2004: 23). As a vital part of its company culture, Sony stresses the importance of human capital for the success of the firm. From executives to assembly-line workers, the philosophy of the co-founding entrepreneur, Morita, was designed to make sure that Sony employees were treated well. 'Sony has a principle of respecting and encouraging one's ability and always tries to bring out the best in a person', Morita once said. 'This is a vital force of Sony' (Frisch, 2004: 24).

However, at the end of 2008, Sony's difficulties, particularly in the electronics business, became so severe that the firm had to decide, against its traditional values, on a drastic lay-off program. Sony announced plans to cut 8,000 jobs in the midst of a financial crisis that had many consumers distancing themselves from the electronics consumer markets in order to save money. In the biggest layoff announced by an Asian firm so far in the financial crisis, the Japan-based electronics firm said it would cut about 4 percent of its 160,000 employee workforce, scale back investments, and pull out of businesses as it aimed to cut USD 1.1 billion in costs from its ailing electronics operations. 'These initiatives are in response to the sudden and rapid changes in the global economic environment', Sony stated in its press release. About 10 percent of the company's fifty-seven plants were shut down. Sony also intended to reduce its investments in the electronics sector by approximately 30 percent in the fiscal year ending March 2010. The cutbacks would save Sony more than USD 1.1 billion a year (Sony, 2008d, f).

As a result of the investment cuts, it became questionable whether and when Sony would gain back its technological leadership position in consumer electronics. At one time, the consumer electronics business helped develop Sony's valuable reputation worldwide. It can be assumed that business success or failure in the consumer electronics segment is of vital importance for the firm's future destiny. In 2012, Sony revealed that it would eliminate 10,000 additional jobs. The announcement followed a corporate realignment that demoted its once-sacred television business. Looking ahead, Sony's new chief executive, Kazuo Hirai Hirai, said Sony would focus more on games, digital imaging, and mobile products (Pham, 2012). Mobile products? This is not a new story.

Already by the second half of the 1990s, Sony had experimented in the mobile phone business but with little success. Therefore, Sony transferred its mobile phone device business to an international joint venture with the Swedish Ericsson Group in 2002 (Sony, 2008b, e). Unfortunately, the international joint venture Sony Ericsson Mobile Communications has never reached a reputation as a technological leader compared to, for example, Apple Inc. Around one decade later, in 2011, Sony took over full control of the international joint venture operation in the course of their revised company strategy to re-enter the smart-phone device business (e. g., launching a new brand series called Xperia) and connect its mobile-gadget offerings with an online network of music, videos, and games. Sony paid Euro 1.05 billion (USD 1.46 billion) in cash for Ericsson's 50 percent share in the international joint venture (Grundberg, 2011). Sony Xperia smart phones are competing against Apple's iPhone and Samsung's Galaxy. And new competitors such as Xiaomi from China are coming up.

Sony's most serious mistake was that it failed to recognize important waves of technological innovation in recent decades, such as digitalization, a shift toward software, and the importance of the Internet. One by one, every sphere where Sony competed – from hardware to software to communications to content – was turned upside-down by disruptive new technology and emerging rival competitors. With its portfolio of music and its foundation in electronics, Sony had the tools to create a version of the iPod long before Apple introduced it in 2001 (Tabuchi, 2012a).

Sony Corp.'s new chief executive, Kazuo Hirai, has vowed to turn things around, telling investors that 'Sony will change' (Pham, 2012).

Chapter review questions

1. In light of the recourse-based view, describe Sony's strengths and weaknesses after its foundation up to the 1990s and compare them to Sony's resource assets as developed during the last two decades.
2. Summarize the major reasons for Sony's current business performance.

3. From today's perspective, do you think it was rather wrong or right to enter the music and entertainment business in the 1980s?
4. Suppose you are in the shoes of Sony's current management, which business fields would you concentrate on and develop further in order to regain competitive strength in the future?

2.6.1.4 The approach of Johanson and Mattsson

Beginning in the mid-1980s, among the first to focus attention on network dynamics in the internationalization of business were Johanson and Mattsson (1985; 1988; 1992). They claimed that firms are embedded in industrial networks and linked to each other through long-lasting relationships that develop complex inter-firm information channels. As a result, the industrial system is composed of firms engaged in supply, production, distribution, and service. The authors describe this system as a *network of relationships* among the firms (Johanson & Mattsson, 1988: 290 – 291).

A firm's internationalization development is to an important extent dependent on its position in the network. Thus, the internationalization characteristics of both the firm and the market influence the process. The firm's market entry resources have different structures if the firm is highly internationalized (e. g., foreign market experience) in relationships than if it is less or not experienced at all. Furthermore, the market assets of other firms in the network have a different structure depending on whether the market has a high or low degree of internationalization. From this assumption, Johanson and Mattsson identify four categories that determine the degree of market internationalization in relation to the degree of firm internationalization. These categories are illustrated in Figure 17 below.

The *early starter* describes firms with few relationships with other enterprises abroad. Competitors, suppliers, and other firms in the domestic as well as in foreign markets have few but important international relationships. The initiative to start foreign operations comes from other parties, such as distributors or important customers located abroad.

The *lonely international* is a firm that is highly internationalized, while its market environment is not. The company has unique knowledge of cultures and institutions abroad developed through relationships in foreign markets. The firm's advanced international expertise compared to other firms gives it a favorable position with easier access to international networks. Initiatives for further internationalization are not developed by other parties in the network since the firm's suppliers, customers, and competitors are not internationalized. The lonely international has the qualifications and resources to promote internationalization for the firms that are engaged in the network. To exploit the advantages of being a 'lonely international', the firm has to coordinate activities in the different national networks, which necessarily requires international integration knowledge (Johanson & Mattsson, 1988: 300 – 302).

The *late starter* describes a firm focused on the home market and forced to internationalize by other players, such as customers or suppliers that are actively involved

		Degree of internationalization of the market	
		Low	High
Degree of internationalization of the firm	Low	The Early Starter	The Late Starter
	High	The Lonely International	The International among Others

Figure 17. Firm and market internationalization degree. Source: Johanson & Mattsson (1988: 298)

in international business (e. g., the follow-the-customer phenomenon). Comparative disadvantages for the late starter come from less international experience. On the other hand, because it is embedded in the network, the late-coming firm is able to gain access to the knowledge and international experience of other firms (Johanson & Mattsson, 1988: 302–303). The descriptions of a *late starter* are in accordance with Matthew's international *latecomer* phenomenon and its derived advantages and disadvantages for the firm in the global business arena (Mathews, 2002: 8, 222).

The fourth category is the *international among others*. In this case, both the firm and its environment are highly internationalized. Market expansion and penetration of an international firm takes place in global networks. The advantage for this firm is that it is able to coordinate operations in international networks in order to react to changes in the market environments. Disadvantages derive from an increased communication and coordination complexity on a global scale. The *international among others* predominantly faces counterparts and competitors who are themselves internationally active in markets that are rather tightly structured. Major position changes in the network will increasingly take place through merger and acquisitions and joint ventures in contrast to the situations of firms in the previously introduced categories (Johanson & Mattsson, 1988: 306).

Johanson and Mattsson (1988: 311) claim that the network approach can distinguish entry strategies that differ with regard to the characteristics and number of relationships the entry firm seeks to establish with other firms in the network. It can be expected that because of the cumulative nature of network processes, the sequential order of activities in international markets is important and should be given more attention in research. From the strategic point of the most interesting research issue is derived the analysis of how to get prepared for international market entry and penetration when the time is ripe. Following the idea of the network concept, preparedness for and the successful implementation of international market entry strategies is largely a matter of having relationships with other firms and institutions embedded in the network.

2.6.1.5 The concept of Johanson and Vahlne

An increasing market dynamism linked with the rapid internationalization processes of firms, particularly witnessed since the 1990s, has led Johanson and Vahlne to review their own concept of psychic distance and conclude that 'we have a situation where old models of internationalization processes are still applied quite fruitfully at the same time as a number of studies have suggested that there is a need for new and network-based models of internationalization. We think it might be worthwhile to reconcile and even integrate the two approaches' (Johanson & Vahlne, 2003: 84). As a result, Johanson and Vahlne have further developed their Uppsala internationalization model of incremental market entry towards an integrated *business network model* for internationalization. They define business networks as sets of interconnected business relationships, in which each exchange relation is between firms and is conceptualized as collective steps. According to this definition, all firms are engaged in a limited set of business relationships with customers, suppliers, and service providing firms (e. g., logistics, finance, and banking) that, in turn, have relationships with other firms (Johanson & Vahlne, 2003: 92).

Hohenthal (2001: 54) claims that there is always a connection of two separate pools of knowledge when a new relationship between actors is created. Through this connection, the firms gain access to each other's knowledge systems (and their international experience), which can be used in other relationships and in the creation of new international business opportunities with less cost than would be required to generate the knowledge by themselves. International experience gives the firm an ability to see and evaluate global business opportunities and thereby reduce the uncertainty associated with commitments to foreign markets. Accumulated knowledge and experience in foreign markets leads to improved overall international business performance (Lou & Peng, 1999: 290).

Johanson and Vahlne (2003: 91) distinguish between market-specific experience and operation experience. The former concerns conditions in the particular market and cannot, without great difficulty, be transferred to other markets. The latter refers to ways of organizing and developing international business operations that can more easily be transferred from market to market. Apparently, the internationalization of a firm is associated with commitment decisions such as cooperative agreements with suppliers, distributors, or customers; acquisitions of competitors; or direct investment in operations and manufacturing abroad. The more specific and the more integrated those activities abroad, the stronger is the firm's dependence on them and, as a consequence, the higher the corresponding market exit barriers (Johanson & Vahlne, 2003: 91). Within a business network perspective, market entry difficulties are not mainly associated with the general market surroundings in a country. The challenge is rather in terms of specific customer or supplier firms' characteristics due to language, ethics, and cultural obstacles, such as different perspectives on avoiding business uncertainty and short versus long-term business performance views (Hofstede, 2001: 145, 351; Johanson & Vahlne, 2003: 91–92).

Consequently, Johanson and Vahlne (2003: 96) combine the incremental internationalization process and the network models, assuming there is one set of business-related managerial issues that is relationship-specific and another set of challenges associated with country-specific institutional and cultural barriers. On the way to internationalization, the enterprise has to overcome these challenges. International expansion is a result of the firm's establishment of relationships with other industry actors, such as suppliers and customers. Success in international business significantly depends on the company's ability to build a network, which, for its part, depends on the firm's learning openness and experience in developing it. Subsequent foreign entries benefit from the learning and experience gained from previous operations. Experienced managers who are familiar with international business help the company overcome difficulties related to entry activities in new markets (Li, 1995: 347). Johanson and Vahlne (2003: 93–94) distinguish between *three types of network learning*, which acquire extraordinary importance with regard to prosperous internationalization activities.

Three types of network learning

First, firms do business in customer-supplier relationships. They learn partner-specific behaviors, such as willingness and ability to maintain and develop the relationship (e. g., order forecasting reliability, flexibility, and keeping promises related to the business). As a result, they learn about each other and how to coordinate their activities in ways that strengthen their joint business. Such connection increases the firms' commitment in the foreign market.

Second, experience in relationship development assumes that when interacting in business engagements, the involved partner is learning skills that may be transferred to and used in other business transactions. These skills include how to get in touch with new business network actors (e. g., customers and suppliers) as well as expertise on knowing how to develop and deepen relationships with them.

> *Third,* coordinating experience concerns several supplier relationships, for example concerning new product developments or just-in-time delivery schedules. It also concerns coordination between a supplier and a customer in order to make both parties' value chain activities more efficient. All of these connect and intensify the relationships of the business network (Johanson & Vahlne, 2003: 93–94).

International business experience is not the result of positive international business outcomes only. Negative experiences gained from a firm's failure concerning its foreign market entry are also of significant value for the management and develop the entire internationalization competence of a firm. Experience, whether negative or positive, thus seems to be important in the triggering, creation, and development of the international market entry processes (Hohenthal, 2001: 206).

As a consequence of relationship learning, the firm acquires expertise on how to build new business relationships and how to connect them to each other. The relationship development experience is likely to be useful also when the enterprise approaches strategic relationships (Johanson and Vahlne, 2003: 94). For instance, joint ventures may be made in order to secure technological resources or to gain the strategic advantage of the cooperating partners through shared distribution channels relative to their competitors. Foreign market expansion is a matter first of developing the firm's relationships in the specific market, second of establishing and developing supporting relationships (e. g., local politicians and government), and third of cultivating connections that are similar or connected to the focal one. In order to support a strategic relationship with a partner, the firm might be forced to develop a relationship in another country, thereby entering that foreign market (Johanson & Vahlne, 2003: 94, 97).

Mathews (2002: 45) similarly argues that firms possess a unique set of relationships that contribute to their own resources and capabilities. An enterprise is able to improve or enhance its capabilities by attracting and sharing resources with other firms with which it shares connections. A network perspective of the economy and its players, which can accommodate the perspectives of firms developing complementary strategies and accessing more mobile resources, needs to be contrasted with the conventional view that sees enterprises as atomistic entities engaged in arm's length transactions with each other, mediated through the price system. Those firms are viewed only as production entities with transparent technology in the form of a production function that converts input and output. However, markets have become increasingly integrated (e. g., electronics in vehicles), industries have become digitalized, and value added activities are more complex. Therefore, the conventional view of a (manufacturing) firm and its internationalization processes needs to be replaced with an inter-disciplinary perspective and the firm's location in networks.

The creation of knowledge through technological learning is crucial to gaining a competitive advantage in international business. Interactions with reliable business partners provide important insight into other firms' research and how those products develop over time in the international markets. The functions and the design of products and services used to meet local customer expectations can be more easily observed through interlinks with foreign business partners. Thus, the development of future products and services can be adapted to better meet local market conditions. The main characteristic of those interlinked firms is their engagement in a global 'lattice' construction, with accelerated global expansion as the key goal. Firms that develop a corporate culture and organizational structures that ensure the effective integration of technological and administrative learning from their international interfaces will boost their performance in international business (Zahra, 2005: 20 – 22; Zahra, Ireland, & Hitt, 2000: 925). As a result, the resource-based view turns out to be a suitable ground for understanding the dynamics of international competition. Seeing the emerging global economy as networks of interlinked enterprises provides a fresh perspective on the process of internationalization (Mathews, 2002: 46, 217; Sharma & Blomstermo, 2003: 739 – 740).

2.6.1.6 Review of inter-organizational network positioning approach

The network concept draws particular attention to the social and cognitive ties that are formed among actors (e. g., suppliers, customers, service providers, banks, etc.) engaged in international business. The rapid growth of new entrants in the global arena leads to the conclusion that enterprises do not necessarily internationalize incrementally as claimed in the Uppsala approach (Johanson & Vahlne, 1977: 23 – 32). Against the background of globalization, international firms make increasing use of their global networks. While traditional foreign-market entry research describes how firms decide on markets and appropriate entry modes *on their own*, the network approach concentrates on how existing actors influence the entry of new firms into networks that provide the base for business activities abroad (Björkman & Forsgren, 2000: 13).

Firms maintain a range of bilateral relationships, and researchers who favor the network approach need to include a variety of variables in their analysis. Thus, the measurement and evaluation of a firm's business performance within the context of international relationships and their individual impact on the firm's performance in terms of its foreign market entry success are methodologically enormously complex and are, therefore, challenging (Samiee & Walters, 2006: 597). Further conceptual difficulties are measuring the ownership control and the efficiency and effectiveness of bilateral relationships in networks (Jones & Coviello, 2002: 9).

Network research tends to focus on the actor's behavior in oligopolistic business-to-business market surroundings (Dunning, 1995a: 473). The resource dependence theory, which is derived from the resource-based view, emphasizes resource exchanges, such as in international joint ventures, as the central feature of these relationships (Newbert, 2007: 139). According to this perspective, groups and organizations gain power over each other by controlling valued resources. In parallel, there is always the risk of opportunistic behavior from the participating players in the industry network. This causes network instabilities as a considerable number of firms involved in joint ventures experience failures, much to their regret (Das & Teng, 2000: 78; Glaister, Husan, & Buckley, 2003: 83; Schuler, 2001: 13). While descriptions of individual examples through case studies of business reality are often satisfactory, the corresponding research results are hard to generalize and future predictions tend to be vague. Consequently, the theoretical potential of drawing conclusions about common patterns of internationalization in global networks is challenging and requires intensive and costly research (Björkman & Forsgren, 2000: 14).

Since the 1990s, the network approach of internationalization has been amplified. Innovative, young, and usually small firms often start their foreign business early in their establishment. Therefore, the phenomenon of rapid and not necessarily gradual internationalization processes entered the academic literature. The appearance of these types of firms and the influence of their 'entrepreneurs' have led to a second stream of the network approach that specifically focuses on social ties of bilateral personal relationships in networks (Ellis, 2011: 100).

Chapter review questions

1. According to the inter-organizational network approach, how does a firm gain competitive advantage?
2. What are the major differences between the Uppsala and the network concept?
3. Explain the advantages and disadvantages of intensive network engagements.

2.6.1.7 The case study of Haier (China) – Learning by imitation

Haier's origins go back to Qingdao Refrigerator Company, which started operations in the 1920s. In 1949, the firm became a government-owned company; and in 1984, Zhang Ruimin, who is still chairman and CEO, took over leadership of Haier. That same year, based on an international joint venture with the German firm Liebherr, Haier began to produce refrigerators, which were called 'Qingdao Liebherr' (manufacturing around 80 units per month, indicating an average failure rate of 20 percent). In Chinese, Liebherr is pronounced 'Li-Bu-Hai-Er', thus the last two syllables contribute the current firm name, Haier (Munich_Innovation_Group, 2012). Since that time, Haier has been transformed from an insolvent collectively owned factory to a global home appliance manufacturer (Haier, 2014).

In the 1990s, Haier, which is headquartered in Qingdao, started exporting refrigerators to Europe, based on contract manufacturing for well-known multinational brands including Liebherr. In parallel, it acquired various smaller Chinese companies. Haier concentrated on further improving its technological expertise through joint ventures with companies such as Mitsubishi (Japan) and Merloni from Italy. CEO Zhang Ruimin said about the firm's strategy,

'First we observe and digest. Then we imitate. In the end, we understand it well enough to design it independently' *(Frynas & Mellahi, 2011: 178)*.

Today, Haier employs more than 70,000 people; and its products are sold in more than 100 countries (Munich_Innovation_Group, 2012: 19). Haier's home appliance business consists of 1) washing machines, 2) water heaters, and 3) services (e. g., after-sales, e-commerce, distribution, and logistics). The organization of the firm is designed around the three strategic business units illustrated in Figure 18 (Haier, 2014a). Haier pursues a related diversification strategy.

In recent years, Haier has strengthen its research and development activities, resulting in 10,167 patents in 2013 (Haier, 2014a, c). One of the most important subsidiaries of Haier Group Corporation is Haier Electronics Group Co., Ltd., which is listed in Hong Kong. Haier Electronics is engaged in the research, design, development, and manufacturing of washing machines and water heaters. In 2010, emphasizing their customer-oriented service approach, Haier launched a global brand called 'Goodaymart' (Haier_Electronics, 2014). Sales – as recorded since 2004 – indicate a sharp increase between 2009 and 2013, while net income remains at a marginal level (Haier Electronics Group Co., 2005; Haier Electronics Group Co., 2010, 2013).

Relative to its competitors from Japan and South Korea, Haier is an international latecomer that seeks to increase its global market shares within the shortest possible time, which is, however, costly as the marginal net income for the years from 2004 to 2013 illustrate (compare Figure 19).

One of the major reasons for Haier's rather marginal net income is the firm undertook various foreign direct investments through greenfield investments and acquisitions, such as of the Italian refrigerator assembler Meneghetti in 2001. In the same year, Haier established a plant in the US. The acquisition of the washing machine, refrigerator, and consumer electric appliance business of Sanyo Electric Co., Ltd., from Japan manifests a further milestone in the course of Haier's progressive internationalization (Haier, 2012). In 2015, Haier communicated its ambitious plans for customer integrated 'e-commerce in transit' sales concepts by providing on-demand services integrating sales, distribution, installation, and after-sales services through direct web-based communication channels with its consumers (Haier, 2015b). As per September 2015, Haier is running eight research and development centers, twenty-nine manufacturing bases, and sixteen so-called industrial parks in Europe, North America, Asia, the Middle East, and Africa (Haier, 2015a).

Chapter review questions

1. Describe how Haier modified its market entry strategies from 1984 until the present.
2. Applying your knowledge about the resource-based view, describe Haier's resource strengths and weaknesses during the 1980s and today.

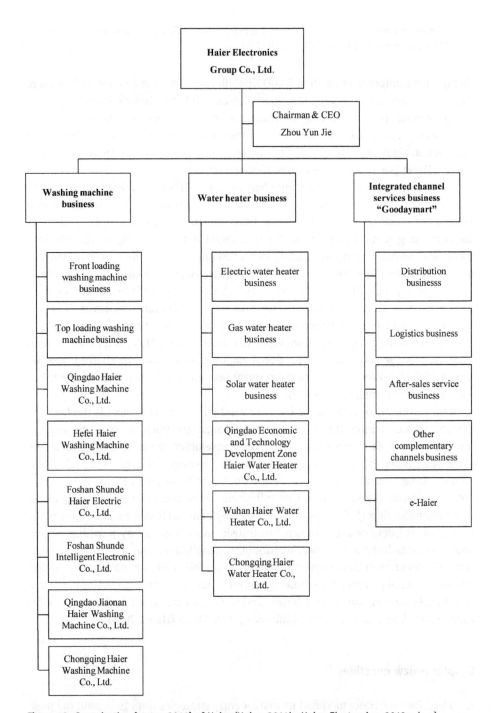

Figure 18. Organization [status 2014] of Haier (Haier, 2014b; Haier_Electronics, 2012a, b, c)

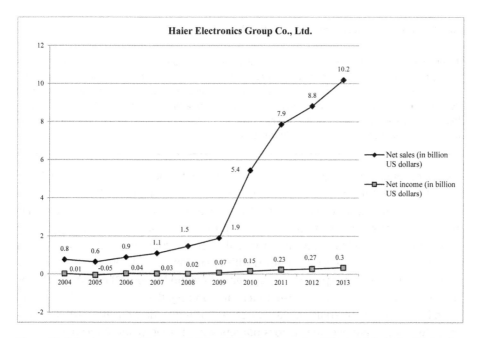

Figure 19. Net sales and net income of Haier Electronics Group for 2004 to 2013 (Haier Electronics Group Co., 2005; Haier Electronics Group Co., 2007, 2008, 2010, 2012, 2013)

3. Suppose you are a member of Haier's management, develop a strategic concept for the future in terms of the firm's product, marketing, and internationalization strategies.

2.6.2 Interpersonal relationships approach

2.6.2.1 Early internationalization of the firm

The digitalization of various industries, up and coming e-commerce, improved and faster logistics, and liberalized trade patterns has permanently fostered new business opportunities for smaller firms with limited conventional resources. The phenomenon of rapid internationalization of relatively young firms has directed the focus of scholarly research to the role and influence of the entrepreneur in the firm's international activities (Oviatt & Mc Dougall, 1994: 49; Shrader, Oviatt, & Mc Dougall, 2000: 1235).

Firms that are able to internationalize rapidly often have established personal relationships with firms abroad. Consequently, they are intensively embedded in international business structures (Hohenthal, 2001: 25). Thus, members of the international network value relationships rather than discrete and contractual, formalized transactions (Coviello & Munro, 1997: 365).

How to define an 'early internationalizer'

The emergence of digitalized service-based industries in particular has further supported the business opportunities of small- and medium-sized enterprises to internationalize rapidly after inception. The changing pattern of internationalization, especially among small firms, has been increasingly discussed in the literature. However, definitions that describe the phenomena of firms that internationalize in the early stages after the firm's founding are rather heterogeneous than unified in the literature (Lopez, Kundu, & Ciravegna, 2009: 1230).

One of the most cited definitions stems from Oviatt and McDougall (Oviatt & Mc Dougall, 1994: 49, 94), who describe an international new venture (INV) as a business organization that 'from inception, seeks to derive significant competitive advantage from the use of resources in the sale of outputs in multiple countries'. Further INV definitions, to name just a few, are from Zahra et al. (2000: 928), who specify INVs as firms competing in several countries with operations in different international regions and targeting multiple market segments. Coviello (2006: 713) describes INVs as 'different' from conception because from near founding, they have a global focus and commit resources to international activities. According to Madsen (2013: 70), INVs coordinate value chain activities across borders within three years of inception.

In addition to INV, another differentiating term emerged in the literature: the 'born global'. INV and born global deal with the same phenomenon: a category of firms that implement their international business from their foundation. They develop their internationalization knowledge through an 'absorptive capability', usually fostered and developed by their entrepreneurs, who use their versatile and diversified personal relationship ties in foreign markets. These firms are usually found in new technological-based service businesses with a strong customer orientation linked to the utmost flexibility in order to adapt their market entry strategy to the needs of the local market circumstances (Sharma & Blomstermo, 2003: 749–750).

Grant (1996: 121) emphasizes the role of the individual as the primary actor in knowledge creation and the principal repository of knowledge. According to this logic, a firm's potentials to immediately launch international business engagements are fostered by the firm's people, in particular the entrepreneur, who is often, but not always, the founder and business owner (Zahra et al., 2005: 21). Entrepreneurial capabilities may result in finding ways to create value beyond the established competitors and usually conventional, resource-rich industry incumbents. Competitive advantages in the global marketplace are mainly derived from the particular intangible assets of the young and early internationalizing firm (e. g., organizational cultures and personal relationships). Consequently, the success of the firm is influenced by the ability of the entrepreneur to mobilize and dynamically combine external and internal resources and adapt them to changes in the environment. Particularly, personal contacts and social interaction play an extraordinary role when it comes to market entry decisions – especially where complex technological products with a high service value are concerned (Axelsson & Easton, 1992: 33; Ellis, 2000: 462). Dynamic capabilities allow a flexible reconfiguration of the firm's asset structures in terms of product portfolio, process efficiency, and personal and organizational experience (Zuchella & Scabini, 2007: 172–173).

International entrepreneurship has been identified as involving firm activity that crosses national borders. Consequently, it is a combination of innovative, proactive, and risk-seeking behavior intended to create value in organizations (Jones & Coviello, 2002: 4; McDougall & Oviatt, 2000: 903; Young et al., 2003: 33). McDougall and Oviatt (2003: 7) enlarged the definition of international entrepreneurship 'as the discovery, enactment, evaluation, and exploitation of opportunities – across national borders – to create future goods and services'. An integrative model comparing traditional and rather large firms versus modern entrepreneurial small business firms and their diversified internationalization processes was developed by Bell at al. (2003: 351) and is illustrated in Figure 20. The authors claim that firms can follow different pathways of internationalization. These modes include the traditional, the 'born global', and the 'born again global' pathway. The model attempts to explore and seeks to explain any variations in the patterns, pace, and process of internationalization. The authors illustrate contrasting internationalization patterns, including different motivations, aims, strategies, and methods of market entry.

In business reality, internationalization patterns tend to be highly individualistic, situation specific, and unique. Firms with advanced international knowledge tend to launch international business faster and often more efficiently. The internationalization process is significantly dependent on external environmental conditions as well as on a firm's internal circumstances, including resource availability, behavioral characteristics, and a global vision of the key personnel. Enterprises may pass periods of rapid internationalization and drawbacks in international business. These periods are influenced by political-legal impacts, the firm's customers, or other actors in the industry network. The focus of the model by Bell et al. (2003: 351–352) is on strategic issues with respect to internationalization concepts of small firms. Additionally, the model provides recommendations for strategy formulation and implementation in order to assist the internationalization process.

2.6.2.2 The dimension of time

In their model, Jones and Coviello (2005: 297) combine the dimension of time, management's behavioral aspects, and the influence of the external environment on the firm's performance. The scholars assume that internationalization is a reflection of time-based behavior, specific to individual entrepreneurs as participants and managers of social systems and networks. Behavioral aspects of the entrepreneur, determined by the decisions and actions that occur at a specific point in time, move to the center of research interest (Jones & Coviello, 2002: 2–3; 2005: 287, 289). The relationship between the entrepreneur, the organization, and the external environment is viewed from a systems perspective and assumes the continued activity of input, process motion, output, and feedback over time, whereby elements of the external

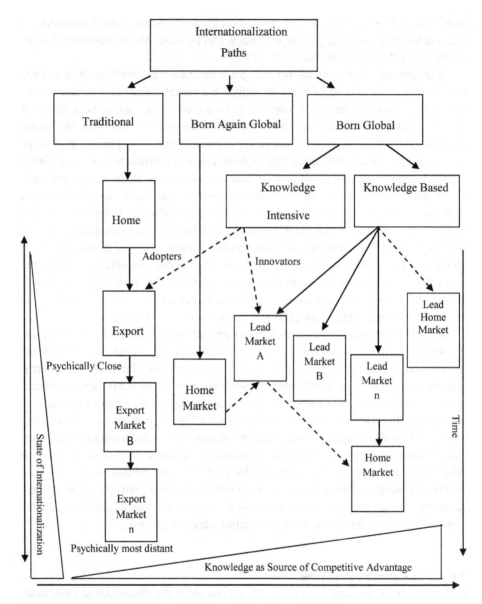

Figure 20. Towards an integrative model of small firm internationalization
Source: modified from Bell et al. (2003), p. 351

environment moderate internationalization behavior. The entrepreneurial influence serves to combine resources and knowledge as part of the strategic and tactical activity of the firm (Jones & Coviello, 2002: 15; Jones & Coviello, 2004: 485).

Entrepreneurial activities include specific decisions and actions that result in or contribute to internationalization. External associations, such as international business links with other firms abroad and corresponding modes of market entry, are seen as part of that interaction (as indicated on two dimensions, time and country distance). Cross-border activity may commence or terminate at any time, thus leading to a complex pattern of internationalization decisions, processes, and activities. Enterprises with an open, responsive interactivity with the external foreign business community will internationalize more rapidly and successfully than those whose boundaries are relatively impermeable. Consequently, internationalization is a process of behavior that emerges as a firm's unique response to internal and external influences and is particularly driven by the entrepreneur. Time is a fundamental component of internationalization in that each firm has a history comprised of significant internationalization events occurring at specific points in time. For example, the establishment of a new type of cross-border link, such as the start of an export activity, represents a milestone in the firm's chronology of internationalization (Jones & Coviello, 2002: 16–17).

The internationalization process is understood as 'value-creating-events' (Jones & Coviello, 2005: 297). As illustrated in Figure 21, the entrepreneur's level of innovativeness, risk tolerance, and managerial competence has a significant impact on the firm and its organizational structure. The firm's internationalization behavior is a result of 'fingerprint pattern' and profiles over a period of time. The 'fingerprint' of internationalization behavior includes the functional diversity (decision of entry mode choice) and country diversity (geographic, economic, and cultural distance) in relation to time. 'Fingerprint' patterns give a static impression at a specific point in time, whereas profiles identify changes over a period of time. Thus, the firm's internationalization process (e. g., market entry organization) mirrors the entrepreneurial behavior and the firm's organization (organic vs. mechanistic). Internationalization can be seen as a firm-level entrepreneurial behavior manifested by events and outcomes in relation to time. Internationalization behavior influences the firm's performance expressed in financial data (profit or loss as indicators of market success) or non-financial assets (degree of organizational learning). Different 'fingerprint' patterns of internationalization behavior evolve over time, and firm performance will impact future behavior through an iterative process of further organizational learning.

Reuber and Fischer (1999: 31) build on the relationship of time and the 'stock of experience', which influence the international new venture's performance. Experience includes things that happen or events that occur during a specific time period. A particular event can have both a positive and negative impact on the international business of the firm. For instance, the loss of a key customer might reduce the sales revenue in the short term. This loss may result in better long-term performance if the firm is able to learn from its experience, for example through improvement of product quality or service.

Hurmerinta-Peltomaki (2003: 219, 224) claims that traditional internationalization models describe a firm's export activities as a linear and predictable pattern on a simple, orderly, or progressive path, which is often an unrealistic notion. Consideration should be given to the idea that particular events or experiences in the past may cause a firm's reorientation, moving the foreign trade activities in a nega-

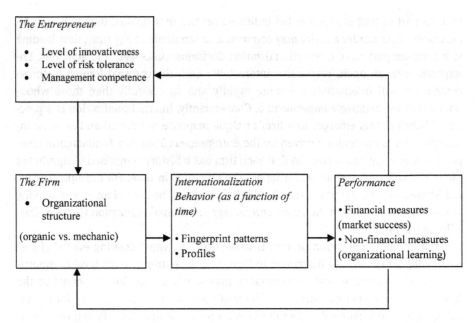

Figure 21. Internationalization: conceptualization of an entrepreneurial process of behavior in time
Source: Jones and Coviello (2005), p. 297

tive direction and causing export involvement to decrease or even to be interrupted. Thus, experience over a period of time may cause strategic reorientation that alters or stops the international activities of the firm. Time enables us to understand various organizational processes, in particular those of decision making and learning from positive and negative business episodes. During decision making, the owner or manager intentionally attempts, in the present, to connect the past to the future by assessing the relevance of his/her experience to the future. Experience is the antecedent of present and future activities, and it is this property that makes it relevant and interesting (Butler, 1995: 925; Reuber & Fischer, 1999: 30).

The past experience dimension, on both the organizational (enterprise) and the individual (entrepreneur) level should be taken into account when describing a firm's internationalization process. Thus, cyclical, experience-based internationalization on an individual level affects internationalization on an organizational level. Cyclical internationalization may also be perceived on an organizational level in a forward-backward-forward movement. For example, the enterprise is able to utilize its past export experience to continue the internationalization process at present and in the future (Hurmerinta-Peltomäki, 2003: 226–230).

The dimensions of time in international business have not been emphasized adequately in conventional concepts of internationalization so far. As illustrated in Figure 22, the direction of development in research on the internationalization process evidently proceeds from the upper left-hand corner (positive direction-linear) towards the lower right-hand corner (no fixed direction-cyclical) (Hurmerinta-Peltomä-

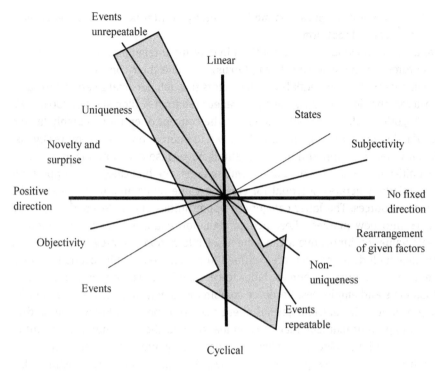

Figure 22. Dimension of time in internationalization concepts research.
Source: Hurmerinta-Peltomäki (2003), p. 226

ki, 2003: 225–226). Traditional research on internationalization is mostly based on a linear idea of time; that is, the models consist of several identifiable and distinct successive stages. A higher stage of international activities indicates a greater foreign involvement (Leonidou & Katsikeas, 1996: 527). The challenge in this context is to understand internationalization as a process that is highly dynamic and time dependent. However, paradoxically almost all internationalization models are static in nature; for example, models fail to conceive each export stage as a continuum of episodes and micro-steps (Leonidou & Katsikeas, 1996: 527). This is one explanation as to why 'stages models' on internationalization are commonly used because permanent changes between the stages are difficult to perceive by researchers. It could be said that two dimensions of time are relevant to the development of internationalization concepts: linear, which describes the human understanding of time as a forward-going line in a positive direction (past-present-future), and cyclical time, which reflects the business reality, but where there is no fixed direction or arrow. This allows for the description of a backward direction of internationalization (Hurmerinta-Peltomäki, 2003: 226–227).

2.6.2.3 Towards a conceptualized model typology of international new ventures and born global firms

Due to a lack of previous or fixed routines in entering foreign markets, international new ventures (or the synonym, born globals) combine their conventional resource disadvantages with the potentials of other actors through personal relationships usually fostered and developed by the entrepreneur (Sharma & Blomstermo, 2003: 248).

DiGregorio et al. (2008: 190) emphasize the concept of entrepreneurship 'as the nexus of individuals and opportunities' applied to international new ventures by distinguishing between opportunities that entail novel resource combinations versus opportunities that entail novel market combinations. The first category of opportunities essentially generates potential for creating value by combining internationally dispersed resources. The latter category of opportunities entails leveraging existing resources into new markets. Resource combination chances refer to the potential to create value via innovative arrangements of international strategic factors. Such factors may include assets that are confined to certain geographic locations, for example access to natural resources, labor force qualifications, and consciousness of the customers and employees. Resource combinations may also involve cross-border pooling of innovative entrepreneurial talent and corresponding knowledge, and/or access to important markets. Market combinations, on the other hand, entail introducing a particular product or service from one country into one or more other countries. Introducing this new perspective enables the delineation of two distinct phenomena: first, the creation of international ventures and second, the process of internationalization of recently established ventures. DiGregorio et al. (2008: 191–192) categorizes firms into four typologies (compare Figure 23).

Quadrant I – Domestic New Venture
The first quadrant contains new venture firms that have a strictly domestic orientation. That means no international sales or resource combination occurs. Such firms cannot be defined as an international new venture but, instead, are a domestic joint venture.

Quadrant II – Accelerated International Sales
International new venture firms categorized in this segment begin international sales at an early stage but do not combine resources across borders. These firms concentrate their resources locally and are typically founded in response to local opportunities. They rapidly expand their market scope to include international markets in order to take advantage of their domestically based resources to exploit differences between local and foreign markets in terms of quality or cost.

Quadrant III – Cross-Border Resource Integration
International new venture firms take advantage of geographically dispersed resources and the diverse knowledge embedded within those resources. The combination of resources across national borders is the main basis for gaining competitive advant-

age. Because they are embedded in international networks, their opportunities to improve the product quality, service, innovation potentials, or cost structures are enhanced. Existing business models in one market are transferred into another.

Quadrant IV – International Resource and Market Combination
Firms located in this segment depend on cross-border interactions for their tangible and intangible resources in order to realize market opportunities. Competitive advantage is developed by careful management of the risks associated with multiple entries into foreign markets. For these firms, internationalization is a means of creating new value via cross-border resource combination and capturing existing value via international sales (DiGregorio et al., 2008: 191–192).

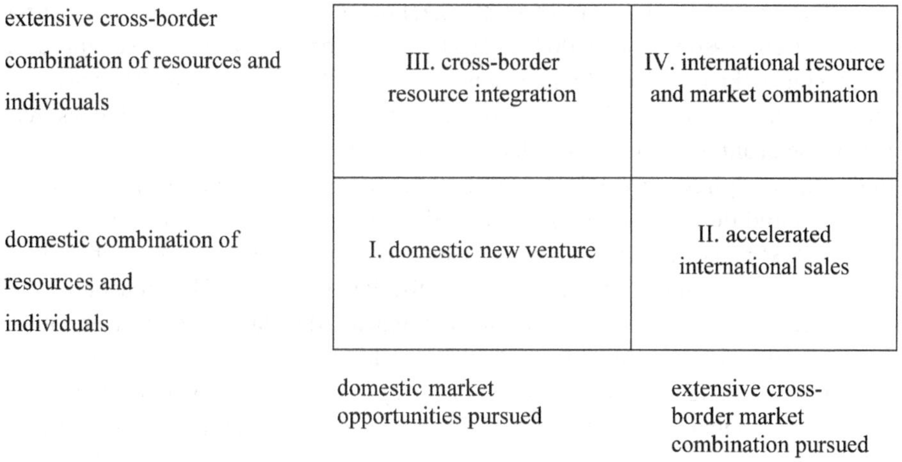

extensive cross-border combination of resources and individuals	III. cross-border resource integration	IV. international resource and market combination
domestic combination of resources and individuals	I. domestic new venture	II. accelerated international sales
	domestic market opportunities pursued	extensive cross-border market combination pursued

Figure 23. Typology of new ventures. Source: Di Gregorio et al. (2008), p. 191

International new ventures emerge when resources abroad are combined without necessarily coordinating value chain activities internationally as witnessed for multinational enterprises. For example, an international new venture is created by combining a resource such as technology or a business model from one country with resources and/or markets in another country. International new ventures arise from leveraging domestic resources into foreign markets or to exploit new foreign resource combinations. While Oviatt and McDougall (1994: 45) focus on internationalization soon after a firm's inception, the concept of Di Gegorio et al. (2008: 191–194) concentrates on the emergence process of an international new venture. The importance concerning external opportunities of foreign resources (e.g., material procurement, knowledge, and technology transfer), which help to improve the firm's performance in domestic and foreign markets, has been ignored so far. Entrepreneurs of young firms seeking to internationalize should intensively and permanently search for foreign resource opportunities.

Gabrielsson et al. (2008: 385–388) propose a born global firm definition that includes various aspects. A firm should have a global market potential and entrepreneurial competence that enables rapid internationalization. Furthermore, a firm should have a distinct differentiation strategy and products with either an unique technology, superior design, unique service know-how, or other highly specialized competence. Born globals understand foreign markets as a chance to explore and create new knowledge regarding products with global market potentials. The establishment of a successful start-up firm needs a global vision linked with reasonable risk awareness. The time factor should be regarded along with two dimensions: precocity (early internationalization) and speed (effectiveness). All-in-all, these types of firms show a broad entrepreneurial scope, high intensity in the business focus, and rapid growth (Gabrielsson et al., 2008: 386–388; Kuemmerle, 2002: 99).

In order to overcome the conceptualization weakness of the entrepreneurial models, Gabrielsson et al. (2008: 391) attempt to develop a combined approach that includes the born global phenomenon and its behavior over time. They describe the firm's development in different stages and the reasons it proceeds as it does. As a result, the evolution process is divided into three phases: first, the introduction and initial launch phase; second, growth and resource accumulation; and third, the break-out and desired strategies phase as described in more detail below.

The first phase, the introduction, describes the period when born globals have limited resources and an undeveloped organizational structure. They rely on unique and mostly tacit knowledge to achieve competitive advantage. The most important resources are the firm founder(s) and other employee resource (knowledge) capabilities and inimitable skills. Combined with entrepreneurship, these abilities may lead to the development of products with global market potential. Firm growth mostly depends on the distribution channel strategy and the relationships chosen—for example, a long-term sales contract concluded with a multinational enterprise and further relationships created through personal relationships of the entrepreneur. Organizational learning is important for the success of the born global, especially knowledge about foreign markets (Gabrielsson et al., 2008: 391–395).

Phase two describes growth and resource accumulation. Business success depends on the product and service itself and the ability to place it on the market. Knowledge rests on the ability to learn from partners, suppliers, and customers, as well as collected success and failure experiences (Gabrielsson et al., 2008: 396).

Phase three, the break-out and desired strategies phase, describes the period where the born global decides on a strategy based on its previous learning and experience in order to arrange its own position in the markets and its industry network. The strategic reorientation is influenced by the desire for independence from global players and the control of its own actions. A fundamental global vision and devotion are necessary as well as the availability of a client portfolio, which allows the development of international success to continue. At this stage, a born global may develop and continuously grow to become a 'normal multinational enterprise' in the future (Gabrielsson et al., 2008: 400).

2.6.2.4 The phenomenon of the 'born again global'

The limited focus on the start-up phase of new venture firms led (Bell et al., 2003: 340) to an expansion of the discussion of the 'born again global' phenomenon. This term describes firms that have become well established in their domestic market with apparently no great motivation to internationalize, but which have suddenly embraced rapid and dedicated internationalization. Born again global firms fail to conform to the conventional stage models of small firms' internationalization process concepts, which concentrate on the initial phase from the firm's inception.

The radical change in internationalization behavior of the born again global firm may be triggered by a critical incident or several events happening at the same time. These incidents may include a change of ownership or management, a decision to follow a main customer to foreign markets, or the introduction of Internet-based distribution channels. Especially a change of ownership or management has significant influence on the internationalization path of born again global firms. Not only top management representatives with an international vision but also other human resources of the firm with special international expertise (for example, embedded in the firm's sales or purchasing department) influence the company's internationalization re-launch. Furthermore, additional financial resources and new opportunities may come up due to access to new international industry networks and, consequently, more amplified knowledge (Bell et al., 2003: 345–346).

The motivation of born again global firms to internationalize is, in comparison to born globals, rather reactive; they only respond to a critical event. Business goals of born again global firms include the utilization of new industry relationships and corresponding emerging resources. Born again global firms show, after the initial reactive event, a more systematic and structured approach to internationalization than born global (international new venture) firms. They also tend to originate from traditional industries rather than from high technology and service sectors. It might be assumed that born again global firms have a better position from which to finance rapid internationalization because they have secure revenues from their home market. These firms have a certain stock of financial resources and knowledge from the 'critical incident' at their disposal. However, international business success will not become reality if the firm faces difficulties in the domestic market (Bell et al., 2003: 347–353).

The born again global concept may also apply well to service intensive organizations because these firms will remain in the domestic market until the business idea and the service quality has been verified as successful and able to be culturally adapted abroad. Another explanation of the born again global firm phenomenon is that these firms initially tried to internationalize but failed. Thus, they decided to build up a supporting domestic infrastructure that would allow them to internationalize quickly and successfully at a later time (Bell et al., 2003: 351–353; Gabrielsson et al., 2008: 386). An entrepreneurial person may also be able to bring organizational change and innovation to established enterprises. These changes in strategies and knowledge may enable the corporation to form new capabilities and sources of innovation and creativity. Two different approaches derive from this: first, 'corporate entrepreneurship' and second, 'dispersed corporate entrepreneurship', also known as 'intrapreneurship' (Zuchella & Scabini, 2007: 69–70, 113). These approaches will be introduced in the following chapter.

2.6.2.5 Individual and corporate international entrepreneurship

When born global firms have grown successfully over time and thus have become mature and carry out various cross-border activities, the variability of the term 'entrepreneurship' is increased. Corporate entrepreneurship is characterized by a new division in an established company that identifies and develops new business opportunities for the firm. The department or division acts autonomously, has a relatively flat hierarchical structure, but has strong internal integration with high availability of resources and support from management. In contrast to this, the term dispersed corporate entrepreneurship (intrapreneurship) assumes that every employee has the potential to behave in an entrepreneurial way. Thus, entrepreneurial groups are formed and deal with normal managerial tasks. This entrepreneurial culture within the company culture serves as a basis for any activity, including among others the firm's internationalization movements (Zuchella & Scabini, 2007: 113). The phenomenon of rapid internationalization is often a result of a firm's internal projects carried out by team members with entrepreneurial and international spirit ('international intrapreneurship') (Cavusgil & Knight, 2015: 11).

There are several ways that entrepreneurial activities can take place either inside or outside of a firm. Developing them inside the firm would involve organizational structures and managerial capabilities. Outside development would include another business stakeholder – for example, long-term contractual relationships with a supplying firm. Entrepreneurial activities increasingly become the focus of international subsidiaries of mature and rather large enterprises. These subsidiaries are controlled by the firm's headquarters but act proactively and find new resources and chances to expand their business. Over time, they develop their own unique capabilities and personal bilateral relationships. The local environment makes local managers alert to new opportunities and creates an entrepreneurial orientation within the subsidiary. As a result, the local subsidiaries act independently for the most part in pursuing opportunities and develop an organizational culture that sets particular international goals and strategic directions. This development of entrepreneurial subsidiaries can be seen in connection with the need for local market responsiveness. To what extent the subsidiary can determine independent actions, roles, and objectives, or whether these issues have to be strictly in accordance with the goals of the headquarters seems to be important. The self-determined and autonomous approach facilitates local entrepreneurship. It ensures exposure to different resources, local knowledge, and close contact with markets and their customers. Entrepreneurial subsidiaries allow further development of adapted solutions and more effective management in the course of the firm's internationalization process (Zuchella & Scabini, 2007: 113–117).

If the role of the firm's international subsidiary is more independent and innovative, it develops and implements better performing strategies because it is closer to the local markets. Moreover, this role supports the employee's motivation to be innovative and entrepreneurial in the future. It can be assumed that turbulent, complex, and dynamic environments better foster entrepreneurship due to the pressure for the firm to be competitive through permanent innovation and improvement. Nevertheless, there is still a need for coordination and integration of companies in order to avoid duplication of efforts. The multinational firm needs to monitor and evaluate the subsidiary in strategic and financial terms, which cannot be done without managerial and organization efforts that entail corresponding costs (Zuchella & Scabini, 2007: 118).

2.6.2.6 Review of the international new venture, born global, and entrepreneurial concepts

Entrepreneurship and its impact on a firm's internationalization concepts are recent and upcoming research topics. The different contributions in this field have their roots in many disciplines (e.g., business administration and social sciences, psychology), but generally accepted definitions and unified theoretical frameworks are still missing (Holmquist, 2003: 74; Zuchella & Scabini, 2007: 57).

Success in international business is dependent upon the embedding of the entrepreneur in cross-border institutional structures comprising national and international networks (Young et al., 2003: 36). Coviello (2015: 23) claims that further research is necessary concerning the entrepreneurial characteristics and behavioral qualities that drive international new ventures. In addition to the role and influence of the entrepreneur, international new venture models take into account various other influential factors (e.g., the factor of time, internationalization processes, and internal and external environmental surroundings of the firm). The weight of a single businessman or entrepreneur when making internationalization decisions seems significant in small- and medium-sized companies. This influence is, however, rather restricted or even legally restrained in larger or multinational companies. The impact of the owner on internationalization decisions is fundamentally stronger in hierarchical cultures with a relatively high degree of top-down decision power than in less hierarchical firm cultures.

Rialp-Criado et al. (2002: 10) critically mention diversified denominations such as international new venture, born global, instant international, and so forth, which describe the same phenomenon of internationalization but increase the confusion and complexity of the theoretical concept. They further argue that the term 'global' is too 'optimistic' to be suitable for most firms and their degree of international scope. Therefore, the authors recommend using the term 'international new venture'. In the corresponding literature, there are variations in the definitions regarding the time span until an international new venture records the first international sales after its establishment and how much this contributes to the total sales. Oviatt and McDougall (1997: 86) define a period of six years as a standard time span. Madsen (2013: 70) requires 'coordinated value chain activities across borders within three years after inception'. Liesch et al. (2007: 852) categorize a firm as 'born global' when it 'internationalizes rapidly after the firm's establishment'. In comparison, Loane et al. (2007: 493) require 50 percent export ratio, while Karra and Phillips (2004: 1–2) presuppose 'at least 25 percent international sales', and Chetty and Campbell-Hunt (2004: 61) postulate 'rapid engagement in multiple national markets'. Therefore, confusion arises because there are no fixed definitions of the time span concerning the initiation of international business after the firm's establishment and the extent of foreign business in order to arrive at a common basis for empirical research.

Entrepreneurs take considerable risks when they pursue opportunities in international markets. Differences in international business performance among firms arise because of the creativity and modes of exploitation the entrepreneurs might use. Entrepreneurs are also embedded in a social context and in institutional external environments and experience with success and failure influence their internationalization behavior (Zahra et al., 2005: 131, 136).

Loane et al. (2007: 501) argue that entrepreneurship research tends to focus on the owner or key decision maker. In light of project team structures, particularly in knowledge-based industries, this approach needs to be reconsidered. Team members as a collective may have more experience in a greater number of international markets, and their combined networks of contacts are likely to be more extensive than those of a single founder Rapidly internationalizing small- and medium-sized firms are often founded by teams that have more diverse skills and wider personal network relationships (Cooper & Dailly, 1997: 144; Loane, Bell, & Cunningham, 2014: 469). Similarly, Zuchella and Scabini (2007: 172) recommend that the role of individuals, as well as organizations, has to be analyzed in conjunction with their relationship networks.

A firm-specific transformational process, sometimes provoked spontaneously due to severe market or technology changes, causes new organizational structures (Van de Ven & Poole, 1995: 535). Further research is necessary, which may lead to a classification of those environmental conditions that are more supportive of successful international entrepreneurship activities and those with neutral or negative influence (Young et al., 2003: 38). Hypothesis testing of entrepreneurial, international new venture, and time-based approaches tends to be difficult due to limited quantifiable data. For example, it is hard to verify whether a particular time event (e. g., a meeting with visitors who passed the firm's booth at the trade fair by chance and later became international customers) causes changes or routes the international business activities of the firm in a particular direction. Thus, empirical methodology and a structured, dominant theoretical framework are missing in the current status of the literature. Future research is necessary in order to evaluate those determinants of behavioral patterns that describe how firms venture into foreign markets right from inception (Schwens & Kabst, 2008: 15).

Chapter review questions

1. How would you describe the major characteristics of an 'early internationalizing firm'?
2. What are the significant differences between the interpersonal network approach and other internationalization theories?
3. Discuss conceptual overlaps between the resource-based view and the interpersonal network approach in terms of valuable resources, how to overcome resource drawbacks, and how to gain competitive advantages.

2.6.2.7 The case of Xiaomi: An early internationalizer – made in China

Chinese mobile phone maker Xiaomi (which means 'little rice') was founded in April 2010 by Lei Jun. Listed by Forbes as one of China's wealthiest entrepreneurs, Mr. Lei's property was already worth USD 1.7 billion because he had cofounded three successful technology start-ups during and after the late 1990s (Yu, 2014).

The young company of not even five years of age has built up its business by learning from market rulers such as Apple and Nokia. Lei Jun is unmistakably mimicking Steve Jobs in his presentations and is copying Apple's marketing techniques. In addition to acquiring managers from Microsoft and Motorola, signing Hugo Barrara (ex-Google executive) to become a member of Xiaomi's growing international team has taken the company a step further toward going global and becoming a serious market competitor. Currently, the company is estimated to hold a total worth of USD 4 million and has joined the group of leading smart phone vendors in the world: Samsung, Apple, LG, and others. What is even more astonishing is that Xiaomi reached this position by mainly selling its products in Asia at very reasonable price levels (Horvath-Papp, 2015). The firm organization is, relative to its competitors, extremely simple in terms of its business units and managerial hierarchy (compare Figure 24)

Sharp supplies liquid crystal display (LCD) touchscreens and Qualcomm decided to supply processors to Xiaomi's open innovation Miui system. Taiwan's Foxconn, which also makes the iPhone, agreed to assemble the new Xiaomi phones (Yu, 2014). Unlike its competitors, Xiaomi does not spend money on traditional advertising. Xiaomi does not have a major network of its own stores to staff and maintain. Instead, it largely sells its phones directly to consumers through e-commerce distribution channels (Kan, 2014).

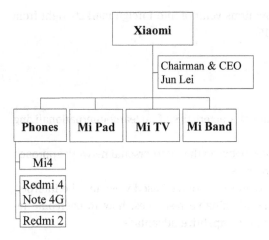

Figure 24. Organization [status 2015] of Xiaomi (Xiaomi, 2015)

2.7 Summary of Internationalization Theories

More than two hundred years ago Adam Smith and David Ricardo (compare Figure 25) were ahead of their time (in terms of reasons that favor liberalized trade patterns among countries) when they launched their trade theories (absolute and comparative advantage). After World War II, trade models were further developed (Heckscher-Ohlin). In addition, these models were amplified by a firm (management) perspective focusing on 'location factors' linked with the question of 'where to initiate international business'. The location concept, despite all its methodological limitations (it is rather a structured approach than a generally applicable theory), has proved to be important. For example, manufacturing relocation activities due to

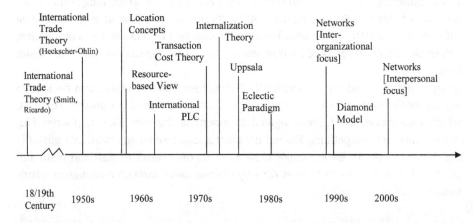

Figure 25. Chronology of the development of internationalization theories, including consideration of the trade theories, the resource-based view, and the transaction cost theory

changing regional differences influencing a firm's value added activities (e. g., development of regional industry networks, local market size, costs, etc.) have been intensively discussed in light of the recent outcomes of globalization. Therefore, very recent contributions to the literature combine *place* and *space* in their discussions. The diamond model by M. E. Porter, first published in 1990, brings traditional location concepts to a national level. Taking a country perspective, the model indicates particular factors as drivers for gaining competitive advantage and is sensitive to issues that are hard for the enterprise to plan for (government and the role of chance).

Model	Representative publications [Year]	Principal contents of the model	Major limitations of the model
Location concepts	originated in traditional trade theories: Smith [1776], Ricardo [1817] Heckscher-Ohlin [1952] Firm perspective: Tesch [1980] Pan and Tse [2000] Rasmussen [2008] Dai et al. [2013] Beugelsdijk [2013]	– supply and demand factors differ among countries and influence the competitiveness of firms – firms' foreign market entry strategies depend on country-specific location factors	– empirical studies about the relative influence of location factors are problematic to perform – difficult to consider all relevant factors due to the model's high complexity
Diamond model	Porter [1990]	– firm competitiveness influenced by country-specific conditions – some firms have better prerequisites for successful international business activities than others because of home market surroundings	– the meaning of competitive advantage is empirically hard to quantify – some model assumptions are rather speculative – lacks precise recommendations about which circumstances allow a firm to gain competitive advantage – tends to neglect other countries and their impact on the home country with respect to the firm's competitiveness

Figure 26. A summary of the principal contents and major limitations of the location concepts and the diamond model

The product life-cycle approach by Vernon (1966, 1972) was developed from the perspective of US-based enterprises and their international business activities for the period beginning after World War II until the 1960s. Against the background of liberalized trade patterns and shortened product and technology life cycles, Vernon's product life-cycle theory became almost outdated for the majority of modern industries and their related economies. Nevertheless, Vernon's model, combining the product's age and varying international market entry concepts, significantly influenced the international management and marketing literature at that time.

Model	Representative publications [Year]	Principal contents of the model	Major limitations of the model
International product life-cycle	Vernon [1966, 1972]	– international market entry and exit strategies depend on the product's positioning in its life-cycle – US economy perspective after WWII – focus on manufacturing industries	– ignores tariff and non-tariff trade barriers as well as behavioral aspects – verification and generalization difficult – neglects threat of product substitution through upcoming nations and their industries – shortened product and technology life cycles cause the model to become almost obsolete

Figure 27. A summary of the principal contents and major limitations of the location concepts and the diamond model

The internalization concept of Buckley and Casson (1976: 109–110), which is based on the transaction cost theory (compare: Coase, 1937, Williamson, 1975, 1985), explained for the first time the nature and development of the MNE (which takes advantage of country-specific market failures). However, the internalization model fails to consider the phenomenon of changing internationalization processes (Johanson and Mattsson, 1988: 307) and the aspect of learning that is emphasized by the Uppsala model, which was introduced at the end of the 1970s.

The Uppsala concept (Johanson and Vahlne, 1977: 23–27) belongs to the most intensively discussed models in the corresponding literature in the last decades. Meanwhile, the model has not proved totally obsolete; but a firm's independent, linear, and forward-directed internationalization approach does not serve as a general theory, particularly against the background of globalized procurement, manufacture, and sales patterns.

At the beginning of the 1980s, the eclectic (OLI) paradigm by Dunning appeared in the literature. The model combines elements of the resource-based view, location concepts, and the internalization theory. The attempt to reflect as much as possible the complex international business environment in the theory served at the same time as major criticism of the eclectic paradigm. The eclectic paradigm shaped the academic discussion of firms' internationalization during the 1980s until the 1990s.

At the end of the 1980s and in particular during the 1990s, more and more findings in empirical research led to the conclusion that firms tend to be embedded in

Model	Representative publications [Year]	Principal contents of the model	Major limitations of the model
Internalization theory	Buckly and Casson [1976] based on the transaction cost theory by Coase [1937] and Williamson [1975]	– focus on transaction costs as main impulse for foreign market entry [hierarchy versus market mechanism] – assumes rational thinking – explains MNE appearance because of organizational capabilities and market imperfections – consideration of the 'knowledge' and 'skill' factors	– transaction costs are hard to quantify – limited attention to behavioral aspects (e. g., entrepreneurial, management preferences) – ignores tariff and non-tariff barriers, legal aspects, and tax policies in the target markets – disregard of 'follow-the-customer' phenomenon

Figure 28. A summary of the principal contents and major limitations of the internalization theory

Model	Representative publications [Year]	Principal contents of the model	Major limitations of the model
Uppsala	Carlson [1966] Forsgren and Johanson, Johanson and Wiedersheim [both 1975] Johanson and Vahlne [1977]	– considers a firm's internationalization as a process – due to a lack of foreign market knowledge, firms internationalize incrementally from physically and culturally close foreign markets to more distant countries – stepwise and orderly utilization of outward going international business operations – 'psychic distance' is defined in terms of factors such as differences in language, culture, political systems, etc. – focus on experience, knowledge, and self-learning	– 'psychic distance' is perceived differently by operating managers – panel focus on large Swedish firms – restricted to the initial stages of internationalization – reactive character leaving little room for entrepreneurial choice – internationalization is not always linear and a continuous process; firms have the opportunity to recall their foreign engagement – the concept concentrates on experiential learning through commitment decisions but ignores imitative learning and the phenomenon of 'early internationalizers'

Figure 29. A summary of the principal contents and major limitations of the Uppsala concept

supplier-customer-competitor networks. Consequently, firms do not decide their internationalization activities independently. For example, the fact that a firm has to

Model	Representative publications [Year]	Principal contents of the model	Major limitations of the model
Eclectic para-digm	Dunning [1979, 1980, 1983, 1988, 1993, 1994, 1995, 2000, 2001] Dunning and Dilyard [1999] Dunning, Park and Beldona [2007]	– consideration of (O)wnership (resource-based view), (L)ocation (concepts), (I) nternalization (transaction cost theory) factors – multi-causal (OLI) reasons influence the market entry strategy of the firm consisting of (1) 'international contracts' (O – available) (2) export (OI – available) (3) foreign direct investment (OLI – available)	– overlapping 'conglomeration of variables' – high model complexity – empirical verification of crucial variables difficult – predictions tend to be vague

Figure 30. A summary of the principal contents and major limitations of the eclectic paradigm

'follow its important customer abroad' (as witnessed by increasingly globalized value added activities) in order to remain a supplier is definitely not an independent decision of the firm. Alternatively, a competitor's movements towards other regions in the world may force a firm to follow and to enter a certain foreign market ('follow the competitor'). In contrast to Uppsala, which emphasizes 'self-learning', the network literature indicates a common denominator: the development and transfer of knowledge through active and/or imitator learning from other actors (e. g., suppliers, customers, competitors) in the industry network. The inter-organizational network theory is based on the assumption that a firm's changing internationalization situation is the result of its institutional positioning (as a result of bilateral relationships with other actors) in a network. Industry network structures change over time, which leads to a network reconfiguration of the involved firms (e.g., instabilities lead to the termination of a joint venture).

Since the middle of the 1990s, due to the phenomenon of small and young firms that immediately internationalize following their foundation, there have been an increasing number of articles that deal with the factor of time and the behavioral aspects of internationalization. Research on behavioral aspects deals with the role of the entrepreneur and/or the team in international new ventures (born globals). All of this research disagrees with the Uppsala model, which claims an incremental internationalization path from neighboring markets to more distant markets utilizing accumulated experience and learning.

Early internationalization concepts focus on personal relationships, and the internationalization process is viewed as 'value-creating-events' (Jones and Coviello, 2005: 297). Internationalization performance is understood as the result of human behavior (e. g., open mindset, innovative, global mindset) in a context of time

Model	Representative publications [Year]	Principal contents of the model	Major limitations of the model
Network Model [inter-organizational]	Johanson and Mattson [1988] Kogut and Zander [1993] Hohenthal [2001] Bjorkman and Forsgren [2000] Hakansson and Johanson [2001] Johanson and Vahlne [2003, 2009, 2010] Mathews, Hu and Wu [2011] Gadde, Hjelmgren and Skarp [2012]	– assumption that a firm's international business success or failure is a result of its positioning in a network of firms or institutions and their connections to each other – networks are a set of relationships among suppliers, manufacturers, merchandisers, customers, and other stakeholders – learning and knowledge transfer within the networks has particular importance – competitive advantage is achieved through dynamic capabilities fostered in networks – emerging global economy as networks of interlinked firms	– empirically hard to test due to the complexity of international networks and their influencing variables – need for industry- specific insights, which is challenging to realize from a researcher's 'outsider perspective' – tends to focus on oligopoly (B-to-B) markets – research results (e. g., through firm case studies) are hard to generalize – empirical research often tends to supply 'spotlights' of network structures because longitudinal fact-finding research is time consuming and therefore expensive

Figure 31. A summary of the principal contents and major limitations of the network concept (interorganizational approach)

(e. g., taking the opportunity at the right time). New internationalization concepts focus on learning through personal relationships (e. g., the entrepreneur and the firm's team and their relationship to suppliers, customers, and other stakeholders), which significantly influence the internationalization activities of the firm. The extent and the quality of personal relationships change over time. Consequently, the behavioral characteristics of the people involved in international business have a vital impact on the firms' internationalization path (Hurmerinta-Peltomaki, 2003: 226).

In the next chapter, the most relevant modes of market entry are explained and discussed along with their individual strengths and weaknesses.

Model	Representative publications [Year]	Principal contents of the model	Major limitations of the model
Network Model [interpersonal] 'early internatio-nalizers'	Oviatt & Mc Dougall [1994, 2000] Jones & Coviello [2002, 2005] Zahra, Ireland and Hitt [2000] Sharma & Blomstermo [2003] Bell, McNaughton, Young and Crick [2003] Hurmerinta-Peltomäki [2003] Liesch, Steen, Middle-ton, Weerawardena [2007] DiGregorio, Musteen and Thomas [2008] Gabrielsson, Kirpalani, Dimitratos, Solberg and Zuchella [2008] Madsen [2013] Cavusgil and Knight [2015]	– rapid internationalization after firm inception fostered by the entre-preneur's behavior (risk awareness, innovative-ness, and managerial international compe-tence) – internationalization as a systems perspective of personal relations-hips and the factor of time – success in international business is dependent upon the embedding of the entrepreneur and his/her team in cross-border personal rela-tionships – internationalization is not always a linear and forward-going process but rather is highly dynamic and cyclical as a reflection of time	– concepts tend to focus on small firms – research tends to focus on the owner or key decision maker – model is influenced by sociological, psycho-logical, and business aspects, which leads to an enormous com-plexity – empirical verification is difficult – hard to get a stand-ardized and structured model – length of internatio-nalizing time horizon is defined differently – impact of a particular event in time during internationalization process is difficult to prove

Figure 32. A summary of the principal contents and major limitations of the network concept (interpersonal approach)

Bibliography

Abegglen, J. C., & Stalk, G. J. (1985) *Kaisha: the Japanese corporation*. New York: Basic Books.

Autio, E., Sapienza, H. J., & Almeida, J. G. (2000) Effects of age at entry, knowledge intensity, and imitability on international growth. *Academy of Management Journal*, 43: 909–924.

Axelsson, B., & Easton, G. (1992) *Industrial networks. A new view of reality*. London and New York: Routledge.

Bandelk, N. (2002) Embedded economics: Social relations as determinants of foreign direct investment in central and eastern Europe. *Social Forces*, 81(2): 411–444.

Barkema, H. G., Bell, J. H. J., & Pennings, J. M. (1996) Foreign entry, cultural barriers, and learning. *Strategic Management Journal*, 17: 151–166.

Barkema, H. G., & Drogendijk, R. (2007) Internationalising in small, incremental or larger steps? *Journal of International Business Studies*, 38: 1132–1148.

Barney, J. (1991) Firm resources and sustained competitive advantage. *Journal of Management*, 17: 99–120.

Bastian, N. (2006) Sharp lässt Loewe an der langen Leine, *Handelsblatt*. March 09th, 2006.

Belderbos, R., & Zou, J. (2006) Foreign investment, divestment and relocation by Japanese electronics firms in East Asia. *Asian Economic Journal*, 20(1): 1–27.

Bell, J., McNaughton, R., Young, S., & Crick, D. (2003) Towards an integrative model of small firm internationalization. *Journal of International Entrepreneurship*, 1: 339–362.

Beugelsdijk, S., Mudambi, R., & Andersson, U. (2013) MNE's as border-crossing multi-location enterprises: The role of discountinuities in geographic space. *Journal of International Business Studies*, 44(5).

bfai_Bundesagentur_für_Außenwirtschaft (2007) Japanische LCD-Fernsehgeräte künftig aus Polen. Retrieved March 20, 2007 from http://www.bfai.de/fdb-SE,MKT20061113105133

Bilby, E. (2013) China has until June 7 to negotiate a deal with the European Union on state subsidies for solar panels and mobile telephone networks or face possible punitive measures, the EU's trade chief said on Wednesday. Retrieved March 26, 2013 from http://www.reuters.com/article/2013/02/27/us-euro-summit-eu-china-idUSBRE91Q0s O20130227

Björkman, I., & Forsgren, M. (2000) Nordic international business research. A review of its development. *International Studies of Management and Organization*, 30 (1): 6–25.

Brakman, S., Garretsen, H., Van Marrewijk, C., & Van Witteloostuijn, A. (2006) *Nations and firms in the global economy – an introduction to international economics and business*. Cambridge: Cambridge University Press.

Brown, W. S. (1976) Islands of conscious power; MNCs in the theory of the firm. *MSU Business Topics*, 24: 37–45.

Bruton, G. D., Ahlstrom, D., & Li, H. L. (2010) Institutional theory and entrepreneurship: Where are we now and where do we need to move in the future? *Entrepreneurship Theory and Practice*, 34(3): 421–440.

Buckley, P., & Casson, M. C. (2009) The internalisation theory of the multinational enterprise: A review of the progress of a research agenda after 30 years. *Journal of International Business Studies*, 40(9): 1563–1580.

Buckley, P. J., & Casson, M. (1976) *The future of the multinational enterprise*. London: Macmillan Press.

Buckley, P. J., & Casson, M. C. (1998) Analyzing foreign market entry strategies: Extending the internalization approach. *Journal of International Business Studies*, 29(3): 539–561.

Butler, R. (1995) Time in organizations: its experience, explanations and effects. *Organization Studies*, 16 (6): 925–950.

Carlson, S. (1966) *International business research*. Uppsala: Acta Universitatis Upsaliensis.

Carlson, S. (1975) *How foreign is foreign trade?* Uppsala: Uppsala University.

Caves, M. (1982) *Multinational enterprise and economic analysis*. Cambridge: Cambridge University Press.

Cavusgil, S. T., & Knight, G. (2015) The born global firm: An entrepreneurial and capabilities perspective on early and rapid internationalization *Journal of International Business Studies*, 46(1): 3–16.

Chaffin, J. (2013) EU and China settle trade fight over solar panels. Retrieved November 06, 2013 from http://www.ft.com/cms/s/0/4e468c26-f6ab-11e2–8620–00144feabdc0.html#axzz2jsA BuvXJ

Chang, S. J. (1995) International expansion strategy of Japanese firms: capability building through sequential entry. *Academy of Management Journal*, 38 (2): 383–407.

Changhong (2013) Changhong: company profile. Retrieved December 18, 2013 from http://www.changhongeurope.com/company-profile

Chen, M. (2004) *Asian management systems*. London: Thomson Learning.

Chetty, S., & Campbell-Hunt, C. (2004) A strategic approach to internationalization: A traditional versus a 'born global' approach. *Journal of International Marketing*, 12(1): 57–81.

Child, J., & Yan, Y. (1999) Investment and control in international joint ventures: the case of China. *Journal of World Business*, 34 (1): 3–15.

Churchill, G. (1967) Production technology, imperfect competition, and the theroy of location: A theoretical approach. *Southern Economic Journal:* 86–100.

Coase, R. H. (1937) The nature of the firm. *Economica*, 4: 386–405.

Cooper, A., & Dailly, C. (1997) Entrepreneurial teams. In D. L. Sexton, & R. W. Smilor (Eds.), *Entrepreneurship 2000*. Chicago: Upstart.

Coviello, N. (2015) Re-thinking research on born globals. *Journal of International Business Studies*, 46(1): 17–26.

Coviello, N., & Munro, H. (1997) Network relationships and the internationalisation process of small software firms. *International Business Review*, 6(4): 361–386.

Coviello, N. E. (2006) The network dynamics of international new ventures. *Journal of International Business Studies*, 37: 713–731.

Cox, J. (2015) Sony on OLED TV: We're looking into it, but concentrating on 4K LED. Retrieved August 14, 2015 from http://www.whathifi.com/news/sony-oled-tv-were-looking-it-concentrating-4k-led

Czechinvest (2012) The Czech electronics industry. Retrieved December 18, 2013 from http://www.czechinvest.org/data/files/electro-95.pdf

Dai, L., Eden, L., & Beamish, P. W. (2013) Place, space, and geographical exposure: Foreign subsidiary survival in conflict zones *Jounal of International Business Studies*, 44(6): 554–578.

Das, T. K., & Teng, B.-S. (2000) Instabilities of strategic alliances: An internal tensions perspective. *Organization Science*, 11(1): 77–101.

Davidson, W. H., & McFertidge, D. G. (1985) Key characteristics in the choice of international technology transfer mode. *Journal of International Business Studies*, 16(2): 5–21.

Delios, A., & Beamish, P. W. (1999) Ownership strategy of Japanese firms: Transactional, institutional, and experience influences. *Strategic Management Journal*, 20(10): 915–933.

DiGregorio, D., Musteen, M., & Thomas, D. E. (2008) International new ventures: The cross-border nexus of individuals and opportunities. *Journal of World Business*, 43: 186–196.

DisplaySearch (2008a) The influence of Sony's investment in Sharp's LCD TV panel factory. Retrieved September 10, 2008 from http://www.displaysearchblog.com/2008/03/the-influence-of-sonys-investment-in-sharp%e2%80%99 s-lcd-tv-panel-factory

DisplaySearch (2008b) OLED characterization report: Sony XEL-1 promo landing page. Is the OLED Display in Sony's XEL-1 OLED TV as good as it looks? Retrieved May 20, 2008 from http://www.displaysearch.com/cps/rde/xchg/displaysearch/hs.xsl/oled_characterization_report_promo_landing.asp

DisplaySearch. (2010) Display Search IFA conference meeting and presentation, September 03–08, 2011. Berlin, Germany.

Dong, B., Zou, S., & Taylor, C. R. (2008) Factors that influence multinational corporations' control of their operations in foreign markets. An empirical investigation. *Journal of International Marketing*, 16(1): 98–119.

Dunning, J. H. (1973) The determinants of international production. *Oxford Economic Papers*, 25(3): 289–336.

Dunning, J. H. (1979) Explaining changing patterns of international production: in defence of the eclectic theory. *Oxford Bulletin of Economics and Statistics*, 41: 269–295.

Dunning, J. H. (1980a) Toward an eclectic theory of international production: Some empirical tests. *Journal of International Business Studies*, 11(1): 9–31.

Dunning, J. H. (1980b) Towards an eclectic theory of international production: some empirical tests. *Journal of International Business Studies*, 11(1): 9–31.

Dunning, J. H. (1983) Changes in the level and structure of international production: the last one hundred years In M. C. Casson (Ed.), *The Growth of International Business:* 84–139. London: Allen & Unwin.

Dunning, J. H. (1993) *The globalization of business.* London: Routledge.

Dunning, J. H. (1994) Re-evaluating the benefits of foreign direct investment. *Transnational Corporations,* 3 (1): 23–51.

Dunning, J. H. (1995a) Reappraising the eclectic paradigm in an age of alliance capitalism. *Journal of International Business Studies,* 26(3): 461–491.

Dunning, J. H. (1995b) What's wrong – and right – with trade theory? *International Trade Journal,* 9(2): 163–202.

Dunning, J. H. (2000) The eclectic paradigm as an envelope for economic and business theories of MNE activity. *International Business Review,* 9 (2): 163–190.

Dunning, J. H. (2001) The eclectic (OLI) paradigm of international production: past, present and future. *International Journal of the Economics of Business,* 8 (2): 173–190.

Dunning, J. H. (2002) Globalization and the theory of MNE activity. In J. H. Dunning (Ed.), *The selected essays of John H. Dunning: Theories and paradigms of international business activity,* Vol. 1: 381–407. Cheltenham: Elgar.

Dunning, J. H., Cantwell, J. A., & Corley, T. A. B. (1986) The theory of international production: Some historical antecedents. In P. Hertner, & G. Jones (Eds.), *Multinationals: Theory and history:* 19–41. Aldershot: Gower.

Dunning, J. H., & Dilyard, J. R. (1999) Towards a general paradigm of foreign direct and foreign portfolio investment. *Transnational Corporations,* 8(1): 1–52.

Dunning, J. H., Pak, Y. S., & Beldona, S. (2007) Foreign ownership strategies of UK and US international franchisors: An exploratory application of Dunning's envelope paradigm. *International Business Review,* 16(5): 531–548.

Easton, G., & Araujo, L. (1994) Market exchange, social structures and time. *European Journal of Marketing,* 28(3): 3–84.

Economic_Review (2013) Interview with the president of Samsung Electronics Poland: Europe can be delivered within five days Retrieved December 18, 2013 from http://www.econovill.com/ar chives/127450

Eisenhardt, K. M., & Martin, J. (2000) Dynamic capabilities: what are they? *Strategic Management Journal,* 21(Special issue 10–11): 1105–1121.

Ellis, P. (2000) Social ties and foreign market entry. *Journal of International Business Studies,* 31: 443–469.

Ellis, P. D. (2011) Social ties and international entrepreneurship: Opportunities and constraints affecting firm internationalization. *Journal of International Business Studies,* 42(1): 99–127.

Eriksson, K., Johanson, J., Maikgard, A., & Sharma, D. D. (1997) Experiential knowledge and cost in the internationalization process. *Journal of International Business Studies,* 28: 337–360.

Erramilli, M. K., Agarwal, S., & Dev, C. S. (2002) Choice between non-equity entry modes: An organizational capability perspective. *Journal of International Business Studies,* 33(2): 223–242.

Esterhuizen, D. (2006) An evaluation of the competitiveness of the South African agribusiness sector. Retrieved July 15, 2007 from www.http://upetd.up.ac.za/thesis/available/etd-12082006–144349/unrestricted/00front.pdf

EU_Japan (2010) Sony Barcelona Tec technology center manufacturing LCD TV sets for Europe sold. Retrieved August 14, 2015 from http://eu-japan.com/2010/09/sony-barcelona-tec/

European_Union (2013) Member countries of the European Union. Retrieved December 23, 2013 from http://europa.eu/about-eu/countries/member-countries/index_en.htm

Fahy, J. (2002) A resource-based analysis of sustainable competitive advantage in a global environment. *International Business Review,* 11: 57–78.

Finanznachrichten.de (2007) LG.Philips LCD module plant in Poland begins mass production. Retrieved June 06, 2007 from http://www.finanznachrichten.de/p.asp?id=7999402

Forsgren, M. (2002) The concept of learning in the Uppsala internationalization process model: a critical review. *International Business Review*, 11: 257–277.

Forsgren, M., & Johanson, J. (1975) *Internationell företagskonomi*. Stockholm: Norstedts.

Frisch, A. (2004) *The story of Sony*. Minnesota: Smart Apple Media.

Frynas, J. G., & Mellahi, K. (2011) *Global strategic management*. New York: Oxford University Press.

Fu, X., & Zhang, J. (2011) Technology transfer, indigenous innovation and leapfrogging in green technology: The solar-PV industry in China and India. *Journal of Chinese Economic and Business Studies*, 9(4 – Special Issue:China's Drive Towards an Innovative Nation): 329–347.

Fujitsu (2005) Sharp and Fujitsu announce agreement on transfer of Fujitsu's LCD business. Retrieved September 09, 2008 from http://www.fujitsu.com/global/news/pr/archives/month/2005/20050207–02.html

Gabrielsson, M., Kirpalani, V. H. M., Dimitratos, P., Solberg, C. A., & Zuchella, A. (2008) Propositions to help advance the theory. *International Business Review*, 17(4): 385–401.

Gadde, L.-E., Hjelmgren, D., & Skarp, F. (2012) Interactive resource development in new business relationships. *Journal of Business Research*, 65(2): 210–217.

Glaister, K. W., Husan, R., & Buckley, P. J. (2003) Learning to manage international joint ventures. *International Business Review*, 12: 83–108.

Glover, J. L., Champion, D., Daniels, K. J., & Dainty, A. J. D. (2014) An institutional theory perspective on sustainable practices across the dairy supply chain. *International Journal of Production Economics*, 152: 102–111.

Gorenje (2015) Gorenje Group performance improves notably in 2014. Retrieved March 18th, 2015 from http://www.gorenjegroup.com/en/media/press-releases/2015/03/6720-Gorenje-Group-performance-improves-notably-in-2014

Grant, R. M. (1991a) Porter's 'competitive advantage of nations': an assessment. *Strategic Management Journal*, 12(7): 535–548.

Grant, R. M. (1991b) The resource-based theory of competitive advantage. Implications for strategy formulation. *California Management Review*, 33(3): 114–135.

Grant, R. M. (1996) Toward a knowledge-based theory of the firm. *Strategic Management Journal*, 17: 109–122.

Grant, R. M. (2000) The resource-based theory of competitive advantage. *California Management Review:* 114–135.

Grundberg, S. (2011) Sony buys Ericsson stake in handset joint venture. Retrieved August 15, 2015 from http://www.wsj.com/articles/SB10001424052970203554104577001062067170178

Gulati, R., Nohria, N., & Zaheer, A. (2000) Strategic networks. *Strategic Management Journal*, 21: 203–215.

Hadjikhani, A. (1997) A note on the criticisms against the internationalization process model. *Management International Review*, 37(Special Issue): 43–66.

Haier (2012) Haier and Sanyo sign final agreement to aquire washing machines, refrigerator and other consumer electric appliance businesses of Sanyo Electric Co., Ltd. Retrieved September 18, 2015 from http://www.haier.com/my/newspress/announcement/201203/t20120330_120921.shtml

Haier (2014a) Corporate development. Retrieved January 12, 2015 from http://www.haier.net/en/investor_relations/haier/cd/

Haier (2014b) Group chart. Retrieved November 26, 2014 from http://www.haier.net/en/investor_relations/haier/gc/

Haier (2014c) White goods group. Retrieved November 26, 2014 from http://www.haier.net/en/haier_industries/201110/t20111018_81797.shtml

Haier (2015a) About Haier. Retrieved September 19, 2015 from http://www.haier.com/my/header/
201202/t20120203_102568.shtml

Haier (2015b) Haier to announce its business focus for 2015. Retrieved September 18, 2015 from
http://www.haier.com/my/newspress/pressreleases/201502/t20150217_262012.shtml

Haier Electronics Group Co., L. (2005) Annual report 2005. Retrieved May 4, 2015 from http://www.
haier.net/en/investor_relations/1169/finance_reports/

Haier Electronics Group Co., L. (2007) Annual report 2007. Retrieved May 4, 2015 from http://www.
haier.net/en/investor_relations/1169/finance_reports/

Haier Electronics Group Co., L. (2008) Annual report 2008. Retrieved May 4, 2015 from http://
www.haier.net/en/investor_relations/1169/finance_reports/

Haier Electronics Group Co., L. (2010) Annual report 2010. Retrieved May 4, 2015 from http://www.
haier.net/en/investor_relations/1169/finance_reports/

Haier Electronics Group Co., L. (2012) Annual report 2012 Retrieved May 4, 2015 from http://www.
haier.net/en/investor_relations/1169/finance_reports/

Haier Electronics Group Co., L. (2013) Annual report 2013. Retrieved May 4, 2015 from www.haier-
elec.com.hk/image/pdf/report/20140520101417118.pdf

Haier_Electronics (2012a) Corporate structure. Retrieved November 26, 2014 from http://www.
haier-elec.com.hk/index.php?route=information/information&information_id=3

Haier_Electronics (2012b) Directors and senior management. Retrieved November 26, 2014 from
http://www.haier-elec.com.hk/index.php?route=information/corebusiness&information_id=7

Haier_Electronics (2012c) Integrated channel services. Retrieved November 26, 2014 from http://
www.haier-elec.com.hk/index.php?route=information/corebusiness&information_id=7

Haier_Electronics (2014) Corporate information. Retrieved October 19, 2014 from http://www.haier-
elec.com.hk/index.php?route=information/information&information_id=6

Håkansson, H., & Johanson, J. (2001) *Business network learning.* Oxford: Pergamon.

Hashai, N., & Almor, T. (2004) Gradually internationalizing born global firms: an oxymoron?
International Business Review, 13(13): 465–483.

Hill, C. W. L. (1990) Cooperation, opportunism, and the invisible hand: Implications for transaction
cost theory. *Academy of Management Review,* 15: 500–513.

Hill, C. W. L. (2005) *Competing in the global marketplace.* Boston: McGraw-Hill/Irwin.

Hitt, M. A., Ireland, R. D., & Hoskisson, R. E. (2015) *Strategic management. Competitiveness and
globalization* (11. Ed. ed.). Stamford, Conn.: Cengage Learning.

Hoetker, G., & Mellewigt, T. (2009) Choice and performance of governance mechanisms: Matching
alliance governance to asset type. *Strategic Management Journal,* 30: 1025–1044.

Hofstede, G. (2001) *Culture's consequences – comparing values, behaviours, institutions and
organization across nations* (2nd ed. ed.). California: Sage Publications Inc.

Hohenthal, J. (2001) *The creation of international business relationships.* Uppsala University,
Uppsala.

Holmquist, C. (2003) *Is the medium really the message? Moving perspective from the
entrepreneurial actor to the entrepreneurial action. New movements in entrepreneurship.*
Cheltenham: Edwards Elgar.

Hon_Hai (2013) Welcome to Foxconn Slovakia. Retrieved December 18, 2013 from http://www.fox
connslovakia.sk/index.php?page=english

Horvath-Papp, M. (2015) Xiaomi. Business strategy in a global context. Retrieved September 19,
2015 from http://www.chinaroom.eu/news/xiaomi-business-strategy-global-context

Hurmerinta-Peltomäki, L. (2003) Time and internationalisation. Theoretical challenges set by rapid
internationalisation. *Journal of International Entrepreneurship,* 1: 217–236.

Ihlwan, M. (2006) Samsung and Sony's win-win LCD venture. Retrieved September 09, 2008 from
http://www.businessweek.com/globalbiz/content/nov2006/gb20061128_546338.htm?chan=
tc&campaign_id=rss_tech

Imai, K. (1987) The corporate network in Japan. *Japanese Economic Studies*, 16: 1–37.

IMF (2013) World economic outlook database by countries. Retrieved November 30, 2013 from http://www.imf.org/external/pubs/ft/weo/2013/02/weodata/weorept.aspx?sy=2002&ey=2013&scsm=1&ssd=1&sort=country&ds=.&br=0&pr1.x=54&pr1.y=10&c=918 %2C964 %2C968 %2C922 %2C935 %2C936 %2C174 %2C944 %2C926&s=NGDP_R%2CNGDP_RPCH%2CNGDPRPC%2CNGAP_NPGDP%2CPCPIPCH%2CLUR%2CGGXCNL%2CGGXCNL_NGDP%2CGGXWDN%2CGGXWDN_NGDP%2CGGXWDG%2CGGXWDG_NGDP%2CBCA&grp=0&a=

Johanson, J., & Mattsson, L.-G. (1985) Marketing investments and market investments in industrial networks. *International Journal of Research in Marketing*, 2(3): 185–195.

Johanson, J., & Mattsson, L.-G. (1988) Internationalization in industrial systems – a network approach. In N. Hood, & J.-E. Vahlne (Eds.), *Strategies in global competition*: 468–486. New York: Croom Helm.

Johanson, J., & Mattsson, L.-G. (1992) Network positions and strategic action – an analytical framework. In B. Axelsson, & G. Easton (Eds.), *Industrial networks: a new view of reality*. London: Routledge.

Johanson, J., & Vahlne, J.-E. (1977) The internationalization process of the firm: A model of knowledge development and increasing foreign market commitments. *Journal of International Business Studies*, 8(1): 23–32.

Johanson, J., & Vahlne, J.-E. (1990) The mechanism of internationalization. *International Marketing Review*, 7(4): 11–24.

Johanson, J., & Vahlne, J.-E. (2003) Business relationship learning and commitment in the internationalization process. *Journal of International Entrepreneurship* 1: 83–101.

Johanson, J., & Vahlne, J.-E. (2009) The Uppsala internationalization process model revisited: From liability of foreignness to liability of outsidership. *Journal of International Business Studies*, 40(9): 1411–1431.

Johanson, J., & Wiedersheim, P., E. (1975) The internationalization of the firm: four Swedish cases. *Journal of Management Studies*, 12: 305–322.

Jones, M. V. (2001) First steps in internationalisation. Concepts and evidence from a sample of small high-technology firms. *Journal of International Management*, 7: 191–210.

Jones, M. V., & Coviello, N. E. (2002) A time-based contingency model of entrepreneurial internationalisation behaviour. *Working Paper 2002–12*, Haskayne School of Business: 1–60.

Jones, M. V., & Coviello, N. E. (2004) Methodological issues in international entrepreneurship research. *Journal of Business Venturing*, 19: 485–508.

Jones, M. V., & Coviello, N. E. (2005) Internationalisation: Conceptualising an entrepreneurial process of behaviour in time. *Journal of International Business Studies*, 36: 284–303.

Jordan, M. (2012) Sony's fiscal 2012 results: $820 million loss due to floods, earthquakes and exchange rates. Retrieved May 28, 2015 from http://www.engadget.com/2012/05/10/sonys-fiscal-2012-results-820-million-loss-due-to-floods-ear/

Kan, M. (2014) Why are Xiaomi phones so cheap? Retrieved September 19, 2015 from http://www.pcworld.com/article/2156320/why-are-xiaomi-phones-so-cheap.html

Karra, N., & Phillips, N. (2004) *Entrepreneurship goes global*. Ontario: Ivey Business School.

Kita, M. (2001) How the electronics manufacturing service business model can help Japanese corporations revolutionize their factories? *Japan Bank for International Cooperation Review* 4: 1–24.

Kogut, B., & Zander, U. (1993) Knowledge of the firm and the evolutionary theory of multinational corporation. *Journal of International Business Studies*, 24(4): 625–646.

Kotabe, M., & Murray, J. Y. (2004) Global sourcing strategy and sustainable competitive advantage. *Industrial Marketing Management*, 33(1): 7–14.

Koumparoulis, D. N. (2013) PEST analysis: The case of E-shop. *International Journal of Economy, Management and Social Sciences*, 2(2): 31–36.

Kuemmerle, W. (2002) Home base and knowledge management in international new ventures. *Journal of Business Venturing*, 17: 99–122.

Kutschker, M., & Schmid, S. (2011) *Internationales Management*. München: Oldenbourg Wissenschaftsverlag.

Leonidou, L. C., & Katsikeas, C. S. (1996) The export development process: an integrative review of empirical models. *Journal of International Business Studies*, 27(3): 517–551.

LG.PhilipsLCD (2006) LG.Philips LCD signs investment agreement with the Polish government. Retrieved January 05, 2006 from http://www.lgphilips-lcd.com/homeContain/jsp/eng/pr/pr201_j_e.jsp?BOARD_IDX=941&languageSec=E

LG_Electronics (2008) History. Retrieved September 05, 2008 from http://www.lge.com/about/corporate/history.jsp

Li, J. (1995) Foreign entry and survival: Effects of strategic choices on performance in international markets. *Strategic Management Journal*, 16: 333–351.

Liao, J. J., Kickul, J. R., & Ma, H. (2009) Organizational dynamic capability and innovation: An empirical examination of internet firms. *Journal of Small Business Management*, 47(3): 263–286.

Liesch, P. W., Steen, M., Middleton, S., & Weerawardena, J. (2007) *Born to be global: A closer look at the international venturing of Australian born global firms*. Sydney: Australian Business Foundation.

Lin, H.-E., McDonough III, E. F., Lin, S.-J., & Lin, C. Y.-Y. (2012) Managing the exploitation/exploration paradox: The role of a learning capability and innovation ambidexterity. *Journal of Product Innovation Management*, 30(2): 262–278.

Loane, S., Bell, J., & Cunningham, I. (2014) Entrepreneurial founding teams exists in rapidly internationalising SMEs: A double edged sword *International Business Review*, 23: 468–477.

Loane, S., Bell, J. D., & McNaughton, R. (2007) A cross-national study on the impact of management teams on the rapid internationalization of small firms. *Journal of World Business*, 42: 489–504.

Loewe (2013) TV maker Loewe files for bankruptcy. Retrieved Dec 16, 2013 from http://www.industryweek.com/competitiveness/tv-maker-loewe-files-bankruptcy

Loewe_AG (2014) Loewe AG: Veröffentlichung gemäß § 26 Abs. 1 WpHG mit dem Ziel der europaweiten Verbreitung. Retrieved September 7th, 2015 from http://www.dgap.de/dgap/News/pvr/loewe-veroeffentlichung-gemaess-abs-wphg-mit-dem-ziel-der-europaweiten-verbreitung/?companyID=76&newsID=811099

Lopez, L. E., Kundu, S. K., & Ciravegna, L. (2009) Born global or born regional? Evidence from an exploratory study in the Costa Rican software industry. *Journal of International Business Studies*, 40(7): 1228–1238.

Lou, Y., & Peng, M. W. (1999) Learning to compete in a transition economy: experience, environment, and performance. *Journal of International Business Studies*, 30(2): 269–295.

Luostarinen, R. (1980) *Internationalization of the firm. An empirical study of the internationalization of firms with small and open domestic markets with special emphasis on lateral rigidity as a behavioral characteristic in strategic decision-making*. Helsinki: The Helsinki School of Economics.

Madsen, T. K. (2013) Early and rapidly internationalizing ventures: Similarities and differences between classifications' based on the original international new venture and born global literatures. *Journal of International Entrepreneurship*, 11: 65–79.

Makadok, R. (2001) Toward a synthesis of the resource-based and dynamic-capability views of rent creation. *Strategic Management Journal*, 22: 387–401.

Makhija, M. (2003) Comparing the resource-based and market-based views of the firm: Empirical evidence from Czech privatization. *Strategic Management Journal*, 24(5): 433–451.

Mankiw, G. N. (2007) *Macroeconomics* (Sixth Edition ed.). New York: Worth Publishers.

Martin, X., & Salomon, R. (2003) Knowledge transfer capacity and its implications for the theory of the multinational corporation. *Journal of International Business Studies*, 34(4): 356–373.

Mathews, J. A. (2002) *Dragon multinational. A new model for global growth.* New York: Oxford University Press.

Mathews, J. A., Hu, M.-C., & Wu, C.-Y. (2011) Fast-follower industrial dynamics: The case of Taiwan's emergent solar photovoltaic industry. *Industry and Innovation*, 18(2): 177–202.

McCann, P., & Sheppard, S. (2003) The rise, fall and rise again of industrial location theory. *Regional Studies*, 37(6): 649–663.

McDougall, P. P., & Oviatt, B. M. (2000) International entrepreneurship: The intersection of two research paths. *Academy of Management Journal*, 43(5): 902–906.

McDougall, P. P., & Oviatt, B. M. (2003) Some fundamental issues in international entrepreneurship. Retrieved January 22, 2014 from http://www.hajarian.com/esterategic/tarjo meh/88–1/farahzadi.pdf

McIvor, R., Humphreys, P., & Cadden, T. (2006) Supplier involvement in product development in the electronics industry: a case study. *Journal of Engineering and Technology Management*, 23: 374–397.

Meyer, T. (2006) Globale Standortwahl – Einflussfaktoren. In E. Abele (Ed.), *Handbuch globale Produktion:* 36–100. München: Hanser.

Moschek, M. (2007) Sharp startet LCD-Modul Produktion in Polen. Hamburg: Press Release January 04th, 2007.

Müller-Stewens, G., & Lechner, C. (2011) *Strategisches Management. Wie strategische Initiativen zum Wandel führen* (4. Ed. ed.). Stuttgart: Schäffer-Poeschel.

Munich_Innovation_Group (2012) Chinese Champions. Retrieved September 18th, 2015 from http://www.chinese-champions.de/wordpress/wp-content/uploads/Studie_Chinese_Champions.pdf

Nathan, J. (1999) *Sony.* New York: Houghton Mifflin Company.

Naver (2004) Going to Eastern Europe: Samsung SDI Hungary. Big and bigger over the EU market – Samsung's 'production base'. Retrieved December 17, 2013 from http://news.naver.com/ main/read.nhn?mode=LSD&mid=sec&sid1=101&oid=014&aid=0000131670

Newbert, S. L. (2007) Empirical research on the resource-based view of the firm: An assessment and suggestions for future research. *Strategic Management Journal*, 28(2): 121–146.

Newman, J. (2014) Sony quits the PC business. Good! Retrieved August 15th, 2015 from http://time.com/5412/sony-quits-the-pc-business-good/

news1.Korea (2012) Samsung doniniert den TV Markt in Osteuropa. Retrieved December 18, 2013 from http://news1.kr/articles/908623

North, D. C. (1990) *Institutions, institutional change and economic performance.* Cambridge: Cambridge University Press.

OECD (2013) Average annual wages. Retrieved December 19, 2013 from http://stats.oecd.org/ Index.aspx?DataSetCode=AV_AN_WAGE

Olsson, J. (2007) Sharp attracts new investors to Poland. Retrieved June 06, 2007 from http://www.evertiq.com/newsx/default.aspx

Otani (2008) Sony, Sharp form joint venture for 10th-generation liquid crystal display fabrication. Retrieved May 05, 2008 from http://techon.nikkeibp.co.jp/article/HONSHI/20080327/149601/

Oviatt, B. M., & Mc Dougall, P. P. (1994) Toward a theory of international new ventures. *Journal of International Business Studies*, 25(1): 45–64.

Oviatt, B. M., & McDougall, P. P. (1997) Challenges for internationalization process theory: The case of international new ventures. *Academy of Management Executive*, 9 (2 Special Issue): 85–99.

PAIZ (2009) Foreign direct investments in Poland. Retrieved August 15, 2009 from http://www.paiz.gov.pl/index/index.php?id=59112692262234e3fad47fa8eabf03a4

Pan, Y., & Tse, D. K. (2000) The hierarchical model of market entry modes. *Journal of International Business Studies*, 31(4): 535–554.

Parkin, M., Powell, M., & Matthews, K. (2000) *Economics*. Harlow: Addison-Wesley.

Penrose, E. (1959) *The theory of the growth of the firm*. New York: Oxford University Press.

Penrose, E. (1995) *The theory of the growth of the firm* (2nd ed.). Oxford: Oxford University Press.

Peters, M., Siller, L., & Matzler, K. (2011) The resource-based and the market-based approaches to cultural tourism in alpine destinations. *Journal of Sustainable Tourism*, 19(7): 877–893.

Pham, A. (2012) Sony posts a record loss, vows 2012 profit. Retrieved May 28, 2015 from http://articles.latimes.com/2012/may/10/business/la-fi-ct-sony-earns-20120510

Philips. (2004) Annual Report 2004. Eindhoven.

Philips (2011) Philips and TPV to create strong global television company. Retrieved December 17, 2013 from http://www.newscenter.philips.com/main/corpcomms/news/press/2011/20110418_tpv_jointventure.wpd#.UrCGHxA4iM0

PolandBusiness (2007a) Poland Business Networks. Poland not crowding out the competition. Retrieved June 06, 2007 from http://polandbusinessnetwork.pl/news/index.php?contentid=132697

PolandBusiness (2007b) Poland Business Networks. Special economic zones. Retrieved October 11, 2007 from http://business.poland.com/special-economic-zones/

Porter, M. E. (1980) *Competitive strategy*. New York: Free Press.

Porter, M. E. (1990) *The competitive advantage of nations*. New York: The Free Press.

Porter, M. E. (2003) *Competitive advantage: Creating and sustaining superior performance*. New York: Free Press.

Porter, M. E., & Fuller, M. B. (1986) Coalitions and global strategy. In M. E. Porter (Ed.), *Competition in global industries*: 315–343. Boston: Harvard Business School Press.

Porter, M. E., & van der Linde, C. (1995) Toward a new conception of the environment-competitiveness relationship. *Journal of Economic Perspectives*, 9(4): 97–118.

Rasmussen, E. S., Jensen, J. M., & Servais, P. (2008) Location and internationalization: are international firms just as sticky as local firms? In J. Larimo (Ed.), *Perspectives on Internationalization and International Management*. Vaasa: University of Vaasa.

Reuber, A. R., & Fischer, E. (1999) Understanding the consequences of founders experience. *Journal of Small Business Management*, 37(2): 30–45.

Reuters (2013) Panasonic to shut Czech LCD panel production plant. Retrieved December 12, 2013 from http://www.reuters.com/article/2012/10/31/panasonic-idUSL5E8LVB3P20121031

Rialp-Criado, A., Rialp-Criado, J., & Knight, G. A. (2002) The phenomenon of international new ventures, global start-ups, and born globals: What we know after a decade (1992–2002) of exhaustive scientific inquiry?, Vol. No. 200211. Barcelona: Universitat Autonoma de Barcelona.

Robock, S. H., & Simmonds, K. (1989) *International business and multinational enterprises*. Boston: Richard D. Irwin.

Roger, F. (2015) Apple suppliers Sharp, Foxconn in talks for LCD partnership – report. Retrieved September 7th, 2015 from http://appleinsider.com/articles/15/08/24/apple-suppliers-sharp-foxconn-in-talks-for-lcd-partnership—report

Rugman, A. M., & D'Cruz, J. R. (1993) The double diamond model of international competitiveness: the Canadian experience. *Management International Review*, 33(Special Issue 1993/2): 17–93.

Rugman, A. M., & Verbeke, A. (1993) Foreign subsidiaries and multinational strategic management: an extension and correction of Porter's single diamond framework. *Management International Review*, 33(Special Issue 1993/2): 71–84.

Samiee, S. (2008) Global marketing effectiveness via alliances and electronic commerce in business-to-business markets. *Industrial Marketing Management*, 37: 3–8.

Samiee, S., & Walters, P. G. P. (2006) Supplier and customer exchange in international industrial markets: An integrative perspective. *Industrial Marketing Management*, 35(5): 589–599.

Samsung (2014) Affiliated companies. Retrieved October 19, 2014 from http://www.samsung.com/us/aboutsamsung/samsung_group/affiliated_companies/

Samsung (2015) Samsung Profile 1995–2014. Retrieved January 18, 2015 from http://www.samsung.com/us/aboutsamsung/samsung_group/our_performance/

Schuler, R. S. (2001) Human resource issues and activities in international joint ventures. *International Journal of Human Resource Management*, 12(1): 1–52.

Schwens, C., & Kabst, R. (2008) How early internationalizer venture abroad: a review. In R. Moser (Ed.), *Ausländische Direktinvestitionen, Neuere Entwicklungen, Entscheidungsinstrumente und führungsrelevante Folgen*. Wiesbaden: Gabler Edition Wissenschaft.

Sharma, D. D., & Blomstermo, A. (2003) The internationalization process of born globals: A network view. *International Business Review*, 12: 739–753.

Sharp (2004) Loewe and Sharp agree on the enhancement of LCD TV collaboration and Sharp's additional investment. Retrieved August 13, 2008 from http://hiddenwires.co.uk/resourcesnews2004/news20041215–05.html

Sharp (2005) Annual report 2004. Retrieved March 18, 2015 from http://sharp-world.com/corporate/ir/library/annual/past.html

Sharp (2007a) *Sharp Allianzen*. Retrieved August 22, 2007 from http://www.sharp-world.com/corporate/news/index.html

Sharp (2007b) Sharp TV history. Retrieved December 26, 2007 from http://www.sharp-world.com/corporate/info/his/chronology/index.html

Sharp (2008a) *Affiliated companies of Sharp*. Retrieved August 13, 2008 from http://sharp-world.com/corporate/info/ci/consolidated/oversea.html#other

Sharp (2008b) Kameyama plant. Retrieved September 09, 2008 from http://www.sharp-world.com/kameyama/feature/index.html

Sharp (2008c) Sharp and Toshiba to form alliance in liquid crystal display and semiconductor businesses. Retrieved September 09, 2008 from http://sharp-world.com/corporate/news/071221.html

Sharp (2010) Annual report 2009. Retrieved March 18, 2015 from http://sharp-world.com/corporate/ir/library/annual/past.html

Sharp (2011) Annual report 2010. Retrieved March 18, 2015 from http://sharp-world.com/corporate/ir/library/annual/past.html

Sharp (2012) Annual report 2011. Retrieved March 18, 2015 from http://sharp-world.com/corporate/ir/library/annual/past.html

Sharp (2013) Annual report 2012. Retrieved March 18, 2015 from http://sharp-world.com/corporate/ir/library/annual/past.html

Sharp (2014a) Annual report 2013. Retrieved March 18, 2015 from http://sharp-world.com/corporate/ir/library/annual/past.html

Sharp (2014b) Business Activities. Retrieved October 23, 2014 from http://www.sharp-world.com/corporate/info/ci/business/index.html

Sharp (2015a) Annual report 2014. Retrieved March 18, 2015 from http://sharp-world.com/corporate/ir/library/annual/

Sharp (2015b) Notice of extraordinary losses accompanying structure reforms to consumer electronics business in Europe. Retrieved 2015, July 13 from http://sharp-world.com/corporate/ir/topics/pdf/141219.pdf

Shrader, R. C., Oviatt, B. M., & Mc Dougall, P. P. (2000) How new ventures exploit trade-offs among international risk factors: Lessons for the accelerated internationalization of the 21st century. *Academy of Management Journal*, 43(6): 1227–1247.

Slovak_Investment. (2012) Electrical engineering industry: Slovak Investment and Trade Development Agency.

SolarOne, H. (2010) Solarfun Power Holdings, newly starts by the name of 'Hanwha SolarOne' in 2011. Retrieved November 18, 2013 from http://www.hanwha-solarone.com/de/news/com pany-news/company-news-002/113-company-news-005

Sony (2004) Annual report 2003. Retrieved January 18, 2015 from http://www.sony.net/SonyInfo/ IR/financial/ar/Archive.html

Sony (2005) Annual report 2004. Retrieved January 18, 2015 from http://www.sony.net/SonyInfo/ IR/financial/ar/Archive.html

Sony (2006a) Annual report 2005. Retrieved January 18, 2015 from http://www.sony.net/SonyInfo/ IR/financial/ar/Archive.html

Sony (2006b) Annual report 2006. Retrieved from http://www.sony.net/SonyInfo/IR/financial/ar/Ar chive.html

Sony (2006c) Samsung and Sony sign final contract regarding production line for world's most advanced generation liquid crystal display panel. Retrieved from http://www.samsung.com/ us/news/newsRead.do?news_group=productnews=businessproduct=lcd&news_seq=3218

Sony (2007a) Annual report 2006. Retrieved January 18, 2015 from http://www.sony.net/SonyInfo/ IR/financial/ar/Archive.html

Sony (2007b) Sony's new BRAVIA LCD TV factory in Nitra, Slovakia, starts mass production. Retrieved February 01, 2008 from http://www.sony-europe.com/view/ShowPressRelease.ac tion?section=ODW+SS+en_..

Sony (2008a) Annual report 2007. Retrieved January 18, 2015 from http://www.sony.net/SonyInfo/ IR/financial/ar/Archive.html

Sony (2008b) History. Retrieved July 18, 2008 from http://www.sony.net/Fun/SH/1–34/h4.html

Sony (2008c) History. Supporting the electronics business. Retrieved July 18, 2008 from http:// www.sony.net/Fun/SH/1–32/h2.html

Sony (2008d) Sony business and financial overview. Retrieved September 14, 2008 from //http:// www.sony.net/SonyInfo/IR/financial/ar/2007/qfhh7c00000d7q0j-att/SonyAR07–08.pdf

Sony (2008e) Sony Corporation. Retrieved July 18, 2008 from http://www.sony.net/SonyInfo/Corpo rateInfo/Subsidiaries/index.html

Sony (2008f) Sony cuts jobs, investment. Retrieved August 19, 2008 from http://www.redorbit. com/news/technology/1608487/sony_cuts_jobs_investments/index.html?source=r_technol ogy

Sony (2009) Annual report 2008. Retrieved January 18, 2015 from http://www.sony.net/SonyInfo/ IR/financial/ar/Archive.html

Sony (2010) Annual report 2009. Retrieved January 18, 2015 from http://www.sony.net/SonyInfo/ IR/financial/ar/Archive.html

Sony (2011) Annual report 2010. Retrieved January 18, 2015 from http://www.sony.net/SonyInfo/ IR/financial/ar/Archive.html

Sony (2012a) Annual report 2011. Retrieved January 18, 2015 from http://www.sony.net/SonyInfo/ IR/financial/ar/Archive.html

Sony (2012b) Sharp and Sony to terminate joint venture to produce and sell large-sized LCD panels and modules. Retrieved August 15th, 2015 from http://www.sony.net/SonyInfo/News/ Press/201205/12–0524E/

Sony (2012c) Sony establishes new management structure- to drive revitalization and growth of electronics businesses and deliver compelling user experiences as "One Sony" -.

Sony (2013a) About Sony. Sony manufacturing in Europe. Retrieved December 18, 2013 from http://www.sony-europe.com/article/id/1170434888571

Sony (2013b) Annual report 2012. Retrieved January 18, 2015 from http://www.sony.net/SonyInfo/ IR/financial/ar/Archive.html

Sony (2014) Annual report 2013. Retrieved January 18, 2015 from http://www.sony.net/SonyInfo/ IR/financial/ar/Archive.html

Sony (2015) Division. Retrieved July 3, 2015 from http://www.sony.net/SonyInfo/CorporateInfo/ Data/organization.html

Sony_Financial_Holdings (2014) About Sony Financial Group. Retrieved October 19, 2014 from http://www.sonyfh.co.jp/en/company/about_group.html

Sony_Pictures (2014) Division. Retrieved November 26, 2014 from http://www.sonypictures.com/ corp/divisions.html

Stöttinger, B., & Schlegelmilch, B. B. (2000) Psychic distance: a concept past its due date? International Marketing Review, 17(2): 169–173.

Svejnar, J. (2002) Transition economies: Performance and challenges. The Journal of Economic Perspectives, 16(1): 3–28.

Tabuchi, H. (2012a) How the tech parade passed Sony by. Retrieved May 28, 2015 from http:// www.nytimes.com/2012/04/15/technology/how-sony-fell-behind-in-the-tech-parade.html?_r=0

Tabuchi, H. (2012b) Japan's electronics behemoths speak of dire times ahead. Retrieved May 28, 2015 from http://www.nytimes.com/2012/11/02/business/global/sony-sharp-and-panasonic-re port-significant-losses.html

TCL (2004) Press Release, TCL and Thomson – Finalization of other definitive agreements and dispatch of shareholders' cicular relating to the establishment of TTE Corporation. Retrieved April 15, 2008 from http://www.tclhk.com/tclhk/admin/upload/ir/press/ep0462.pdf

TCL (2007a) About us, manufacturing plants. Retrieved November 06, 2007 from http://www.tclhk. com/2007/en/aboutus/production.asp

TCL (2007b) Insolvency filing by a major subsidiary. Retrieved May 24, 2007 from http://www. tclhk.com/tclhk/admin/upload/ir/announcements/ec070524.pdf

Teece, D. J. (2000) Managing intellectual capital. New York: Oxford University Press.

Teece, D. J., Pisano, G., & Shuen, A. (1997) Dynamic capabilities and strategic management. Strategic Management Journal, 18 (7): 509–533.

Tesch, P. (1980) Die Bestimmungsgründe des internationalen Handels und der Direktinvestition. Berlin: Duncker & Humblot.

Toshiba (2013) Toshiba sell its Poland factory to Taiwanese Compal Electronics. Retrieved from http://www.wbj.pl/article-64216-toshiba-sells-ots-polish-tv-unit.html

UNCTAD (2010) Inward and outward foreign direct investment stock, annual, 1980–2009. Retrieved December 12, 2010 from www.http://unctadstat.unctad.org

Vahlne, J.-E., & Ivarsson, I. (2014) The globalization of Swedish MNEs: Empirical evidence and theoretical explanations. Journal of International Business Studies, 45(3): 227–247.

Van de Ven, A. H., & Poole, M. S. (1995) Explaining development and change in organizations. The Academy of Management Review, 20 (3): 510–540.

Vernon, R. (1966) International investment and international trade in the product cycle. Quarterly Journal of Economics, 80: 190–207.

Vernon, R. (1972) International trade: the product life cycle approach. In L. T. Wells (Ed.), The product life cycle and international trade. Boston: Harvard University.

Walter, A., Müller, T. A., Helfert, G., & Ritter, T. (2003) Functions of industrial supplier relationships and their impact on relationship quality. Industrial Marketing Management, 32: 159–169.

WarsawVoice (2006) Busy zones. Retrieved June 06, 2007 from http://www.warsawvoice.pl/printAr ticle.php?a=11861

Welch, L. S., & Luostarinen, R. (1988) Internationalization: evolution of a concept. Journal of General Management, 34: 34–55.

Welge, K. M., & Holtbrügge, D. (2015) Internationales Management (5. Ed. ed.). Stuttgart: Schäffer-Poeschel Verlag.

WeltOnline (2008) Endlich darf auch Sony einmal triumphieren. Retrieved July 15, 2008 from
http://www.welt.de/meinung/article1522979/Endlich_darf_auch_Sony_einmal_triumphieren.
html

Wernerfelt, B. (1984) A resource based view of the firm. *Strategic Management Journal*, 5(2):
171–180.

Wheelen, T. L., & Hunger, J. D. (2010) *Strategic management and business policy. Achieving
sustainability* (12. Ed. ed.). Boston: Pearson Education Ltd.

Williamson, O. (1991) Comparative Economic Organization: The Analysis of Discrete Structural
Alternatives. *Administrative Science Quarterly*, 269(36): 269–296.

Williamson, O. E. (1975) *Markets and hierarchies – analysis and antitrust implications*. New York:
The Free Press

Williamson, O. E. (1985) *The economic institutions of capitalism. Firms, markets, relational
contracting*. New York: The Free Press.

Williamson, O. E. (1999) Strategy research: Governance and competence perspectives. *Strategic
Management Journal*, 20(12): 1087–1108.

Windeler, A. (2005) Netzwerktheorien: Vor einer rationalen Wende? In J. Zentes, B. Swoboda, & D.
Morschett (Eds.), *Kooperationen, Allianzen und Netzwerke*. Wiesbaden: Gabler Verlag.

World_Bank (2013) Foreign direct investment, net inflows (% of GDP). Retrieved November 30,
2013 from http://search.worldbank.org/quickview?name=%3Cem%3EForeign%3C%2Fem%3E+
%3Cem%3Edirect%3C%2Fem%3E+%3Cem%3Einvestment%3C%2Fem%3E%2C+net+inflows+%
28%25+of+GDP%29&id=BX.KLT.DINV.WD.GD.ZS&type=Indicators&cube_no=2&qterm=foreign
+direct+investment

WTO (2013) Statistics database. Retrieved November 30, 2013 from http://stat.wto.org/Statistical
Program/WSDBStatProgramSeries.aspx?Language=E

Wu, C.-Y., & Mathews, J. A. (2012) Knowledge flows in the solar photovoltaic industry: Insights
from patenting by Taiwan, Korea, and China. *Research Policy*, 41: 524–540.

Wu, J., & Wu, Z. (2014) Local and international knowledge search and product innovation: The
moderating role of technology boundary spanning. *International Business Review*, 23(3):
542–551.

Xiaomi (2015) Retrieved April 14, 2015 from http://www.mi.com/en/index.html

Young, S., Dimitratos, P., & Dana, L.-P. (2003) International entrepreneurship research: What scope
for international business theories? *Journal of International Entrepreneurship*, 1: 31–42.

Yu, H. (2014) How Xiaomi wooed the best suppliers. Retrieved September 20, 2015 from http://
www.ft.com/cms/s/0/6a675fe2-a9c6–11e3-adab-00144feab7de.html#axzz3mGf5zPPV

Zahra, S. A. (2005) A theory of international new ventures: A decade of research. *Journal of
International Business Studies*, 36: 20–28.

Zahra, S. A., Ireland, R. D., & Hitt, M. A. (2000) International expansion by new venture firms:
International diversity, mode of market entry, technological learning, and performance.
Academy of Management Journal, 43(5): 925–950.

Zahra, S. A., Korri, J. S., & Yu, J. (2005) Cognition and international entrepreneurship: Implications
for research on international opportunity recognition and exploitation. *International Business
Review*, 14: 129–146.

Zajac, E. J., & Olsen, C. P. (1993) From transaction cost to transactional value analysis:
Implications for the study of interorganizational strategies. *Journal of Management Studies*,
30: 131–145.

Zhao, H., Luo, Y., & Suh, T. (2004) Transaction cost determinants and ownership-based entry
mode choice: a meta-analytical review. *Journal of International Business Studies*, 35(6):
524–544.

Zuchella, A., & Scabini, P. (2007) *International entrepreneurship, theoretical foundations and
practises*. London: Palgrave Macmillan.

3 Market Entry Strategies

3.1 About Strategy and Internationalization

The term strategy goes back to Chandler, who defined strategy 'as the determination of the basic long-term goals and objectives of an enterprise and the adoption of courses of action and allocation of resources necessary for carrying out these goals' (Chandler, 1962: 23). Consequently, strategic management is a set of managerial decisions and actions that determine the long-run performance of a firm. Therefore, strategic management emphasizes monitoring and evaluating of external opportunities and threats in light of an organization's internal resource strengths and weaknesses. The strategy of a corporation involves a comprehensive master plan stating how the corporation will achieve its mission and objectives and maximize its competitive advantages (Wheelen & Hunger, 2010: 53, 67). The concept of strategic management is focused primarily on the development of long-term corporate success. Strategies, due to external or internal circumstances, sometimes cannot be realized as planned. In this case, the strategy needs to be modified. Emergent and deliberate strategies create the firm's realized strategy (Mintzberg, Lampel, Quinn, & Ghoshal, 2003: 5). Strategy indicates a complex bundle of planned activities for the attainment of long-term business objectives that also should consider emergent decision and action patterns. Optimal allocation of the firm's entrepreneurial and management capabilities is of vital importance for effective strategy implementation (Kutschker & Schmid, 2006: 798).

Larger firms, such as multinational enterprises, usually follow three types of strategies that are hierarchically linked to the firm's corporate level, strategic business unit (SBU) level, and functional (department) level. On the top management level (corporate level), there are directional strategies that can be categorized as growth, stability, and retrenchment strategies. A growth strategy, as the term itself indicates, is launched in order to increase the firm's turnover and profits through expansion. A stability strategy is implemented after the acquisition of another firm, so organizational integration of the acquired business activities is required. A retrenchment strategy is realized through the shutdown or outsourcing of businesses that continuously accumulate losses, and there is little hope that these poorly performing business units will recover in the future.

In more detail, growth strategies are realized by expanding business activities in the current industry through enlargement of the current product portfolio or manufacturing depth (horizontal, vertical, backward, or forward integration) in related industries (concentric diversification) or in unrelated industries (conglomerate diversification). Porter's concept of competitive strategies, such as cost leadership, differentiation, and niche strategies, is found in the firm's strategic business units (SBUs) (Porter, 1999: 32–38; Wheelen & Hunger, 2010: 67).

Strategies on the functional level are embedded in the firm's operating departments, such as purchasing (e. g., parallel or multiple sourcing strategies), marketing strategies (e. g., penetration versus skimming strategy, push versus pull strategy, shower versus waterfall strategy), R&D (technological leadership versus followership strategy), and operations strategies (e. g., individual versus serial production or mass production). A functional strategy implements and realizes directional and business unit strategies by maximizing the firm's department strengths and effectiveness. Functional strategies are concerned with developing a distinctive competence in order to provide the enterprise and its business units with a competitive advantage (Wheelen & Hunger, 2010: 68).

In light of globalized integrated valued added activities and trade and capital flow patterns, a firm's growth strategy is often realized through enlargement of its business by means of geographic expansion into foreign markets. As a result, the firm is engaged in internationalization processes because its products and services are transferred across national boundaries. The firm's management selects the country and relevant actors; where or with whom the transaction should be performed; and the corresponding international exchange transaction modality, which is called a firm's market entry strategy or, synonymously, market entry mode (Andersen & Buvik, 2002: 347–348). An entry mode refers to the institutional or organizational arrangement chosen by the firm for its business activities in target foreign markets (Hollensen, Boyd, & Ulrich, 2011: 7). The international business activity can range from manufacturing of goods, to servicing customers, to sourcing various inputs (Holtbrügge & Baron, 2013: 239; Welch, Benito, & Petersen, 2007: 18). When entering new markets, the operating management is confronted with various challenges that usually come along with more or less known societal, ecological, economic, legal-political, expertise (S. E.E.L.E), environmental surroundings of the firm. Thus, there should be various advantages from international business activities that cause firms to consider taking the risk of entering foreign markets. What motivates a firm to internationalize? The following are the main reasons.

1. **Demand-oriented factors:** Foreign market entry because of its attractiveness in terms of market volume and growth rates, which provide additional sales volumes, in addition to (often) saturated home markets.
2. **Supply-oriented factors:** Access to rare and valuable resources found in foreign markets, such as qualified and motivated employees, raw materials, knowledge, technological expertise, infrastructure, and others.
3. **Follow-the-customer necessity:** To avoid the risk of being dropped from the procurement list of an important customer, the supplier needs to follow its customer, which is engaged in a foreign target market.
4. **Follow-the-competitor necessity:** To avoid leaving the competitors either with all the sales opportunities or all the investment benefits provided in a regional industry cluster in foreign markets, the firm must join the competitors in the foreign markets.

5. **Financial reasons:** To realize the advantages of foreign markets because of investment incentives (tax reductions, subsidies), large multinationals can make use of cross-stock listing, less costly debt financing because of lower interest rates, and the higher liquidity of the foreign markets.

As is clear from the reasons presented above, a firm does not always make its decision about whether, where, and how to internalize independently but often makes the decision as a result of its bilateral relationships with other actors in its relevant industry network.

The strategic decision process in the course of entering foreign markets is relatively complex, and the outcomes of foreign business normally have a vital impact on a firm's destiny. In other words, the decision regarding the foreign entry mode strategy is one of the most critical for the management. Among others, it is usually costly to change the mode of entry once it is established due to its long-term consequences for the firm (Brouthers & Hennart, 2007: 396; Pedersen, Petersen, & Benito, 2002: 340).

The choice of which foreign country to enter commits a firm to operating in a certain geographical and sociocultural terrain and signals its future strategic intention to customers, suppliers, competitors, and other stakeholder (Ellis, 2000: 443). The portfolio of international market entry strategies can basically be distinguished among *contractual forms* (e. g., exports, franchising, original equipment manufacturing); *cooperative partnerships,* such as international joint ventures; and *foreign direct investments* (e. g., wholly owned subsidiaries). These strategies will be explained in detail in the following sections of the chapter.

3.2 Case Study: The Global Strategy Concept of Samsung

3.2.1 Samsung management philosophy – history and today

The Korean economy is characterized by local-market-dominating *Chaebols* with highly centralized decision structures that consist of many affiliated companies. Compared to large Japanese conglomerates (Keiretsu), Chaebols are generally much younger. The oldest, Samsung, was established in Taegu in 1938 (Chen, 2004: 144) by Byung-Chull Lee (Samsung, 2007). Unlike Chaebols such as LG Electronics, which was founded in 1947, Samsung's origin goes back to the period of Japanese occupation of the Korean peninsula.

Confucian heritage is still readily visible in South Korea; and the influence of Confucian values on management is significant, which is particularly the case for the most conservative and powerful conglomerate Samsung. Although Buddhism has generally been accepted as a religion in South Korea and has become an integral part of the lives of Koreans, there is a major difference between Buddhism and Confucianism: Buddhism is understood and practiced as pure religion; and it recognizes heaven, hell, and transmigration. It teaches that anyone can enjoy the life of heaven if he or she lives a virtuous and honest life in this world. Heaven is the reward for what a person has done on earth. In comparison, Confucianism, as originally observed in China, is understood more as a philosophy with moral teachings than as a religion. It is involved in the world, rather than emphasizing the afterlife (Chang & Chang, 1994: 10).

The five cardinal values of Confucianism: filial piety and respect, the submission of wife to husband, strict seniority in social order, mutual trust in human relations, and absolute loyalty to the ruler still permeate the Korean society. Nevertheless, today, particularly among the younger and urban population, traditional Confucian ethics, such as family or the collectively oriented values of the East, have mixed with the pragmatic and economic goal-oriented values of the West. Behavior based on Confucianism has changed for reasons that include the influence of Christianity, which came to Korea in 1884 (today Catholics represent around one third of the population), and, to some extent, because of the US presence since the Korean Civil War.

Traditional hierarchical roles have changed. Today, scholars and civil servants are at the top; farmers, second; artisans, third; and merchants, last, which has made it possible for businessmen and engineers to prosper in the new industrial society (compare: Kim, 1997: 68; Tu, 1984).

In Korea, as in most of the other Asian countries, education is greatly emphasized. For this reason, Korean parents sacrifice their lives for the education of their children. The clan plays an important role in social and economic relations. It is not uncommon for a core of Korean firms to be staffed by family members, distant relatives, people from the hometown, or graduates of the same university; and it is not unusual for firms to be managed like quasi-family units (Kim, 1997: 69). Harmonious interpersonal consensus-based relations are emphasized. Interpersonal relationships are defined in terms of social status, such as gender, age, and position in the society. Social etiquette is well defined when it comes to interactions among people. Harmony, which refers to respect for other people and a comfortable atmosphere, plays a very important role in Korea, where people try to avoid or minimize face-to-face conflicts. Harmonious interpersonal relationships are mainly built on seniority. Harmony is reached through cultivation and adaptation of one's self (Rowley, Sohn, & Bae, 2002: 72–73).

The emphasis on personal loyalty to those of higher rank is of vital importance—for example, when working at Samsung. A supervisor can practice massive criticism to a subordinate, while the other way around, unconditional loyalty, obedience, and untiring deployment of labor are expected. This is in accordance with the strict discipline already practised first at school and later at work as well as in the entire social life. Discipline combined with loyalty, moral obligation, severity, and benevolence contribute to business competitiveness (Chen, 2004: 42). It is of vital importance that these attitudes, which reflect the company culture, are respected and shown by each Samsung employee in daily life at work. Samsung staff members do not argue in front of their boss and, instead, are 'action-oriented' and busy (in order to realize the boss's order). Despite the challenges and mental pressure at work, Koreans have a positive attitude towards the future that favors realizing the permanently increasing business goals launched by the Samsung management (Kim, 1997: 68–69).

The Korean culture is fundamentally influenced to a greater degree by historical and philosophical Chinese thought than, for example, is the case in Japan. The philosophical values of old Chinese military strategists were transferred to the business community. The Chinese expression 'Shang Chang Ru Zhan Chang' is translated to mean 'the marketplace is a battlefield' (Chen, 2004: 33). Several Asian business leaders have attached great importance to classical Chinese military strategies. Many of the principles behind these strategies are commonly applied to business activities, of which Samsung serves as example.

According to the idea of paternalistic leadership, Chaebols are controlled by their founders or owners (Samsung: Chairman Lee Kun-hee) and their families, who usually have enormous influence not only on the organizational culture but also on business strategies. In business, decision processes, and strategies, the Samsung management is target and goal oriented. Consequently, the company pursues a permanent trade-off between the regional advantages and weaknesses at plant locations around the globe. The management of the Samsung headquarters (located in Seoul) is free to intervene in any subsidiary at any time. According to Rowley et al., military structure contributes heavily to ideas about how business organizations should be designed and operated. This orientation influences behavior, predisposing companies to emphasize hierarchical command, a result-oriented 'can-do spirit', and competition among the employees (Rowley et al., 2002: 75). The hierarchical work atmosphere at Samsung was described by one Samsung employee as follows.

> There are a lot of unscheduled and sudden orders with an urgent due date from the top management and CEO. Even if managers do make a false decision or mistake or give inappropriate orders, employees do not reject it or speak out loud to say it is wrong. Koreans are quite used to being told and directed by managers (or teachers) about what they should do ever since they were teenagers at school and, therefore, very often have a lack of creativity and are afraid of trying new things and breaking rules (Glowik, 2007c).

Koreans rely heavily on personal relationship networks that are embedded in blood relations, growing up in the same region, similar academic background, or the university attended. According to an empirical study by Chang and Chang (1994: 51), Koreans have most confidence in members of their own family, followed by high school classmates and people from the same region. In contrast, Koreans do not trust Korean strangers and foreign people. Due to their long history as a relatively homogeneous ethnic group, Koreans have a high level of communication based on shared contexts (high-context society). They like to convey information through nonverbal cues embedded in physical settings or internalized in particular personal relationships (Rowley et al., 2002: 74).

The Western scientist Hofstede (2001: 215) describes Korea as one of the most collectivist countries in the world. However, Asian scholars like L. Kim (1997: 69) indicate that Koreans are more individualistic than, for example, Japanese (Chang & Chang, 1994: 45). Western expatriates of multinational companies often presume collective attitudes in Korean managers but recognize individualistic, even egotistical, forms of behavior. Koreans have a strong tendency to distinguish themselves from others and show collectivist behavior only to people of the 'in-group'. Among Koreans, communication is more personalized and smoothly synchronized, which is the opposite in the case of communication with 'out-group' members (Rowley et al., 2002: 73).

From the Korean point of view, the success or failure of business reflects one's 'own face' and directly influences the survival of the private family and, consequently, the prosperity of the whole nation (Chen, 2004: 33). According to Kim and Bae (2004: 139), compared with Western enterprises, Korean firms give more weight to human nature – for example, personality, behavior and company-culture integration – than the purely job-related competence of an employee – for example, performance, achievements, and expertise (Kim and Bae, 2004: 139). This attitude differs from Western cultures, where company performance (expressed rationally in profit or loss figures) and private life are perceived as separate matters. Koreans see the company's prosperity as a private matter and, consequently, view it more emotionally. In the case of Samsung, this is reflected in the strong motivation of the employees. As one Samsung staff member commented to me during an interview in Seoul:

> A task or project is to be done by a due date; all team members are devoted to completing the job as fast as possible by dividing the work. The strengths of Asian-based companies are personal relationships and networks, team work, and self-sacrifice. In Europe, work and personal life are completely separate and isolated. After work, employees do not go together for a further casual discussion. Work time is very rigid and inflexible. At 06:00 p.m., no one is present at work because they have gone home. Europeans have long vacations.
>
> 'The person in charge is on holiday for three weeks; therefore, the job cannot be done at the moment. Please wait'. When a Korean business partner listens to such information on the phone and is confronted with such a situation, he or she is speechless. Speed is the key in the twenty-first century, especially in high-technology industries such as the electronics business (Glowik, 2007c).

If the profit of a business segment tends to drop, countermeasures follow from the Samsung management immediately. These activities contain restructuring programs, reduction of employees, and shut-down of production lines or whole plant facilities as was the case in Wynyard, Great Britain, in 1998; Berlin, Germany, in 2006; Tschernitz, Germany, in 2007; and Goed, Hungary, in 2013 (Samsung, 2014a; Zschiedrich & Glowik, 2005: 323). As the company slimmed down during the financial crisis in Asia from about 1997 to 1999, around 30 percent of the employees lost their jobs (Genser, 2005: 3). In the spring of 1998, approximately fifty middle-level managers in the manufacturing plant in Busan (South Korea) took 'early retirement', which can be regarded as a de facto layoff program (Kim & Bae, 2004: 185). The financial crisis in Asia caused the number of regular production workers in the Busan plant to be decreased from approximately 7,000 to 5,000. Wages were cut by around 10 percent, and benefits like summer vacation allowances were abolished or temporarily restricted. At the end of 2006, several managers at the plasma television set business division in Korea had to leave the company due to a sales performance that was lower than expected by the top management (Kim & Bae, 2004: 185).

Restructuring activities like those described above more closely resemble US conditions than traditional Asian management behavior. The influence of the US after World War II – for example, liberalization from Japanese occupation, military support of South Korea during and after the Civil War (1950 – 1953), and considerable financial aid—have obviously made the country open to Western management styles. Korea's business elite has a preference for Western ways of thinking, which encouraged learning from industrialized countries along with imitation of advanced technology and management. This is connected to traditional behavioral values like positive attitudes towards hard work and lifelong learning, which has contributed to the successful performance of Samsung. Employment fluctuation, for example, is comparatively much lower at Samsung than in most US-based enterprises (rather short-term oriented, e. g., quarterly reports) or in Chinese firms (rapid economic growth). Compared to Japan, the human resource management practice at Samsung could, therefore, be described as a 'semi-lifelong' employment policy (Chen, 2004: 193).

Unlike its biggest rival, LG Electronics, Samsung is a non-union company. The non-union philosophy was influenced by the founder of Samsung, Lee Byung Chul (Kim & Bae, 2004: 183 – 184). Representatives of German trade unions reproached Samsung for selecting production locations based on the volume of subsidies. For instance, after subsidies by the local Berlin government expired in March 2006, production at Samsung SDI Germany was shut down; and 700 employees were dismissed. Samsung SDI Hungary, established in 2002, assumed production from Germany. The Hungarian government supported the investment with considerable tax incentives. A couple of years later, the Hungarian plant was shut down (Jacobs, 2006; Wohllaib, 2006: 1). Nevertheless, Western enterprises do not differ very much in that way. For example, the Finnish Nokia in 2008 closed its mobile phone manufacturing in Bochum, Germany, and transferred it to Rumania, where considerable subsidies were paid. And there is another historical aspect to consider. After the Korean Civil War, Korean Chaebols such as Samsung, LG Electronics, Daewoo, and Hyundai grew successfully because of the fundamental financial support of the South Korean government, among other reasons. Thus, deciding on investment activities based on the size of tax incentives is neither immoral nor exceptional for Korean managers.

3.2.2 Strategic relationship building

Japanese companies made an essential contribution to the construction and development of Samsung. In 1969, a joint venture with Sanyo (Japan) was agreed upon, which later led to the founding of Samsung Electro-Mechanics. Samsung Display Devices is the result of a joint venture with Nippon Electric Company (NEC), Japan, which was established in the same year. The foundation (1969) and development of Samsung Electronics, nowadays one of the most important business divisions of Samsung Group, was supported by Japanese companies that were involved by contributing essential technology and management know-how transfer. As a result, the first black-and-white television set was produced in 1971 by Samsung (Samsung, 2007).

The international joint venture Samsung Corning Precision Materials, which is a manufacturer of high-quality glass parts for the production of displays, resulted from an agreement between Corning Inc., USA (e. g., assembler of today's well-known 'Gorilla glass') and Samsung in 1973. Major production capacities for the glass used in smart phones and television sets are located in South Korea, China, and Taiwan. As a result of the joint venture, Samsung Display will secure LCD screen glass supplies from Corning until 2023. Corning holds the joint venture majority ownership position-ing (Corning, 2013). The international joint venture between Corning and Samsung has been further developed over decades and serves as one of the rather rare existing examples of successful and long-term Western-Asian international joint ventures.

Samsung's continued relationship-seeking efforts brought it into collaborative arrangements with the world's technologically leading firms. For example, in 1994, it was announced that Samsung and the Japanese NEC would share development ef-forts at a cost in excess of USD one billion to bring a 256 M DRAM to market in the late 1990s (Lynskey & Yonekura, 2002: 282). In 2001, Samsung and NEC agreed upon a new joint venture called Samsung NEC Mobile Display OLED. The main target of the joint venture was to join efforts to develop the OLED business. Samsung and NEC can rely on their long-term experience in running joint ventures, which has been devel-oped for decades. Over time, various additional technological alliances have helped develop Samsung into one of the leading firms in consumer electronics. Samsung's top management has continuously searched for new market potentials for the future and strengthened its efforts to establish selected alliances, such as with Nokia (2007, mobile phone technologies), Limo (2006, Linux-Platform), IBM (2006, industrial print solution), and Bang and Olufsen (2004, home cinema systems), just to mention some of Samsung's alliances (Samsung, 2008b).

Since the 1990s, the competition between South Korea and Japan in the field of electronics has become intense. Although South Korea's electronics industry, which grew by introducing Japanese technologies, was behind that of Japan in the initial phase, South Korean companies, with Samsung as a representative, made innova-tions on the basis of digestion and assimilation. For example, in 2004, Samsung and Sony decided to establish the joint venture S-LCD Corporation and shared the output from the 'seventh-generation' LCD factory (Genser, 2005: 3). At this time, Sam-sung was technologically already ahead of Sony in flat panel production. Samsung's newly gained position as a serious rival was one of the major reasons that Sony did not prolong the joint venture with Samsung and, instead, started to collaborate in-tensively with Sharp in the LCD panel television set business (Otani, 2008). As a re-sult, Samsung acquired all of Sony's shares of S-LCD Corporation in 2011, making S-LCD a wholly owned subsidiary of Samsung. Meanwhile, in terms of capacity and technology, Samsung successfully exceeded several Japanese firms in the fields of display panels, smart phones, and semiconductor production (Kim, 1997: 193; Sony, 2011).

In 2007, Samsung signed an alliance agreement with LG Electronics, its biggest rival and the 'ever number two' of the Korean electronics industry and competitor in the global display market. Samsung and LG decided 'to join forces to challenge the market' as was stated in the corresponding press release (CDRinf, 2007). The firms pledged to cooperate in various fields, ranging from patents and joint research and development to cross-purchasing of panels from each other. The alliance, fur-thermore, contains a mutual component supply providing selected products, and seeks to standardize panels, equipment, and materials. In addition to this, both panel manufacturing giants have reached an agreement to proceed in the future with a 'small-to-large' joint development strategy for the display industry through the project of Eight Win-Win Partnership, which concentrates on 'patent cooperation, mutual vertical integration, and joint research and development activities'. Korea's commerce and industry minister, Kim Young-Ju, said the following during a meeting of anti-trust regulators:

> The alliance should not be seen as setting the stage for collusion or price fixing. The companies are not seeking mergers or a cartel to fix prices. South Korea should ease tight antitrust rules to help local firms compete with foreign rivals through strategic tie-ups. Samsung and LG jointly account for some 40 percent of the global market for display panels, about the same as Taiwan; and Japan takes up the remaining 20 percent. The moves are seen as a way to battle aggressive competition by Japanese rivals and alliances among Japanese and Taiwanese companies. Japan's Sharp Electronics and Taiwan's Chi Mei Optoelectronics (CMO) and Chunghwa Picture Tubes agreed to share patents last year. But Samsung and LG depend heavily on Japanese parts for their product (CDRinf, 2007).

In recent years, Samsung has accelerated its relationship efforts with other firms doing business in promising future markets, such as batteries (e. g., electric cars) and medical devices. For example, in 2008, Samsung established an international joint venture called SB LiMotive Co. Ltd. with the German Robert Bosch GmbH for the development, production, and sales of lithium-ion battery systems. Robert Bosch GmbH and Samsung SDI each invested 50 percent in that international equity joint venture. The management and the supervisory board consisted of an equal number of appointed members from both enterprises (Samsung, 2008a, b). The knowledge developed and acquired from the joint venture of Bosch and Samsung is applicable for batteries used in electronics devices and cars. However, in 2012, Bosch withdrew its stake in the joint venture due to 'strategic differences' with its joint venture partner (Hammerschmidt, 2012). Probably, Bosch became aware of the risk that Samsung would gain car battery as well as electric car management knowledge, which would help Samsung become a powerful competitor to Bosch in the promising future electric car business.

As a consequence of the international joint venture termination with Bosch, Samsung SDI announced the acquisition of the battery pack division of Magna Steyr International in 2015, which will further solidify the company's foothold in the automotive market. The agreement to buy Magna Steyr includes all 264 employees as well as the current business contracts and all production and development sites. The division is based out of Austria and builds battery packs for electrified vehicles. With the acquisition, Samsung will focus on growing customers in the electrified vehicle markets in North America, Europe, and China. By 2020, Samsung predicts that this market will reach 7.7 million vehicles worldwide. Capacity enlargements are currently underway for a new Samsung plant in China. After its opening at the end of 2015, the factory will be capable of supplying batteries for more than 40,000 electrified vehicles (Shelton, 2015). Samsung SDI currently supplies cells to BMW for its i3 and i8 plug-in cars (Gastelu, 2015).

Interestingly and less known in Western countries, Samsung had already held a foothold in the automotive industry since the end of the 1990s when Samsung agreed with the Japanese Nissan to build a version of the Maxima, called the SM5, which went on sale in 1998. As a result of the Asian financial crisis, which affected Nissan too, Renault from France acquired around 43 percent share of Nissan and, as a consequence, Renault Samsung Motors was established. As per 2015, Samsung holds 20 percent of Renault Samsung Motors (Gastelu, 2015).

3.2.3 Diversified organization

A corporate strategy mirrors organizational processes that are inseparable from the structure, behavior, and culture of the company (Andrews, 2003: 73). Company growth in industries unrelated to the current business through diversification strategies is a significant characteristic of all Korean Chaebols. Historically, diversification strategies have been widely advocated and supported by the Korean government. Samsung entered into wood textiles and sugar in the 1950s ; fertilizer and paper production started in the '60s ; construction, electronic components, heavy industry, petrochemicals, and shipbuilding were entered in the '70s ; and aircrafts, bioengineering, and semiconductors were introduced in the '80s (Chen, 2004: 187–188). More recently, Samsung entered medical devices (healthcare) and automotive industries.

Samsung's strategic advantage in today's business lies in its highly diversified activities, which allow aggressive market entry and penetration strategies because temporary losses in foreign markets are compensated by a continued flow of revenues in the native country, where the company has a dominant position. Although the financial, legal, and organizational encouragement by the Korean government to strengthen the Korean Chaebols is lower nowadays than in earlier decades, Chaebols still have several advantages due to their size and importance for the country's economy. Samsung has a quasi-monopoly position in many areas. For instance, there is the luxury Hotel Shilla in the capital of Seoul. Samsung Everland, a large entertainment and amusement park, follows the US example of Walt Disney (Samsung, 2004). Cheil Communications, South Korea's largest advertising agency, as well as insurance and credit card businesses, petrochemicals, construction, and others also belong to Samsung Group. In recent years, in addition to its strengthened electronics business, Samsung has become involved in automotive and the promising healthcare-related industries (e. g., medical devices).

Another characteristic of Korean Chaebols is the mutual shareholder participation of the diversified businesses, and the Samsung Group serves as an excellent case. As illustrated in Figure 34, Samsung Electronics holds the highest shareholder percentages in the other business units, which underlines its important role for Sam-

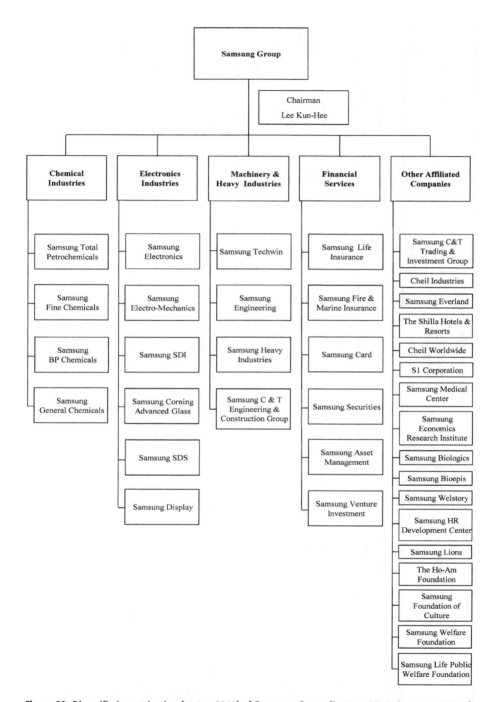

Figure 33. Diversified organization [status 2014] of Samsung Group (Dutton, 2014; Samsung, 2014a)

Shareholder [in percentage]

Company Affiliates	President Lee & Family	Samsung Electronics	Samsung Card	Samsung Everland	Samsung Life Insurance	Samsung Fire & Marine Insurance	Samsung C&T	Samsung SDI	Samsung Electro-Mechanics
Samsung Electronics	4.8					1.3	4.1		
Samsung SDI		20.4							
Samsung Electro-Mechanics		23.7							
Samsung SDS		35.5					18.3		8.4
Samsung Display		84.8						15.2	
Semes		91.0							
Steco		51.0							
Samsung Life Insurance	30.1			1.6					
Samsung Fire & Marine Insurance	3.1	1.3			10.4				
Samsung Card		37.5					2.5		3.8
Samsung Venture									17.0
Samsung Heavy Industries		17.6							2.4
Samsung Total		3.9					38.7	10.7	10.5
Samsung Petrochemical		13.0					27.3		

Continued

Company Affiliates	Shareholder [in percentage]								
	President Lee & Family	Samsung Electronics	Samsung Card	Samsung Everland	Samsung Life Insurance	Samsung Fire & Marine Insurance	Samsung C&T	Samsung SDI	Samsung Electro-Mechanics
Samsung Fine Chemicals		8.4					5.6	11.5	
Samsung Techwin		25.5					4.3		
Samsung C&T	1.6				5.2			7.4	
Samsung Engineering								5.1	
Samsung Everland	41.8		5.0				1.5	4.0	4.0
Hotel Shilla		5.1							
Cheil Worldwide		2.6					12.6		
S-1 corporation								11.0	
Samsung Medicine		68.5							
Samsung Biologics		42.1					10.5		

Figure 34. Mutual capital participation of the diversified business units of Samsung Group (status 2014). Source: Developed by the author based on 2013 and 2014 annual reports and further firm-related information of Samsung

sung Group. In other words, due to its strategic importance, if the electronics business suffers, the entire Samsung organization may start swinging.

Lee Kun-hee, chairman of Samsung Group, and his family own less than 5 percent of the shares of Samsung Electronics directly. Nevertheless, they are able to control Samsung Electronics because of the circular equity structure within Samsung Group, such as Samsung Everland, Samsung C&T, and Samsung Insurance. The total shares in these companies held by Lee and his family are worth about Euro 10 billion (status 2012). Lee and his family exercise absolute management authority (Han, Liem, & Lee, 2013: 4).

Samsung realizes various advantages accruing from these diversified product lines. One obvious benefit is the resulting diversified business risk. Because the company's products spread out into many fields, it is more effectively able to cope with the ups and downs in particular product markets; and this helps the company to develop its sales performance, which reflects the company's growth strategy in the global markets. Another advantage is the cross-product component sharing, which is important when different products are converging onto the same platforms (Chen & Li, 2007: 77). Large manufacturing facilitates help spread the costs of research and development and allow realization of overall economies of scale effects.

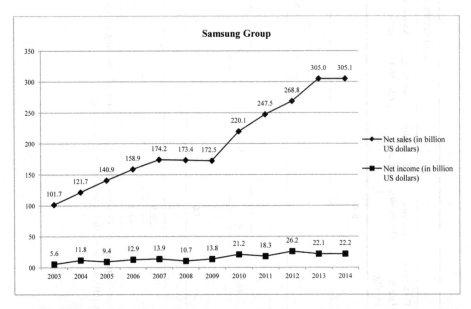

Figure 35. Net sales and net income of Samsung Group for the period 2003 to 2014 (Samsung, 2015)

Successful growth provides the chance to take advantage of the experience curve in order to reduce the per-unit costs of products sold. The sales development of Samsung Group has shown an outstanding sales performance over the last years relative to its competitors. However – for example, compared to the industry benchmark in terms of profit margins, which is currently Apple Inc. (USA) – Samsung's management has not been able to expand net income with the same growth rates. What might be the reason for this shortfall? First, Samsung is embedded in various and diversified business fields and owns facilities that have enormous fixed costs. Thus, taking the risk of running overcapacities, the firm becomes vulnerable in the case of economic downturns in the worldwide markets. In this situation, Samsung sells its products at relatively marginal price levels in order 'to feed the production lines' (bfai, 2007). Second, the electronics industry, which is the core business of Samsung Group, is highly price competitive. Permanent product innovations are necessary to secure the firm's business destiny for the future. The corresponding investment volume in research and development as well as large-scale manufacturing capacities has been increased in recent years.

There is no doubt – relative to its Japanese rivals, such as Sony, Sharp, and Panasonic – that Samsung has reached a more stable and prospective business performance during the last years. Samsung has concentrated on its core competence, the electronics business. The firm invested early in LCD/LED displays and smart phone production capacities at a time when the market potential had been neglected by others. In addition, Samsung Electronics has been expanded in several vertically integrated business segments. The complete manufacturing capacities of television sets, semi-conductors, and mobile phones belong to the most important strategic business segments of Samsung (BBC, 2008; Samsung_Electronics, 2008). Samsung's vertical integration is described in more detail in the following section.

3.2.4 The strategy of vertical integration of Samsung Electronics

Samsung Electronics is the flagship company of Samsung Group, which is composed of 516 companies worldwide. Out of 516, 195 are full fledged Samsung Electronics subsidiaries, meaning they are incorporated entities of which Samsung Electronics owns more than a 50 percent share. In addition, Samsung Electronics controls an additional 63 companies that make components for its subsidiaries, although it does not own a majority share in them. Smart phones, television sets, and more than 260 additional products under the Samsung Electronics brand are produced and sold through Samsung Group's network (Han et al., 2013: 3).

The strength of Samsung Electronics is the company's efficient use of its worldwide vertically integrated research and development, procurement, manufacturing, and sales network. Vertical integration means a firm utilizes an internal transfer within the organization of intermediate parts that a firm produces for its own use, such as materials, components, semi- or completely assembled products, and services. A firm may integrate backward and start generating value added activities it previously procured from outside suppliers. Alternatively, a firm may integrate forward and start integrating products and services, such as a sales and distribution or after-sales service, in order to be closer to the firm's customers and their 'voices'.

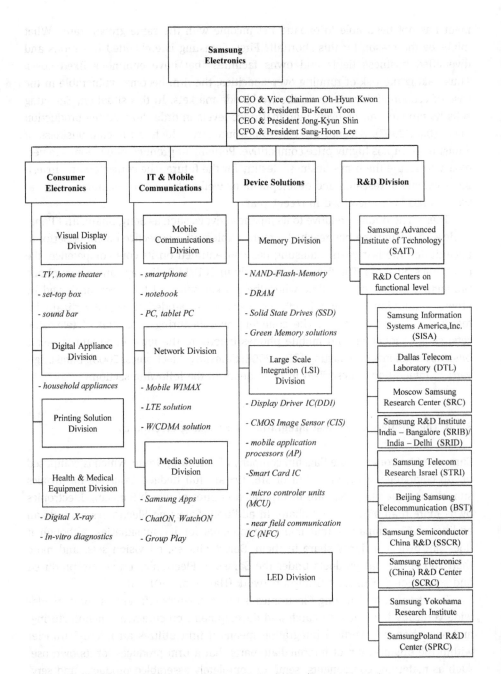

Figure 36. Organization [status 2014] of Samsung Electronics (Samsung, 2014b, c; Samsung_Electronics, 2014b)

Both of these processes represent methods of a firm's growth strategy (Penrose, 1995: 145).

After the Korean Civil War, during the second half of the 1950s, the Korean government started to route Chaebols into particular industries without building the infrastructure of component suppliers or supporting services. Since the Chaebols found it difficult to purchase or otherwise secure the necessary materials and components and the Korean government pushed domestic firms to industrialize, there were clear and seemingly inevitable reasons to integrate vertically. Differences in the Chaebols' use of vertical integration stem from the distinct characteristics of the industries the conglomerates are involved with (Chang, 2003: 113–118). For example, in the case of smart phones and television sets, Samsung Electronics controls almost all stages from research and development, to manufacture, up to worldwide sales and distribution. In comparison to Western enterprises, such as Philips or Apple, the Korean firm indicates a much deeper grade of vertical integration. Figure 37 illustrates the vertically integrated value added activities of Samsung Electronics regarding a state-of-the art LED television set.

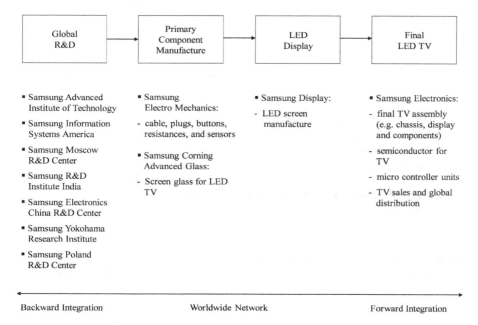

Figure 37. Samsung's vertical integration in terms of value added activities of an LED television set

As illustrated above, Samsung Electronics is closely interlinked with Samsung Display, a manufacturer and key supplier of displays for television sets. Samsung Display can rely on Samsung Corning, which produces the screen glass for the displays. Samsung Electro Mechanics delivers components for the display assembly. An LCD/ LED television set is based on a combination of display and semiconductor technology. Firms like Samsung, with a strong background in both display and semiconductor technologies, are in a comfortable position to manufacture state-of-the art television sets (Kim, 1997: 144). Vertical integration helps Samsung maintain better quality control and delivery punctuality than the company could achieve through outsourcing. Furthermore, vertical integration means that the fruits of research and development in one stage of production are more likely to be shared with other stages, thereby increasing the overall competitiveness of both upstream and downstream operations. Nowadays, the main part of Samsung Electronics' sales is conducted directly with the customers who serve as the firm's major information source in terms of the design and desired product features. Through its vertical integration, Samsung Electronics is able to launch its products more rapidly on the global markets than most of its competitors (Chang, 2003: 120 – 121; Kim, 1997: 144; Worstall, 2013).

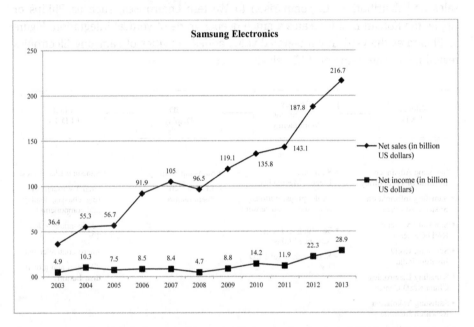

Figure 38. Net sales and net income of Samsung Electronics for the period 2003 – 2013 (Samsung_Electronics, 2004, 2005, 2006, 2007, 2008, 2009, 2010, 2011, 2012, 2013, 2014a)

As illustrated in Figure 38, Samsung Electronics performs well in terms of net sales and net income and is much better positioned than most of its Japanese competitors. Nevertheless, vertical integration also comes along with potential challenges. One of the potential hazards to efficiency comes from vertically integrated suppliers who lack the incentive to be more efficient or innovative because they have captive in-house customers (Mahoney, 1992: 559). This lack of incentive can be severe in the case of Chaebol affiliates because large portions of their sales are transferred internally (Chang, 2003: 122). One's own component production may be less efficient relative to its procurement from outside supply sources. Internal price discussions can lead to wasted time and effort (Roberto, 2009).

In the worst case, financially troubled affiliates can survive only with support from their parent company, which guarantees production volumes. The internal charges between the company units are higher prices than the market average. To create a homogeneous group culture and facilitate the inter-group transfer of personnel, Chaebols use the same level of benefits for all business units, which are often too generous for poorly performing businesses, and support unprofitable affiliates via various forms of internal transactions (Chang, 2003: 122–123). The permanent challenge for Chaebols like Samsung is favoritism, which leads to buying from within and hinders competition as well as the input of fresh, innovative business ideas from group outsiders. The top management of Samsung obviously recognized this danger and started to run each business unit as a separate profit center, which supports competition with outside suppliers for orders up to a certain budget. In some cases, up to one third or more of product demand is procured from Samsung's outside sources, even if it could be supplied in-house.

The system of component production and supply for Samsung Electronics is made up of five layers. The first layer is composed of Samsung Group subsidiaries and accounts for around ten percent of the value of the components purchased by Samsung Electronics. The second layer is made up of transnational electronics component suppliers who have independent technical capability. The US-based Qualcomm, which has a CDMA patent, and 3Com, which has a wireless patent, are examples of companies in this layer. The third layer comprises suppliers to which Samsung Electronics outsources parts production that it could produce by itself but chooses not to for cost or production capacity reasons. These companies – such as Taiwanese AU Optronics for example – supply small-scale LCD panels. The fourth layer is composed of domestic subcontractors that supply parts that Samsung Electronics could not produce itself, such as mobile phone cases manufactured by Intops LED Company Ltd. The final layer in the supply chain is composed of smaller low-cost parts (Han et al., 2013: 6).

Samsung Electronics does not procure and manufacture components only for its in-house uses. It also serves as a vertically integrated, specialised, and large-scale supplier for its major competitors, such as Sony (DRAM, NAND flash, LCD panels), Apple Inc. (mobile processor, DRAM, NAND flash), Dell (DRAM, flat panels, lithium-ion batteries), and Hewlett-Packard (DRAM, flat panels, lithium-ion batteries). Having control over the NAND and controller has major implications both for performance and reliability. Samsung has knowledge of various nuances of these components and can tweak them along each step in the development process to ensure that they work together perfectly. Manufacturers of generic SSD controllers have to worry about supporting multiple NAND specifications (from varying manufacturers who each have different manufacturing processes), while Samsung's proprietary SSD controller is engineered solely to work with its own NAND – which means engineers can focus all of their efforts towards one common specification. As the most integrated SSD manufacturer in the industry, Samsung controls all of the most crucial design elements of an SSD: NAND, Controller, DRAM, and Firmware. Working together, these components are responsible for a crucial task –storing, stable operating, and protecting precious data (Samsung, 2014d).

As a vertically integrated supplier, Samsung is able to achieve economies of scale and protect its position as a consumer electronics giant by leveraging its ability to produce component parts and assemble its products in a large-scale and cost-efficient process. Samsung Electronics relies on other companies mainly in terms of software applications – for example, Google, which supplies the operating system for smart phones and delivers related applications (Apps). In contrast to Samsung, Apple Inc. is a vertically integrated specialized buyer. Apple Inc. represents four companies in one – a hardware company, a software company, a service company, and a retail company. It controls all the critical parts of its value chain, but leaves the manufacturing process of its electronics components to other companies, such as Samsung. Consequently, Apple Inc. is rather a design company, not a manufacturing company like Samsung Electronics (Vergara, 2012). Samsung's supplier positioning also poses another risk. The firm finds itself competing with its customers – which are, in parallel, competitors. About a third of Samsung's revenue comes from companies that compete with it in producing television sets, smart phones, computers, printers, and other items (Ramstad, 2009).

3.2.5 International business expansion

As South Korean electronics firms gradually strengthened their presence and expanded their market shares overseas, import restrictions regarding goods from Korea increased in key markets such as the United States and the European Union. By the end of the 1980s, there were restrictions in the form of antidumping duties, quotas, and quality standard restraints on Korea's major export producers of color television sets, including Samsung. (Cherry, 2001: 65). As a result, Korean Chaebols strengthened their foreign direct investment activities, and overseas expansion through foreign direct investment has been impressive in the case of Samsung Electronics.

During the 1970s, the firm concentrated its manufacturing capacities on its home market, South Korea. The first foreign direct investment outside Korea was done in Mexico and Thailand (1988). In Europe, Samsung built its first television set manufacturing plant in Hungary in 1989. Meanwhile, China, as a manufacturing platform, has played an outstanding role for Samsung. Particularly at the beginning of the 1990s, Samsung Electronics established several manufacturing locations for a wide range of products (e.g., television sets, audio, telecommunication, etc.) in China. The manufacturing capacity expansion, including the foreign direct investment activities of Samsung Electronics, as well as additional details, such as the year of establishment and the manufactured products, are illustrated in Figure 39 for the period 1969 to 2013.

In recent times, such as in 2002, taking advantage of a favorable investment environment (e. g., relatively low costs combined with subsidies from the government), Slovakia was selected as a new investment location for building television set manufacturing capacities in Europe. In 2008 and 2009, Samsung invested in Russia, Vietnam, and Poland, while 'coming back to Asia' when it established LCD (2012) and semiconductor (2013) manufacturing capacities in China. Straight from its foundation, the Samsung management obviously has invested in locations where it has forecast promising business opportunities instead of paying too much attention to geographical distance or perceived cultural differences.

Traditional internationalization theories like the Uppsala approach assume that firms follow a linear, incremental internationalization chain pattern (Johanson & Vahlne, 1977: 23 – 26; Luostarinen, 1980, 200 – 201). Interestingly, Samsung has developed its international business, from its beginning, in contrast to the traditional internationalization theories. As can be seen, in the business expansion route of Samsung Electronics, the firm did not follow an incremental, linear investment path from nearby countries located in Asia to more distant countries such as those overseas. Instead, through various joint venture and strategic alliances, Samsung Electronics has gained knowledge from its relationship partners, which rather reflects major characteristics of the network theory of internationalization.

3.2.6 Product design, research, and development

Samsung Electronics has continuously increased its efforts to seek a reputation as a premium brand manufacturer. In this regard, Samsung's advertising campaigns have increased considerably. In Europe, Samsung is rather known for its electronics products but plays a minor role in other businesses, such as heavy industry, insurance, credit cards, and others. Samsung Electronics' annual budget for worldwide promotion expenditures amounts to around one billion Euro. Such a large advertising budget allows for market-specific and professional campaigns. Additionally, the company does extensive sports sponsoring. In Europe, Samsung's brand awareness has particularly increased during the last decade. One of the reasons for this is the company's strategy of single brand marketing, which includes a diversified electronics product range of smart phones, television sets, and other items.

A company that provides a full product range obtains attention and, consequently, easier access to the end consumer. This is an advantage in mass markets such as consumer electronics with relatively standardized products and intense price competition. As a high-technology company that produces various types of products in different segments (e. g., mobile media, semiconductors, home applications), Samsung has to consider that the designing process is one of the fundamental activities in creating value. Since high-tech products are changing rapidly, the corresponding crea-

Region	Country	Plant	Established	Product Portfolio
Asia	Korea	Suwon, Kyonggi-do	1969	CTV, DVDP, video, microwave oven, washing machine, camcorder, MP3, air conditioner
Asia	Korea	Kumi Complex 1, Kyongsang-buk-do	1980	Printer
Asia	Korea	Kiheng Complex (R&D), Yongin-gun, Kyonggi-Do	1980	Semiconductor, TFT-LCD, vending machine
America	Mexico	Samsung Mexicana S.A. de C.V. (SAMEX), Tijuana	1988	Television set, monitor
Asia	Thailand	Thai Samsung Electronics Co., Ltd. (TSE), Sriracha	1988	Television set, washing machine, refrigerator, air conditioner, microwave oven
Asia	Korea	Kwangju Complex	1989	Refrigerator, vacuum cleaner, vending machine, motor compressor
Asia	Malaysia	Samsung Electronics Malaysia Sdn. Bhd (SEMA)	1989	Microwave oven
Europe	Hungary	Hungary Samsung Electronics Hungarian Co., Ltd. (SEH)	1989	Television set, monitor
Asia	Korea	Onyang Complex, Asan-gun, Chungchongnam-do	1990	Semiconductor
Asia	Indonesia	P.T. Samsung Electronics Indonesia (SEIN), CiKarang	1991	Video cassette recorder, optical disc drive (ODD)
Asia	China	Samsung Electronics Co., Ltd., Hulzhou (SEHZ)	1992	Audio
Asia	China	Tianjin Samsung Electronics Co., Ltd. (TSEC)	1993	Video cassette recorder, digital video disk recordable
Asia	China	Shandong Samsung Tele-communications Co., Ltd. (SST), Weihai	1993	Fax machine, printer
Asia	China	Samsung Electronics Suzhou Semiconductor (SESS), Suzhou	1994	Semiconductor
Asia	China	Tianjin Tongguang Samsung Electronics Co., Ltd. (TTSEC)	1994	Television set
America	Brazil	Samsung Electronica da Amazona Ltda. (SEDA), Manaus, São Paulo	1995	Monitor, hand-held products
America	Mexico	Samsung Electronics Mexico S.A. de C.V. (SEM)	1995	Random electricity fluctuation, multiple wave oscillator
Asia	China	Suzhou Samsung Electronics, Suzhou	1995	Random electricity fluctuation, multiple wave oscillator
Asia	India	Samsung India Electronics Ltd. (SIEL), New Delhi	1995	Television set, microwave oven
Asia	Malaysia	Samsung Electronics Display (M)SDN, Bhd. (SDMA), Seremban	1995	Monitor, microwave oven
Asia	Vietnam	Samsung Vina Electronics Co., Ltd. (SAVINA), Ho Chi Min	1995	Television set, monitor

Continued

Region	Country	Plant	Established	Product Portfolio
America	USA	Samsung Austin Semiconductor L.L.C. (SAS)	1996	Dynamic random access memory
Asia	Korea	Kumi Complex 2, Kyongsang-buk-do	1996	Cellular phone, optical cable component
Asia	China	Tianjin Samsung Electronics Display Co., Ltd. (TSED)	1997	Monitor
Asia	Korea	Chonan Complex, Chungchong-nam	1997	Thin film transistor (TFT)-liquid crystal display (LCD)
Asia	Korea	Hwasung Complex, Hwasung, Kyonggi-do	2000	Semiconductor
Asia	China	Tianjin Samsung Tele-communications Company (TSTC), Tianjin	2001	Hand-held programmer
Asia	Philippines	Samsung Electronics Manufacturing Corporation (SEPhil), Calamba	2001	Optical disc drive (ODD)
Asia	China	Shanghai Bell, Samsung Mobile Communications Co., Ltd. (SSM), Shanghai	2002	Code division multiple access, business support system
Asia	China	Samsung Electronics LCD Suzhou Co., Ltd., Suzhou	2002	Liquid crystal display (LCD)
Asia	China	Shenzhen Samsung Kejian Mobile Telecommunications Technology Co., Ltd. (SSKMT)	2002	Hand-held programmer
Europe	Slovakia	Slovakia Samsung Electronics Slovakia (SESK), Glanta	2002	Television set
Asia	China	Tangjung Complex (Sony) Asan, Chungchongnam-do	2002	Thin film transistor (TFT)-liquid crystal display (LCD)
Asia	Vietnam	Samsung Electronics, Yentrung Commune, Yenphong Dist., Bacninh Province	2008	Electronics components manufacture
Europe	Russia	Pervyi Severnyi Proezd Vladenie 1, Koryakovo Village Borovskii District Kaluga, 249002, Russia	2008	Television set
Europe	Poland	Samsung Electronics Poland Manufacturing ul. Mickiewicza 52, 64–510 Wronki	2009	Refrigerators, washing machines
Asia	China	Samsung (China) Semiconductor Co., Ltd. A12F, City Gate, 1 Jinye Rd., Xi'an, China	2012	Semiconductor manufacture
Asia	China	No.318, Fangzhou Rd Suzhou Industrial Park Suzhou, 215123	2013	Liquid crystal display (LCD)

Figure 39. Expansion of Samsung Electronics' worldwide factory network. Source: Collected by the author as exhibited at Samsung Electronics' main entrance hall in Seoul, South Korea

tion of designs is needed in order to compete in the global market (Korea_Associates, 2012: 14). For its product designs, Samsung is running product design centers located in the following countries (compare illustration).

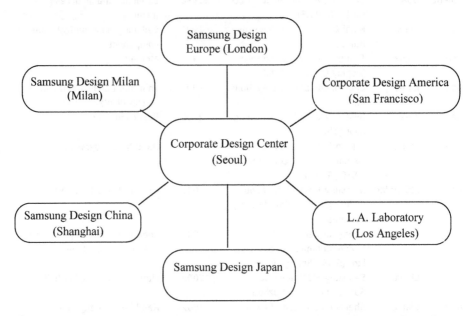

Figure 40. Samsung's worldwide network of product design units. Source: Samsung Electronics (2006: 52) and Korea Associates (2012: 14)

For advanced and research-intensive products, Samsung Electronics still concentrates on its home base in South Korea. In addition to the Samsung Advanced Institute of Technology (SAIT) located in South Korea, the network is completed by local research and development centers in various locations around the world (Lynskey & Yonekura, 2002: 283). The technological results are transferred to the headquarters in Seoul, which collects data from similar research units around the world and prepares fine-tuned economies of scale production scenarios for various Samsung factories around the globe. More specifically, the Samsung Electronics research and development activities are organized in three layers. (The first two layers are core to technology development and product planning.)

(1) The Samsung Advanced Institute of Technology (SAIT) ensures Samsung's technological competitiveness in core business areas, identifies growth engines for the future, and oversees the securing and management of technology including patents.

(2) The research and development centers of each business focus on technology that is expected to deliver the most promising long-term results. Each division of Samsung Electronics has its own research department, but all of these can outsource projects both to SAIT and to third-party institutions.

(3) Divisional product development teams, working with design centers, are responsible for commercializing products scheduled to launch in the market within one or two years.

Samsung Electronics spends about Euro 6 to 10 billion per annum on research and development, which equals about 7 percent of gross earnings. In smart phones, research and design is taking place in multiple centers, with the 'solution divisions' in Korea preparing products for external customers like Apple and for its internal customers in Samsung (Korea_Associates, 2012).

Center description	Research and development areas	Region
Samsung Information Systems America, Inc. (SISA)	Strategic parts and components, core technologies	America
Dallas Telecom Laboratory (DTL)	Technologies and products for next generation telecommunications systems	America
Samsung Electronics Research Institute (SERI)	Mobile phones and digital TV software	Europe
Moscow Samsung Research Center (SRC)	Optics, software algorithms, and other new technologies	CIS
Samsung Electronics India Software Operations (SISO)	System software for digital products, protocols for wired/wireless networks, and handsets	Asia-Pacific
Samsung Telecom Research Israel (STRI)	Hebrew software for mobile phones	Middle East
Beijing Samsung Telecommunication (BST)	Mobile telecommunications standardization and commercialization for China	Asia-Pacific
Samsung Semiconductor China R&D (SSCR)	Semiconductor packages and solutions	Asia-Pacific
Samsung Electronics China R&D Center (SCRC)	Software, digital TVs, and MP3 players for China	Asia-Pacific
Software, digital TVs, and MP3 players for China	Core next-generation parts and components, digital technologies	Asia-Pacific
Samsung Poland R&D Center (SPRC)	STB SW Platform Dev., EU STB/DTV commercialisation	Europe
Samsung India Software Center (SISC)	S/W Platform and Application Design, Graphic design	Asia-Pacific

Figure 41. Worldwide research and development centers of Samsung Electronics. Source: Korea_Associates (2012: 15)

There is no doubt that Samsung has successfully changed its reputation from a cheap original equipment manufacturer (OEM) to a technology- and marketing-driven company. Samsung's strength is based on its expertise forecasting future market potentials, which comes along with its major strength: very fast market response times. Despite its diversified business portfolio, further strengths of Samsung lay in its vertical manufacturing depth and in the firm's fast knowledge absorbing capabilities of strategically valuable information from customers, suppliers, and competitors' products. The acquired knowledge immediately results in newly developed products and the establishment of vertically integrated economies of scale manufacturing techniques, using regional cost advantages in its own factories – such as those in China and, more recently, in Vietnam. The products are launched through Samsung's global sales network, usually faster than competitors, which allows further experience curve and learning effects.

Additionally, through faster market entry than its competitors, an impression of an innovative technological pioneer (first inventor) is spread, which is in most of Samsung products still not the case (e. g., LCD/LED TV was mainly developed by Sharp, smart phones introduced by Apple, laptops by Toshiba, Blu-ray by Sony, and so on). Samsung rather holds the position of the 'second first', targeting to learn from the mistakes of the others; but this is done very effectively by the largest Korean Chaebol. This absorptive capability, together with its efficient forecasting and market timing, establishes Samsung as a true industry benchmark in high-technology industries.

Chapter review questions

1. Describe the major characteristics of the management philosophy of the South Korean Chaebol Samsung and the culturally based strengths and weaknesses in terms of developing the business.
2. Explain the historical reasons for, the current business fields of, and the advantages and disadvantages of the diversification strategy of Samsung Group.
3. Explain the vertical integration strategy of Samsung Electronics and the corresponding opportunities and challenges for the management.
4. Taking today's perspective, do you think Samsung Electronics holds the position of a technological leader or technological follower in the consumer electronics industries?
5. Assuming you are in the shoes of the management, where do you see the future of Samsung Electronics? Explain the reasons for your answer, and provide reasonable arguments.

3.3 Foreign Market Entry Strategies

3.3.1 Contractual modes of market entry

3.3.1.1 Indirect and direct export

Export describes business activities where goods and/or services are sold outside the country in which the major value-added activities took place. Export allows a fast and relatively less risky foreign market entry. The exporter's major risk is a financial risk (importer does not pay for the cargo) that can be reduced by asking for pre-payment before delivery or by using a letter of credit or export credit insurance. By developing the service or manufacturing the products at home and exporting them abroad, the organization is able to realize substantial economies of scale effects from its expanded sales volumes in the foreign markets in addition to its sales in the local market (Hitt, Ireland, & Hoskisson, 2015: 243). Exports help to develop the firm's international business competence and innovative capabilities due to the firm's access to information located in foreign markets. According to Love and Ganotakis (2013: 14), knowledge-intensive service-sector firms are able to gain earlier benefits from their expansion to export markets than manufacturing firms.

Basically, we distinguish between direct and indirect exports. Indirect exports and direct exports describe transactions in which the firm delivers products and/or services to an importing company based on a contractual agreement. Having no, or very little, experience in the business of foreign trade, it is desirable for the firm to initiate its first foreign engagement through so-called indirect exports. This market entry mode is called *indirect* export because an intermediator, with a commission, searches for potential customers (importers) in the target foreign country. The commission is subject to negotiation between the exporter and the intermediator and usually ranges from two to fifteen percent of the contract value. The commission is due after a contract is signed by the exporter and importer. Because the intermediator searches for pre-negotiated agreements with potential importing customers, the exporting firm is not confronted with challenging socio-cultural conditions, such as unfamiliar negotiation behaviors or language barriers. However, intermediators who run their business based on a commission often carry the products of competing firms and, therefore, tend to have divided loyalties (Hill, 2012: 491).

In the case of *direct* exports, the firm undertakes personal relationships with the importing customer abroad. Direct export requires more resources relative to indirect business because of traveling as well as actively managing the negotiations and contracts. The advantages from direct market access and the benefits from gaining valuable first-hand customer information may easily exceed the costs of active export management. Carriers and banks are important participants in the exporter's business-to-business network. The carrier's willingness and degree of resource commitment influence the performance of on-time delivery of the cargo from the exporter to the importer. The bank, through its transfer of timely payments and its fee and loan policy (which is also a result of the bank's resource commitment), has further significant impacts on the importer's and exporter's degree of satisfaction. The mutual resource commitments of the exporting firm, the importer, the bank, and the carrier for a direct export contract are illustrated in Figure 42. A particular form of export without the involvement of a bank is called *barter*. With barters, products and services are mutually exchanged between exporter and importer without financial payments. The volume of the products exchanged may differ depending on the unit value of each product. Barter businesses come about with firms located in rather fragile regions in terms of the economy, infrastructure, and finance.

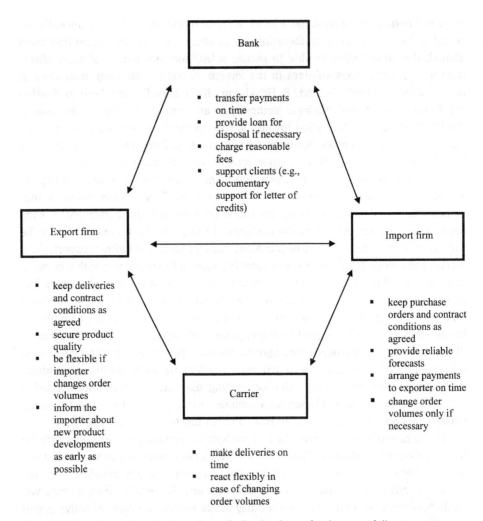

Figure 42. Mutual commitment expectations of relevant players for the case of direct exports

The major challenges for a firm doing export business are cross-border trade barriers. Because of liberalized trade patterns as a result of the General Agreement on Tariffs and Trade (GATT), which became effective in 1948 and was replaced in 1995 by the World Trade Organization (WTO), the average customs import tariffs are lower or disappeared compared to the past. However, nontariff barriers (bureaucratic import documentation), which are more difficult to gain evidence about, may remain a threat for the exporting firm, especially in volatile export target markets where the government of the host country tends to make use of barriers in order to accommodate the domestic industry lobby.

Export easily becomes uneconomical for bulky products and/or long-distance markets, which entail relatively high transportation costs. Furthermore, in light of globalization, firms face the challenges of supply flexibility and efficient management of demand changes in order to gain competitive advantage (Vollmann, Berry, Whybark, & Jacobs, 2005: 588). Exports from geographically distant markets result in a longer transportation lead time and limited response time in case the order is changed by the customer. The after-sales service becomes more difficult and expensive when the manufacturing location is far away from the export sales market. Domestic production and export may not be appropriate if lower cost locations or highly skilled staff for manufacturing and selling the product or service is available abroad or if local manufacturing is supported by infrastructure incentives granted by the local government (Hill, 2012: 491–492).

In the past, products with a relatively high degree of tangibility and a low demand for interaction between producer and final customer were usually exported. In recent years, we have witnessed export activities for products with a high degree of intangibility, such as software development or accounting services. An example is India, known as an exporting country (Blomstermo, Sharma, & Sallis, 2006: 216). E-commerce-based communication, sales, and distribution channels make it possible for an exporter to neither require an intermediator nor be permanently physically present in the target foreign markets. The case study of the upcoming Chinese telecommunication company Xiaomi describes how digital distribution is applied in order to successfully enter foreign markets.

3.3.1.2 Contract manufacturing
3.3.1.2.1 How it works?
In highly competitive and technologically fast changing industrial environments, manufacturers often consider establishing production capacities in a foreign market. The major reasons for market entry through contract manufacturing (synonymous term: original equipment manufacturing) are the following: a firm takes advantage of lower-cost locations and is able to save logistics costs due to local manufacturing in the target foreign market. The original equipment manufacturing (OEM) strategy allows the brand manufacturer a faster market entry abroad via the contracted firm than through foreign direct investments. This is particularly the case in high-technology industries where product innovations, simultaneously launched on a global scale, are of vital importance in order to gain competitive advantage. While the original equipment contractor (OEC) firm concentrates on the production, the brand manufacturer can bundle the resources in its core competencies, such as research and development or marketing. In other words, contract manufacturing is linked to the 'make-or-buy' question (Morschett, 2005: 599, 610). The OEC can combine production for several OEMs and thus realize economies of scale (Plambeck & Taylor, 2005: 133–134). Further incentives for contract manufacturing from the OEM's perspective are improved sensitivity to local customer needs and avoidance of host country import taxes or quota restrictions (Hollensen, 2014: 369).

How does the OEM system work in practice? The OEM (brand manufacturer) searches for a potential firm in the foreign target market that is able to manufacture, based on the OEM's desired cost structure, the technical specification and quality standards of the OEM's products. When the OEM has found a suitable and capable firm, a contract is signed; and the OEC starts production of quantities of the OEM's product. It is important to mention that the OEC puts the OEM's brand name on the product at the end of the assembly process. Because the brand is visible on the product, consumers do not realize the product is assembled by the OEC. However, consumers are usually charged at the same price level (market goodwill of the OEM's brand) as they are used to paying when it is manufactured by the OEM. The lower unit manufacturing costs (because the product is manufactured by the OEC) but higher sales price (as though it was manufactured by the OEM) finally generates higher OEM margins.

According to the conditions (everything is negotiable) between the contracting parties, the OEC may launch individual component assembly operations (semi-products) or manufacture the complete products including services (full operations). Payments by the OEM to the OEC are generally calculated on a per unit basis. In many cases, the OEM contracts with different OECs located at different places around the globe. Thus, the OEM benefits from each OEC's proximity to the market, which results in an increased flexibility to balance the production capacities of each OEC, if necessary (Hollensen, 2014: 369). This close proximity helps to accelerate the OEM's time-to-market responses in case of fluctuating order volumes. Additionally, contract manufacturing enables the OEM to undertake foreign operations without making a final investment commitment in the foreign target market. As a result, the OEM reduces its investment risk through its contractual agreement with the OEC (instead of establishing its own operations). The contract between the OEM and OEC can be terminated at any time – for example, if sales volumes in the target foreign markets shrink (Cole, Mason, Hau, & Yan, 2001: 7).

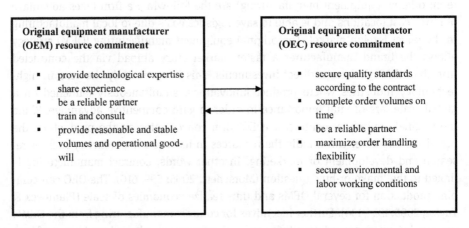

Figure 43. Mutual commitments of OEM and OEC

How about the potential drawbacks of contract manufacturing? Disadvantages for the OEM can derive from the OEM's loss of direct hierarchical control of the manufacturing and administrative (such as quality control) processes. The ongoing fulfillment of quality, based on the technical specification set by the OEM, is of vital importance. In case the OEC does not meet the quality or working condition standards as agreed upon in the contract, this failure may cause serious damage to the OEM's reputation in the markets. Thus, partner selection, contract negotiation, and quality control procedures have great importance (Hollensen, 2014: 369).

Furthermore, there is a risk for the OEM that the cost and desired benefits become unbalanced because of transaction costs related to the contract partner's selection process and negotiation procedures (ex-ante costs) and ex-post costs, such as monitoring and control of delivery punctuality, assembly quantity, and assembly quality (Williamson, 1991: 279). The more OEM activities initiated by the original brand firm, the higher the complexity, which provokes expanded information and communication structures. The original brand manufacturer has to decide which value-added activities (products and services) are transferred to a contracting firm. There is another risk when the OEM outsources activities that contributed to the ability of the OEM in the past to differentiate itself from its competition (Kita, 2001: 1). In the worst case, core competencies of the brand manufacturer are transferred to the OEC. As a result, the OEC acquires knowledge through its absorptive capability, which helps to develop the overall manufacturing and business expertise of the OEC. Thus, after a certain period of time, the OEC may become a competitor to the OEM on the global markets by learning from its OEM contracting partner.

The terms contract manufacturing and outsourcing should be clearly separated. The first serves as a method for increasing the OEM's manufacturing capacities at home by utilizing the OEC's capacities in the foreign target market (manufacturing activities continue at the OEM).

If, however, the OEM decides to terminate the manufacturing of a certain product at its home base and, instead, shifts the entire production to another firm, this is called outsourcing. In contrast to internal sourcing of materials, components, or products and services within a firm, outsourcing is the process of employing an external provider to perform functions that could be performed in-house (Bertrand & Mol, 2013: 751; Potkány, 2008: 53).

Outsourcing enables a firm to flexibly handle its customer-order management. The firm's manufacturing capacities are located outside the firm's hierarchy as an alternative to owning the production facilities. The management is often better able to focus on its core competencies, such as marketing or research and development, to achieve competitive advantage (Cheng, Cantor, Dresner, & Grimm, 2012: 890). Experience curve effects and the specific manufacturing expertise of the contracted firm enables the company to perform tasks more effectively (Caruth, Pane Haden, & Caruth, 2012: 5–6). Outsourcing may help to reduce the fixed costs of the internal manufacturing facilities and thus lower the breakeven point, which helps to improve a firm's return on equity (ROE). Suppose a corporate executive's performance is evaluated on the basis of the contribution to the firm's ROE; the management tends to have a strong incentive to increase outsourcing (Kotabe & Murray, 2004: 7–10).

However, the more the brand manufacturer shifts value-added activities to contracted firms, the less the brand manufacturer is involved in the value-added activities processes. The engineering expertise; technological knowledge; and, finally, the innovation capabilities and quality consciousness of the branded firm incrementally decreases over time. Further potential drawbacks of shifting value-added activities to outside firms are changes in employee morale and erosion of organizational loyalty. An organizational-cultural misfit between the contract partners may lead to a lower product and service quality, which damages the brand manufacturers reputation (Caruth et al., 2012: 6).

In the case of Philips (The Netherlands), it became increasingly difficult to remain efficient and innovative concerning new product developments in the consumer electronics industry. In 2008, Philips announced that it would transfer more than 70 percent of its television set manufacturing orders to contract manufacturers such as TCL Corporation (China), TVP (Taiwan), Hon Hai Precisions (Taiwan), and Funai Electric (Japan). In parallel, these previously rather less-known Asian-based electronics firms strengthened their technological and manufacturing expertise through learning during contract manufacturing relationships with OEMs such as Philips, among other reasons (Digitimes.com, 2008). Around five years later, in 2013, Philips sold the remnants of its audio, video, multimedia, and accessories activities to Japan's Funai Electric for Euro 150 million in cash and a brand-license fee. The Dutch group reported the management targets of becoming primarily a maker of healthcare, medical equipment, and lighting products and, thus, terminated its once-core business of consumer electronics (Van den Oever, 2013). Other 'international latecomers', such as Flextronics of Singapore and Hon Hai Precision Foxconn of Taiwan, successfully used contract manufacturing as a learning tool on their way to becoming major players in the electronics industries (Tung & Wan, 2012: 3–4).

3.3.1.2.2 The case study of Foxconn/Hon Hai Precision Industry Company (Taiwan)

In 1974, the Taiwan-based firm Hon Hai Precision Industry Company, better known in Western markets by the name Foxconn Technology, was founded by Terry Gou (Hon Hai Precision Co., 2013). During the first years of its existence, the company produced channel-changing knobs for television sets. In 1988, it began to invest in mainland China by establishing production locations in several regions of the country and by expanding its business to computer assembly. Nowadays, Foxconn is the largest original equipment manufacturer (OEM) in the world (Yiwei, 2014).

Foxconn manufacturers and delivers components, modules, and services and provides solutions ranging from the design and manufacture of components and system assembly to maintenance and logistics (Hon_Hai_Precision_Company_Ltd., 2013). As the largest contract manufacturer, especially for global consumer electronics companies, Hon Hai Precision Company employs about 1.5 million people in China. The enterprise is the major assembler of PCs for Hewlett Packard, Dell, and Acer; and it manufactures iPhones and iPads for Apple Inc., PlayStations for Sony, the Nintendo Wii, and Amazon's Kindle Fire. Moreover, TVs for Sharp, Sony, and Toshiba are produced at Foxconn factories (Kan, 2012). Foxconn represents one of the largest suppliers for Apple Inc. About 40 percent of its revenue is generated by the OEM partnership with Apple. Apple's relationship with Foxconn is so extensive that the Taiwanese firm has been building factories for the exclusive purpose of assembling Apple products (Kan, 2012). In 2013, sales hit a record high of USD 130.8 billion; and the company's net income rose to about USD 3.5 billion (Agence_France, 2014).

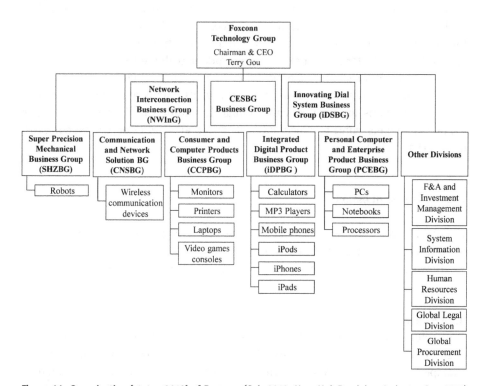

Figure 44. Organization [status 2013] of Foxconn (Cai, 2012; Hon_Hai_Precision_Industry Co., 2013)

Nevertheless, in recent years, several scandals erupted because of labor rights violations at Foxconn factories. In addition to miserable working conditions, including overtime issues, unpaid wages, and accidents, suicides of employees were revealed in the media. Finally, Hon Hai and Apple Inc., the most important buyer of Foxconn products, were forced to implement reforms that included a reduction of working hours, overtime wages, and safety procedures in order to improve the poor reputation of both companies. The Fair Labor Association was hired to control working conditions (O'Toole, 2013). In recent years, Foxconn announced several times that robots would be utilized in the production line in order to raise efficiency and decrease labor costs. This change could also be a chance to distance the company from accidents, suicides, and other conflicts at the factories (Mozur & Luk, 2012).

China Labor Watch released a report about conditions at ten factories in China, including the ones operated by Foxconn, Quanta, Catcher Technology, Samsung, and Compal Electronics. According to Debby Chan, a project manager for the Hong Kong-based Students and Scholars Against Corporate Misbehavior (SACOM), 'We never said that Apple was the worst in the industry. Samsung, HTC, Motorola, Amazon, and Nokia have the same problems' (Kan, 2012).

SACOM has been one of the most vocal advocates for change at Foxconn. The issue was first raised in 2010, when a string of worker suicides prompted former Apple CEO, Steve Jobs, to defend the supplier. In a widely reported email, Jobs said, 'Although every suicide is tragic, Foxconn's suicide rate is well below the China average'. Since then, Apple has taken a more active role in addressing problems at Foxconn factories – for example, by working with the Fair Labor Association to audit facilities for labor violations. While labor groups remain unconvinced that the progress is sufficient, Apple's influence over its suppliers could help improve working conditions in factories across China. In addition to Foxconn, Apple uses 155 other suppliers, some of which have also drawn allegations of poor working conditions (Kan, 2012).

Chapter review question

1. Describe the opportunities and challenges, from the perspective of Apple's management, of working with Foxconn.
2. How do you evaluate Foxconn's potentials for its future business?

3.3.1.3 Licensing

Contractual licensing relationships describe the transfer of knowledge between one licensor and usually various licensees. The licensor, as the owner of knowledge – for example, concerning a product technology – needs to have a registered patent or trademark, which legally protects the licensor from illegal use of its intellectual property. When applied as an international market entry mode, the licensor grants exclusive rights to a licensee located in the target foreign country to use the intellectual property for a defined purpose for a certain period of time as agreed to by both parties in the contract (Aulakh, Jiang, & Li, 2013: 700).

In other words, licensing describes contractual transactions in which the owner of knowledge-based resource assets sells to another organization or individual the right to use these intangible resources for a defined purpose. Under the licensing arrangement, the licensor transfers, but does not give up, this ownership of the knowledge in exchange for the payment of royalties by the licensee (Luostarinen & Welch,

1997: 31–32). The royalty to the licensor, agreed to and documented in the contract, is normally calculated and paid based on each product unit sold by the licensee. License agreements offer the advantage to the licensee of gaining access to advanced, but legally protected, intellectual knowledge. The licensee takes the entrepreneurial risk and undertakes financial investments in facilities for material procurement, manufacturing, marketing, sales, and distribution of the products and services in the target foreign markets where the licensed knowledge is used (compare Figure 45).

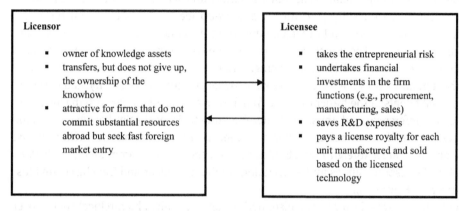

Figure 45. Mutual commitments of licensor and licensee

Licensing can be attractive for rather small firms that have limited financial resources because it allows them to build up operations outside their home country. Furthermore, licensing as an international market entry mode is desirable in industries characterized by relatively short product and technology life cycles, such as high-technology industries.

Potential drawbacks for the licensor come along with the fact of having no control over the operations and quality of the products and services created by the licensee. Innovation can be commercialized quickly with little investment risk. However, the success of a technological innovation in the market is totally dependent on the commitment and effectiveness of the licensees (Grant, 2013: 255). Because of the licensee's operational value-added activities, the licensor is unable to realize experience curve and economies of scale effects. The licensor's reputation can be damaged when the licensee does not appropriately follow the quality, safety, or environmental protection standards agreed to in the contract. In parallel, depending on the licensee's learning capabilities, there is a threat that a new competitor is built up, based on the licensor's knowledge and expertise. Many firms made the mistake of thinking they could maintain control over their knowhow within the framework of a licensing agreement. RCA Corporation, for example, once licensed its color television set technology to Japanese firms. The Japanese companies quickly assimilated the technology, improved on it, and used it to successfully enter worldwide markets, taking substantial market share from RCA (Hill, 2012: 495).

3.3.1.4 Franchising

Franchising is a contractual agreement between a franchisor and usually many franchisees that are legally and financially separated (Hendrikse & Jiang, 2007: 13). Combs et al. (2004: 907) describe the process of franchising as follows: the franchisor sells to the franchisees (typically small business owners) the right to commercialize goods or services under the franchisor's established brand name (market goodwill) and a proven business concept. During the contractual relationship, the franchisor provides ongoing commercial, administrative, and technical assistance. In return, the franchisee typically pays an initial start-up fee, royalties based on the sales, and advertising fees – all of which depend on the conditions agreed to in the franchising contract. The franchise system combines the advantages of ongoing research and development activities, marketing, and economy of scale potentials offered by the franchisor with the regional market knowledge, cultural sensitivity, and entrepreneurial talents of the franchisee. The franchisees are most familiar with the local customer preferences and, thus, can better fine-tune their local sales behavior. From the perspective of the owner of the business concept, franchising allows a relatively fast entry into target foreign markets (Zentes, Morschett, & Schramm-Klein, 2011: 140 – 142). The responsibilities and expectations of the franchisor and franchisee are illustrated in Figure 46).

Potential drawbacks for a franchisor derive from the limited hierarchical control over the franchisee, which is an independent contractor, not an employee of the franchisor. Franchisees can harm the reputation of the franchisor and its business concept if they do not follow the quality, hygiene, and working condition standards specified in the contract. Moreover, the franchisor depends on the franchisee as an information source because the latter has direct contact with the customers. Therefore, market forecasts and necessary product and service modification, which may influence the business concept, depend on the franchisee's information input. Having this in mind, the franchisor can lower the risk of franchisee dependence by simultaneously investing in financial and managerial assets, such as wholly owned operations in the target market (Dunning, Pak, & Beldona, 2007: 545).

Conflicts in the franchisor-franchisee relationship mainly arise from disagreements over objectives such as sales and profits, which may result from poor communication or failure. The potential for conflicts is reduced if franchisor and franchisee view each other as partners in running a business with common objectives and operating procedures. This approach requires a strong common culture with shared values established by means of intense communication between franchisor and franchisee. Another way of reducing disputes is to establish an efficient and transparent monitoring and reporting system between the franchisor and franchisee – for example, real-time access to computer-based inventory and accounting systems (Hollensen, 2014: 379).

However, the more the franchisee is monitored and controlled by the franchisor, the more questionable becomes the *entrepreneurial freedom* of the franchisee, which is usually claimed as one of the driving advantages when promoting franchise con-

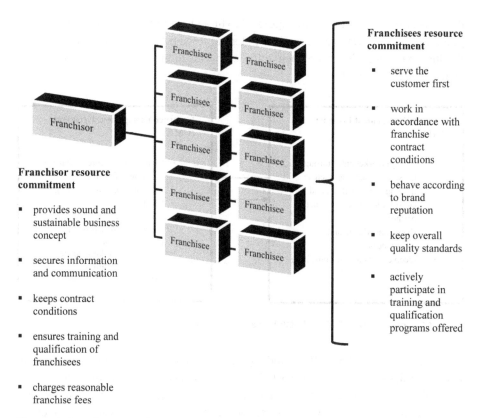

Figure 46. Mutual contractual commitments of franchisor and franchisees

cepts. Because of the franchise start-up fee – which can easily reach, conditional to the business concept, more than one hundred thousand Euros – the dependency of the franchisee on the franchisor seems to be incomparably higher than vice versa from the franchisor's perspective. Thus, as in all contractual relationships, the right selection of a partner, which includes the careful evaluation of the business concept, is of vital importance for the involved parties.

3.3.1.5 Management contracts

Management contracts offer a means through which a firm may use some of its personnel to assist a firm located in a target foreign country for a specified fee and period of time (Wheelen & Hunger, 2010: 262). The management (knowledge) transfer recipient is seeking a contractual partner that is able to run its enterprise and, in parallel, qualifies and trains its staff by providing technical, commercial, and managerial knowledge. At the same time, the transferring firm enters new foreign markets, selling its managerial expertise and bringing in resources that help to improve the competitive positioning of the contract partner abroad, who in return pays fees for the consulting service (compare Figure 47). Through contractual relations with local governments, the firm is able to enter potential foreign markets where the local authorities may have a less than open attitude towards foreign investors (Foscht & Podmenik, 2005: 582–583).

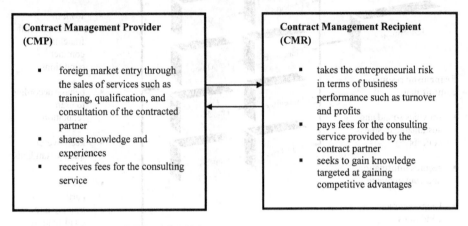

Figure 47. Expectations of CMP and CMR in management contracts

While training the staff, including transfer of managerial and technological knowhow, there is a risk for the CMP that a new competitor is being fostered and developed. In addition, the management supplying firm needs to send qualified personnel, particularly those with cultural sensitivity and language skills. Such a qualified pool of employees is not always readily available. Personal and cultural conflict with locals may arise, depending on the expatriate's characteristics and qualifications for carrying out the contract tasks. Opposing expectations regarding between the contracting firm and the local governments may also provide the basis for conflicts. The local management may have divergent work ethics or show a less motivated learning behavior. Nevertheless, management contracts can be an interesting and profitable market entry mode. In order to successfully realize management contract projects, considerable effort needs to be made in terms of communication at the local level as well as back at the CMP headquarters (Luostarinen & Welch, 1997: 105).

3.3.1.6 Turnkey contracts

Turnkey describes a market entry mode where a firm sells complete operations and supply and distribution chain services: material procurement, assembly, testing, and aftersales service, including warranty support (Henning, 2013: 18). Turnkey operations are usually used in large investment initiatives, such as the design, planning, construction, and building of a large manufacturing plant in a target foreign country. Market entry through turnkey usually includes the start-up of operations as well as necessary training, qualification, and consulting with the local personnel. The firm then 'turns the key over' to the local government in return for an agreed upon payment of use fee (Deresky, 2014: 218). Turnkey operations are attractive for firms that have, for example, specific engineering and complex technological process know-how.

The build, operate, transfer (BOT) concept is a variation of the turnkey operation. Instead of turning the facility (e. g., power plant or toll road) over to the host country when completed, the firm operates the facility for a fixed period of time. During this operating period, the company earns back the investment, plus a profit. At the end of the time period agreed upon with the foreign contract partner, the firm turns the facility over to the contract partner – for example, the local government at little or no cost to the host country (Naisbitt, 1996: 143; Wheelen & Hunger, 2010: 262).

Critical success factors for the turnkey selling firm usually derive from the availability of qualified personnel; a less developed infrastructure; security issues; and limited availability of local suppliers, logistics, and other service firm networks. There may also be a particular risk exposure if the turnkey contract is with the local government of the target foreign country, which is often the case in politically and economically rather fragile countries. The firm may face the threat of contract revocation initiated by the government if differences of opinion related to the project aims and targets arise between the contract partners, which may occur over time (Deresky, 2014: 218).

3.3.2 Cooperative modes of market entry

3.3.2.1 Strategic alliances

Strategic alliances, which belong to the category of cooperative market entry strategies, are formal mechanisms that are established to strengthen the participating firms' competitive positions in the markets. International strategic alliances are working partnerships between firms across national boundaries in the same or different industries. Strategic alliances are agreements between two or more participating organizations that target business objectives that are rather long term (Deresky, 2014: 235). The firm members usually have access to strategically relevant resources, such as client data and distribution channels that are shared between the alliance partners. While vertical strategic alliances display cooperation between suppliers and buyers, horizontal strategic alliances are characterized by cooperation at the same stage of value-added activities. Lateral alliances entail the firms' cooperative sharing of products and services originating in different lines of business (Welge & Holtbrügge, 2015: 118).

Firms agree on cooperative strategies with other industry stakeholders – such as competitors, suppliers, and customers – for various strategic purposes. Firstly, an international strategic alliance may facilitate entry into a foreign market because of the regional expertise and market goodwill of the local firm. The local firm may help secure government and public approval to establish the business. Market entry activities tend to be more efficient because the foreign firm supports entry with its regional marketing expertise and better information access to behavioral aspects, such as purchase attitudes, service expectations, and design tastes of the customers. An alliance, supposing it runs well, is a way to bring together complementary knowledge, such as regional client data, that neither company could easily develop on its own.

Firms seek to establish strategic alliances in order to implement different product branding strategies in the international markets. These strategies include direct extension of an existing brand to the new product, introducing a new brand for a new product, and collaborating with a local brand (of the partner firm) to establish a brand alliance for a new product (Li & He, 2013: 90). For example, Sharp is well known for innovative and quality products in Asia. However, the Japanese firm had been confronted with rather weak brand recognition in Europe. Therefore, in 2002, Sharp's management decided to establish a strategic alliance through capital participation of 8.9 percent with the reputable German Loewe AG. Sharp delivered its innovative liquid crystal display modules, which were assembled and sold by Loewe in the Western markets at much higher prices than Sharp could have reached (Sharp, 2004).

In various markets such as high-technology industries, particularly at the beginning of a new technology life cycle, firms have to decide on common technological or industry standards. At this stage, the firm's management often agrees on strategic alliances in order to implement their favored technological standards for the future. An alliance of companies can look forward to promising earnings due to the fact that the defeated alliances of firms, in terms of another competing technological standard, usually have to license the superior technology. For example in 1979, Philips joined its research and development efforts with Sony for the standardized development and introduction of the 'world audio disc'. The cooperation between Philips and Sony was continued in 1992 (joint development of a DVD industry standard). However, the Sony and Philips partnership finally failed against the high-definition DVD standard of the rival alliance of Toshiba, Hitachi, Pioneer, JVC, Thomson, and Mitsubishi Electric. Panasonic, which supported Sony at the beginning, later joined the rival alliance in the technological battle. In 2008, the alliance group initiator, Sony, with its Blu-ray Disc™ won the competition against its Japanese rival, Toshiba, which was previously the leading firm in developing the high-definition DVD standard (Sony, 2008; WeltOnline, 2008). Just one year later in 2009, Panasonic, Philips, and Sony established, with other Blu-ray Disc™ patent holders, a license that covers essential patents for Blu-ray Disc™. The fees for the new product licenses are US $9.50 for a Blu-ray Disc™ player and US$14.00 for a Blu-ray Disc™ recorder. The per disc license fees for Blu-ray Disc™ will be US$0.11 for a read only disc, US $0.12 for a recordable disc, and US$0.15 for a rewritable disc (one-blue, 2009).

The formal difference, compared to a joint venture, is that a strategic alliance does not come along with a legally independent entity. All firms participating in a strategic alliance remain legally fully responsible for their business. In most cases, a strategic alliance is established as non-equity cooperation, meaning that the partners do not commit mutual financial investments (Hollensen, 2014: 379). However, there are also cases where firms decide to establish a strategic alliance in which one partner acquires a stake in the other partner or where both partners mutually hold equity participations. If the alliance partner is located in a target foreign market, the equity participating firm undertakes a foreign direct investment. Figure 48 illustrates the decisional alternatives of cooperative strategies, distinguishing between strategic alliances and joint ventures and corresponding relevant facets.

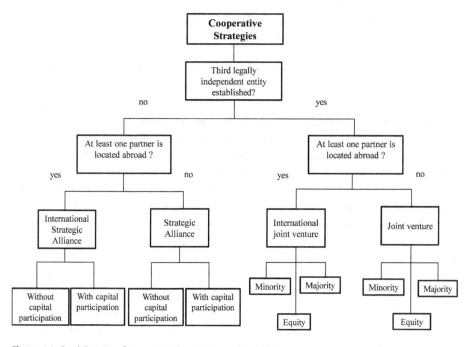

Figure 48. Decision tree for cooperative strategy alternatives

Potential disadvantages from alliance agreements derive from the risk of resource transfer, such as client data, marketing, and technological and managerial knowledge, to the partner firm, which is often, but not necessarily, a competitor. The right partner selection is of vital importance to the success of the alliance. A suitable partner should not exploit the alliance for its own needs. For example, it should not expropriate human resources, such as recruiting highly qualified alliance partner staff through attractive job offers in order to employ them in its own firm. The partner selection process plays a crucial role and includes the collection and analysis of publicly available information regarding potential partners as well as opinions, if available, from other industry stakeholders, such as logistic firms, suppliers, and customers (Hill, 2012: 507).

Against the background of liberalized market structures and the strategic importance of efficient resource allocation and global product launch speed, firms increasingly tend to agree on alliances (Inkpen & Ramaswamy, 2006: 88–89). For sure, the building of a successful alliance partnership belongs to the most complex of management tasks. Synergy effects of the partner firms often are not performing as expected – as many firms involved in international alliances have experienced to their regret.

3.3.2.2 International joint ventures

A joint venture is formed when two or more legally distinct firms decide to own and control a common business – for example, manufacturing and sales of a particular product or service. A joint venture indicates a legally independent entity. The controlling parties, also named joint venture parents, contribute assets and, depending on each party's equity share, the revenue and risks (Rugman & Collinson, 2012: 260–261). An equal joint venture describes the constellation when each party contributes half of the amount of equity, thus sharing the managerial control, risk, and earnings. Majority joint ventures describe the constellation when a firm owns more than fifty percent share of the joint venture and, thus, secures control of strategic-managerial decisions and corresponding resource allocations (Hill, 2012: 507).

A joint venture can be formed between firms that run businesses in the same industry, indicating similar value-added activities (horizontal joint venture). Alternatively, a joint venture can be established between firms that are located at different stages of the industry value-added chain (vertical joint venture), such as a supplier-buyer cooperation. Conglomerate joint ventures describe a constellation when the cooperating firms join different lines of businesses (Kutschker & Schmid, 2006: 862).

An international joint venture (IJV) describes an arrangement where at least one parent organization is headquartered outside the venture's country of operation or if the venture has a significant level of operations in more than just one country. Driven by the fundamental changes that have occurred during recent decades toward internationalization of markets and competition and the increasing costs and complexity of technological developments, IJVs have become an important mode for international market entry (Frayne & Geringer, 2000: 406). The donation and share of resources – such as technological and managerial knowledge, operational capacities, management expertise, and the mutual access of the supplier and customer networks – serve as important advantages for the partner firms.

An IJV can be formed in order to organize research and development and/or manufacturing facilities for the involved partners. This arrangement belongs to the category of an upstream-based partnership. When companies join their marketing, distribution, sales, and after-sales service network, this belongs to downstream-based collaborations. In the case where the joint venture partners have complementary competencies in the value chain (for instance, company A, technology, and company B, brand name), this is an upstream/downstream-based collaboration (Lorange & Roos, 1995: 333).

IJVs are often established under time pressure and fast-changing market environ-ments. Consequently, the qualification development of the venture staff is usually done too quickly or does not take place at all. However, the proper preparation of the venture staff through adequate training programs is of vital importance for the venture lifetime. Cooperative market entry strategies through IJVs are not static con-structs. The factor of time plays an important role for the partner firms, which un-avoidably change their industry network position as the worldwide market circum-stances continuously develop. The network repositioning process (in a positive or negative direction) often develops unnoticed or underestimated by the firms but, in turn, has a decisive influence on the IJV business success.

When a multinational firm's strategic business unit performs less profitably than expected or accumulates losses, the top management has to decide whether to re-structure or even shut down this poorly operating division. Instead of factory clo-sures, there is the alternative of finding another partner with whom the firm can es-tablish a joint venture, hoping that both parties can better manage operations and, thus, improve the business. The transfer of deficiently operating functions to a legal-ly independent joint venture company is perceived less negatively by the public than factory shutdowns, which usually come along with the release of employees. In the course of transferring the business, both parties' top management often emphasize the term 'synergy effects' as a result of the mutual resource commitment. However, synergy effects are often overestimated because both parties, before the joint venture is established, rather hide their individual weaknesses in order to secure a higher in-terest stake ('Who wants to join with a poor performing partner?').

There are several other reasons that firms decide to establish an IJV, such as entry into geographically new markets (Hollensen, 2014: 382). For example, firms no-tice that they lack the necessary market knowledge and brand recognition in the tar-get foreign market. Rather than trying to develop these capabilities internally, the firm may identify another organization that possesses those desired marketing skills. Joint ventures may be helpful when entering a foreign market, particularly where socio-cultural or political-legal differences relative to the home country exist. Coop-eration with a firm in the host country can increase the speed of market entry. The bundle of distribution channels increases sales capacity and allows access to geo-graphically diverse markets. The costs of after-sales service may be reduced, and the service reaction time may be improved. Furthermore, some countries (e.g., India) try to restrict foreign ownership. Governments may create pressure on multi-nationals to establish international joint ventures with local firms.

Global operations in research and development and operations are expensive, but often necessary to achieve competitive advantages. Joint ventures allow partici-pating firms to pool financial capital, human resources, research and development, and operational capacities to gain economies of scale because of joint use of their facilities, thereby reducing the costs per output unit. Pooling the procurement in-creases the bargaining power of the joint venture partners and better provides pre-requisites for standardized platform manufacture. Joint ventures may also be used to build jointly on the technological expertise of two or more firms in developing products that are technologically beyond the capability and resources of the firms acting independently. Complementary technologies provided by the partners can lead to new product or manufacturing process developments. Joint research and development helps to accelerate product innovations (Hollensen, 2014: 379, 382).

Trust is most crucial to the success of an IJV. But how can it be developed? Choose a partner with compatible strategic goals and objectives, and work out with the partner how and to what extent proprietary technology and sensitive information is to be shared. Recognize that most IJVs usually last a couple of years and probably break up once a partner feels it has incorporated the skills and information it needs to go it alone (Deresky, 2014: 244).

When two firms first initiate a relationship and start to interact with each other, trust on both sides might only be present to a limited extent because trustworthy behavior first has to be proved to one another. When the first series of IJV resource transactions are successful and carried out to partners' satisfaction, firms may be willing to increase the size of the resource and accept higher risks, which naturally correlate with greater benefits. This implies that firms gradually gain trust in the relationship when a series of resource exchange episodes within the IJV have been performed successfully. Likewise, it posits that an increase in trust enhances the partners' willingness to increasingly commit to the exchange relationship. Shared values and mutual interests and IJV business objectives entail that both parties have a congruent vision of the direction in which they want to develop their relationship (Lambe, Wittmann, & Spekman, 2001: 11).

Joint ventures between Japanese firms follow a certain pattern that is characterized by the mutual wish over time to create a 'win-win situation'. The long-term time horizon allows partner firms to build up mutual trust and helps to overcome the short-term venture difficulties that come up during the partnership. Experiences collected in one previous joint venture project improve organizational issues and the corresponding business performance of the next venture operation. Moreover, Japanese firms make sure the joint venture management does not operate separately and too independently. The management is integrated into the parent firm's structure and long-term strategic plans. The long-term oriented business relations between Japanese firms mean that the partner firm relations are not interrupted when the venture project comes to an end. Instead, Japanese firms often cooperate on a number of common joint venture projects with one selected partner firm. If a joint venture is ended – because, for example, the market for the corresponding products is no longer there – the cooperation is continued in another project. Panasonic, for example, founded a joint venture with Toshiba in the area of color picture tube manufacture in 2003 (Matsushita, 2003, 2005). In 2006, after the previous cooperation was terminated and the production stopped because the color picture tube sales on the worldwide markets went down, a new joint venture was founded between the two Japanese firms for liquid crystal modules (LCD) and organic light emitting displays (OLED) technology (Toshiba_Matsushita_DT, 2008). Another case is Panasonic, which agreed to a joint venture with Hitachi in 2004 concerning shared research activities, manufacture, and distribution of LCD modules. The cooperation between Panasonic and Hitachi was 'renewed' and continued in 2008 in terms of research, manufacture, and distribution of LCD modules in the Czech Republic. Sharp, in another example, made an agreement with Sony in 1996 for the joint development of flat screen panels. In 2008, the joint project was 'renewed' when both Japanese firms started their common LCD panel manufacturing activities (DisplaySearch, 2008b).

Considering the complexities associated with operating an IJV, flexibility of the IJV parents is required to adapt to continuously changing conditions in the global markets (Zeira & Newburry, 1999: 338). Learning to manage IJVs is multifaceted, and the success of an IJV participating firm assumes a certain ability to absorb knowledge about work-ethics, communication behaviors, and business attitudes from the other IJV partner (Glaister, Husan, & Buckley, 2003: 103; Meschi, 2005: 692). Inter-organizational learning is a process where flexibility and adaptability are consistently important in assimilating the knowledge of the partner firm. Applying external knowledge from the partner organization involves the ability to diffuse knowledge, integrate it into the organization, and generate new knowledge from it (Lane, Salk, & Lyles, 2001: 1156–1157). Commitment to the IJV parent is dependent on the position taken by the other IJV parent. In light of this discussion, there are various reasons for IJV instability that the involved parties should keep in mind and work on when they arise.

- First, one joint venture partner may show opportunistic behavior and attempt to hide proprietary knowledge, such as technological expertise, from the other joint venture participant. This behavior finally causes an IJV failure due to the lack of mutual trust and partners' willingness to learn (Li, 1995: 347; Schuler, 2001: 9).
- Second, tensions are created when either the IJV management or one of the IJV parents redirects its strategic focus, changes key objectives, attempts to reposition in the markets, or undertakes major growth or downsizing without prior appropriate communication to the partner.
- Third, instability occurs when the partners renegotiate contracts (e.g., on technology transfer).
- Fourth, the reconfiguration of the venture's ownership and control structures represents a major source of instability because such amendments cause new bargaining dynamics and/or alter the strategic stakes of the partners (Yan & Zeng, 1999: 407). Lack of appropriate organizational structures, uncertain managerial roles, and indefinite decision authority negatively influence IJV performance (Schuler, 2001: 9). Diverse cultural backgrounds of the IJV partners hinder communication and may cause misunderstanding and reduced motivation of the IJV management (Frayne & Geringer, 2000: 406–407; Müller & Gelbrich, 2004: 367, 381).
- A fifth facet of instability concerns the IJV's relationship with each parent company. The IJV threatens to become unstable when changes take place that affect

the decisional autonomy of the IJV management, such as limitation of their authority (Frayne & Geringer, 2000: 412; Yan & Zeng, 1999: 407).
- Sixth, IJVs are often established in markets where the product is positioned at the declining stage of the technology life cycle. Instead of realizing the business reality, the partners hope that business performance will improve because they have bundled their mutual resources, which is often a fundamental mistake—as many firms experienced to their regret.
- Seventh, IJVs are often founded in order to bring complementary resource assets together. For example, one partner contributes technological and engineering knowhow, and the other partner brings marketing expertise to the venture operations. At first glance, such an approach makes sense. However, engineers and marketers often speak a 'different language' and have different objectives (e. g., technological state-of-the-art versus costs and prices). This communication challenge is increased when engineers and controlling people and marketers have a different language and cultural background due to the different backgrounds of the joint venture parents.
- Finally, major technological product developments on the market, unnoticed by one or both IJV partners, may damage the business performance and provoke disputes, which can lead to the termination of the IJV (Contractor & Lorange, 1988: 25).

To sum up, IJVs represent 'mixed-motive games' in which competitive and cooperative dynamics of the involved partners may occur simultaneously. The significant association of operational control with a partner's achievement of its strategic objectives contributes to competition over resource allocation and pursuit of the unilateral goals of the partner firms (Yan & Gray, 2001: 411). Das and Teng (2000: 94) similarly claim potential different motives, such as cooperation versus competition, rigidity versus flexibility, and short-term versus long-term orientation. These differences create a framework of multiple tensions, which can cause partnership instability and finally the termination of the IJV.

3.3.2.3 Case Study: International Joint Ventures of LG Electronics (South Korea) and Philips (The Netherlands)

3.3.2.3.1 The partners' situation before establishing their international joint ventures

LG Electronics (LG) is the second largest Korean Chaebol in consumer electronics after Samsung. Established in 1958, LG was originally known under the brand Lucky Goldstar. During the 1960s, LG produced Korea's first radios, television sets, refrigerators, washing machines, and air conditioners. In 1995, renamed LG Electronics, the Korean conglomerate acquired the US-based enterprise Zenith. In 2008, LG introduced a new global brand identity: 'stylish design and smart technology in products that fit our consumers' lives' (LG_Electronics, 2005a, b, 2009b). Over the years LG Electronics developed successfully, expanded worldwide, and became a serious competitor in the electronics business. However, the aggressive expansion was financed to a large extent by loans, which resulted in a critical debt-to-equity ratio. As a result of the financial crisis in Asia at the end of the 1990s, LG Electronics faced severe financial difficulties and needed to find external investors (Glowik, 2007b; LG_Electronics, 2008b).

At that time, the traditional and largest European-based electronics company, the Royal Dutch Philips from the Netherlands, was technologically already behind its Korean competitor in television flat panel manufacturing. Philips had a very reputable image with enormous brand recognition among European customers and had a large European sales network, which were the firm's most valuable resource assets. The 1990s was a decade of organizational changes for Philips. The company carried out a major restructuring program, simplifying its organizational structure and reducing the number of business areas (Philips, 2008). In September 2006, Philips sold 80.1 percent of its semiconductor business to a consortium of private equity partners. This laid the foundation for a new independent semiconductor company, called NXP. In September 2007, Philips communicated its Vision 2010 strategic plan to further grow the company with increased profitability targets. As part of Vision 2010, the organizational structure was simplified in January 1, 2008, by forming three sectors: Healthcare, Lighting, and Consumer Lifestyle. With a massive advertising campaign to unveil its new brand promise of 'sense and simplicity', the company confirmed its dedication to offering consumers around the world products that are advanced; easy to use; and, above all, designed to meet their needs (Philips, 2008).

3.3.2.3.2 The foundation of LG.Philips LCD

In August 1999, the management of Philips took the chance to overcome its technological drawback in flat panel display technologies and decided to invest in LG Electronics. Philips paid USD 1.6 billion to LG Electronics and reserved 50 percent of the shares of the newly established joint venture, LG.Philips LCD. The partnership aimed for world leadership in the flat display television set industry. The capital investment was carried out so that Phillips purchased new stock (common shares) against payment to LG Electronics, which kept 98.8 percent of the subsidiary LG LCD shares it held before the transaction was completed (LG.PhilipsLCD, 2005a, b).

The joint venture with LG was not the first time Philips had tried to get into the LCD panel business through a partnership with another firm. Several years before, Philips experimented with developing its own production facilities with limited success. In 1997, Philips attempted to join forces and establish a joint venture with Hosiden Co., Kobe, Japan, a second-tier Japanese LCD manufacturer (Kovar, 1999). However, the joint venture failed and caused losses that reached more than USD 100 million a year (Bondgenoten, 2001).

At the beginning, the international new venture, LG.Philips LCD, was managed by a board of directors composed of six members, three each from LG and Philips. According to a press release dated May 19, 1999,

> The alliance between LG Electronics Inc. and Philips (implemented through selling shares of LG LCD, the global electronic appliances manufacturer) is considered to have an important meaning from the perspective of competition strategy for the highly technical electronics industry, including LCDs. The alliance provides an opportunity for Korea to have absolute superiority in the leading-edge LCD industry because a synergy effect will be generated when the world-class technology of LG's LCD is combined with the market reputation and distribution network of Philips (LG.PhilipsLCD, 2001).

In other words, besides the financial investment of Philips, which helped LG survive at the peak of the financial crisis in Asia, the Korean Chaebol could make use of Philips' exclusive brand and distribution network in Europe and America. Previously, LG's reputation in Europe was linked with a rather cheap, imitative manufacturer's image; and the company name, 'Lucky Goldstar', was rather promoting its low-end image among European consumers.

Headquartered in Seoul, South Korea, the newly established international joint venture, LG.Philips LCD, operated six fabrication facilities in China and South Korea and had approximately 15,000 employees, including those in South Korea. A new production site in Poland, responsible for the manufacture of LCD modules targeting the European market, launched production in 2007 (LG.PhilipsLCD, 2007a, b, c). LG.Philips LCD started to compete mainly against Samsung and

Sharp in the segment that manufactures and supplies thin film transistor liquid crystal display (TFT-LCD) panels. The firm concentrated on TFT-LCD panels in a wide range of sizes and specifications for use in notebook computers, desktop monitors, and television sets (LG.PhilipsLCD, 2008a). On September 6, 2005, LG.Philips LCD announced that it planned to construct a 'back-end' module production plant in Wroclaw, becoming the first global LCD industry player to commence such production in Europe. LG.Philips LCD considered building a production plant by 2011 with an annual capacity of 11 million units and an investment volume total of 429 million Euros. The manufacture of the LCD module began in the middle of 2007, when the construction of the first batch of module lines was completed with an annual capacity of 3 million units (LG.PhilipsLCD, 2006a, c). The vice chairman and CEO of LG.Philips LCD, Bon Joon Koo, said,

> Our planned production facility in Poland is an important step for LG.Philips LCD, as we establish our manufacturing expertise in the geographic center of Europe. With this first major factory outside of Asia, LG.Philips LCD will better serve the rapidly growing European LCD TV market. As we implement our strategic plan for the future, we are proud to broaden the reach of our industry-leading LCD technology and expand our customer intimacy as we bring our products closer to our customers. We are grateful to the Polish government and the city of Wroclaw for their support and cooperation in this great partnership (LG.PhilipsLCD, 2006c).

LG.Philips LCD relied on a worldwide manufacturing network. Major LCD display production plants were located in Asia and Europe, which provided various advantages in terms of manufacturing costs and logistics because of proximity to its regional markets (compare Figure 49).

LG.Philips LCD Manufacturing Locations

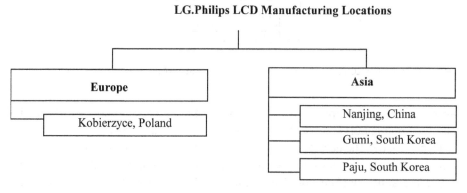

Figure 49. LG Philips LCD manufacturing locations [status 2007]. Source: LG.Philips (2007a)

Global sales were organized by LG.Philips LCD mainly through three distribution clusters in Europe, America, and Asia, which served as a further strength relative to its competitors (compare Figure 50).

The investment of LG.Philips LCD in Kobierzyce (a suburb of Wroclaw) generated further market entry activities through direct foreign investment in Poland. The Jap-

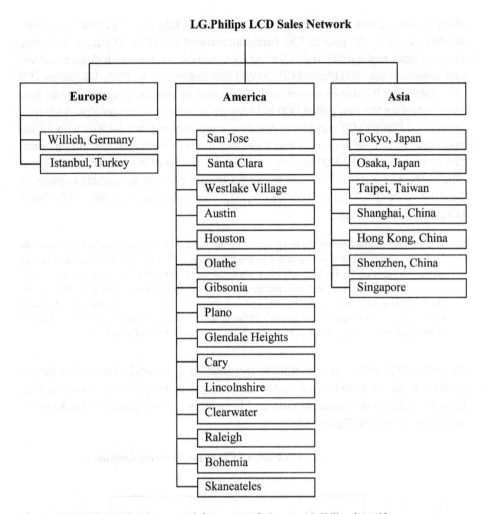

Figure 50. LG.Philips LCD sales network [status 2007]. Source: LG.Philips (2007b)

anese electronics enterprise Toshiba, for example, decided to set up a Polish subsidiary, assembling LCD TVs in Kobierzyce as well. Toshiba also operated an LCD factory in Plymouth, UK. The new Polish plant was scheduled to start operation by mid-2008. About 1,000 employees would manufacture between 1.5 and 2 million 32-inch and larger TVs annually (Johnston, 2006; LG.PhilipsLCD, 2007c). Toshiba's annual production capacity of flat panel TVs in Europe, counting both UK and Polish output, reached around 3 million units by 2009. Toshiba's factory procured large quantities of its LCD panels from the Dutch-Korean joint venture LG.Philips LCD. Toshiba invested 19.9 percent interest in the LG.Philips LCD plant in Poland. The developing industry cluster initiated the market entry of Korean component suppliers (follow the customer phenomenon). Various Korean firms decided to enter the Polish market and invested near the LG.Philips plant. Poland was becoming an important industry cluster in terms of vertically integrated LCD television set manufacturing outside Asia, which at that time was unique. From Poland, the module supply of LG.Philips LCD to other television set assemblers located in Europe was organized as Figure 51 illustrates (Johnston, 2006; LG.PhilipsLCD, 2007c).

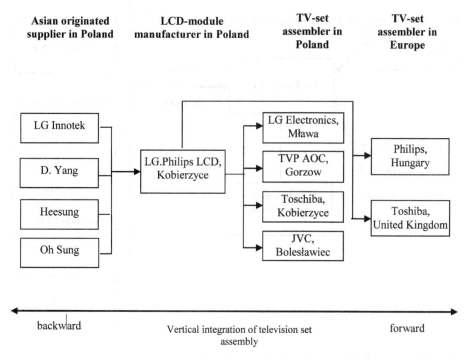

Figure 51. LG.Philips LCD vertical integrated value chain activities in Europe (status February 2008).

In the years following the founding, LG.Philips LCD established various bilateral relationships with other firms doing business in consumer electronics. Stable supplier-customer relationships that secure economies of scale as well as the wish to develop a technological leadership positioning in the LCD business were the main incentives for seeking relationships for LG.Philips LCD. The networking activities of LG.Philips LCD led to the introduction of other partner firms with further distribution channels, competencies, and technological knowledge to the LG.Philips relationship network (compare Figure 52).

Despite a loss in 2001, net income increased in the years following the venture's founding and reached a peak of around USD 1.5 billion in 2004. Overall, the global LCD business developed well, and LG.Philips was able to reap the rewards of it. The net sales of the international joint venture increased annually and reached more than USD 15 billion in 2007 (LG.PhilipsLCD, 2006d). Due to intense competition in the LCD business in the worldwide markets, the net income dropped in 2005 but pro-

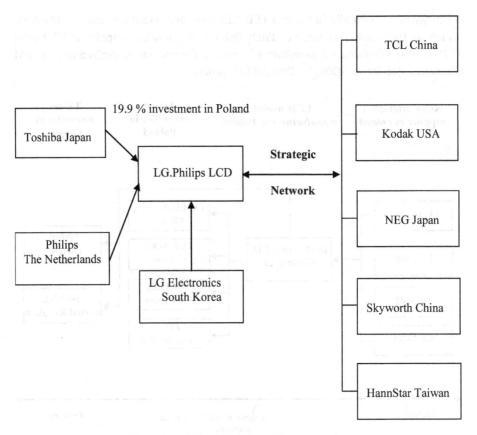

Figure 52. Network embedding of LG.Philips LCD (status February 2008).

gressively developed over the years. The data below illustrate the financial development of the joint venture (LG.PhilipsLCD, 2003, 2006b, 2008b).

3.3.2.3.3 Philips reduces its stake in LG.Philips LCD
On March 3, 2008, LG.Philips LCD changed the name of the firm. The world's second-largest manufacturer of LCDs, which began as a joint venture between South Korea's LG Electronics Inc. and Philips in 1999, was renamed LG Display Corporation nine years later. Despite the promising financial development of the international joint venture, Philips finally decided to terminate its engagement. The Philips name disappeared from the title of the joint venture as result of the stepwise reduction in shares held by Philips. In October 2007, Philips reduced its stake from 32.9 to 19.9 percent, followed by a further reduction in March 2008 to 13.2 percent. As per December 31, 2007, LG Electronics, LG.Philips' largest shareholder, held a 37.9 percent stake. Domestic (Korean) shareholders held 25.3 percent, and overseas investors and others

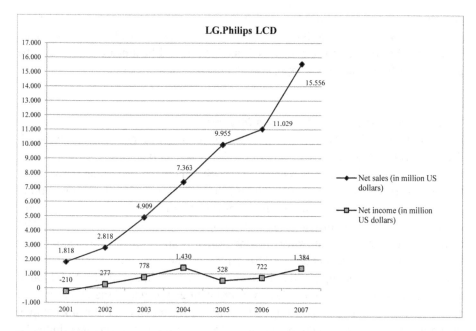

Figure 53. LG.Philips LCD net sales and income for the period 2001 to 2007. Developed based on various firm related sources (LG.Philips LCD, 2003, LG.Philips LCD, 2008b)

held 16.9 percent (LG.PhilipsLCD, 2008c). In April 2008, Mr. Young Soo Kwon, CEO of LG Display, announced,

> Last quarter was a notable quarter for us. Our performance was encouraging despite the season-ally slow market conditions. In addition, we have changed our corporate name from LG.Philips LCD Co., Ltd., to LG Display Co., Ltd., and will transition into a single representative director's organization at the annual general meeting in accordance with the change in corporate gover-nance following the reduction of Philips' equity. The new name reflects our intention to expand our business scope and diversify the business model for sustainable growth in the future. While there were changes in our corporate governance, we remain committed to maintaining our integ-rity and being transparent and consistent, accompanied by our competent directors on the board (LG.PhilipsLCD, 2008c).

From this time onwards, LG Display Co., headquartered in Seoul, South Korea, con-centrated its research and development in Anyang (South Korea) and maintained major module factories in Paju and Gumi (South Korea). In China, the firm establish-ed factories in Nanjing and Guangzhou. The one and only European module assem-bly line remains in Wroclaw, Poland.

Philips announced in February 2008 that it is looking to outsource manufactur-ing for 70 percent of its LCD TVs (in 2006 nearly 60 percent). The company expects to ship 14 million LCD TVs in 2008, with about 10 million units outsourced (Digitimes.-com, 2008). In other words, Philips will further reduce its technological and manu-

facturing involvement in the television set business, taking the increased risk of losing know-how. According to the firm's strategic plan, Philips will strengthen its activities in other business segments, such as lighting and healthcare, in order to be
prepared for future markets (Emphasize_Emerging_Markets, 2007).

3.3.2.3.4 The foundation of LG.Philips Displays

In Amsterdam, on June 11, 2001, Gerard Kleisterlee, president and chief executive officer of Royal Philips Electronics, and John Koo, vice chairman and CEO of LG Electronics, signed a 'definitive agreement' through which the two companies would
merge their respective cathode ray tube (CRT) businesses into a new joint venture
company. The official presentation of the new company was held on July 5, 2001,
in Hong Kong. The fifty-fifty joint venture in display technology concerned all CRT
activities, including glass and key components. With expected annual sales of nearly
USD 6 billion and approximately 36,000 employees, the new company was expected
to have a global leadership position in the CRT market. Philips paid USD 1.1 billion to
LG Electronics. At that time, the joint venture held 25 percent of the global market
share and ranked ahead of Samsung SDI in the CRT business. The following complementary strengths and synergy potentials of the merged entities were mentioned by
both parties' management (LG.PhilipsDisplays, 2001a, b):
- Philips's leadership in television tubes and LG's leadership in monitor tubes;
- LG's geographical leadership in Asia and Philips' brand reputation and distribution network in Europe, China, and America; and
- LG's industrial and manufacturing expertise and Philips' global marketing and
  technological innovation. Further benefits were expected in the areas of purchasing as well as research and development through combining resources and
  economies of scale effects (LG.PhilipsDisplays, 2001b).

Under the terms of the agreement, LG and Philips had equal control of the joint venture. The new company was legally established in the Netherlands, with operational
headquarters in Hong Kong. Philippe Combes, former CEO of Philips Display Components, was appointed to lead the joint venture (LG.PhilipsDisplays, 2001a, b).

The television set market dramatically changed in 2004. While the demand for
conventional cathode ray tubes went down, LCD and plasma sales increased. During
the year 2006, LCD replaced conventional television set sales in Europe. Nevertheless, even in 2005, LG.Philips Displays still pronounced in a press release the bright
future of conventional television sets and that the cathode ray technology would remain a dominant force in display technology, for example, through the introduction
of 'slim tubes' (LG.PhilipsDisplays, 2005a, d). The venture management was totally
wrong when it made such a forecast. Just two years later, in 2007, 26 million LCD
sets were sold in Europe compared to only 10 million CRT-based units (Display-
Search, 2008a; GfK, 2007). CRT manufacturers in general, among them LG.Philips
Display, faced an increasing price pressure, particularly in highly competitive mar-

kets such as Europe. During the course of an increasing risk of running overcapacities, the culturally biased management behavior became increasingly obvious in the Korean-Dutch joint venture. Mr. David Kang, a manager of LG Electronics, explained his joint venture work experience to me,

> There is a considerably different understanding among Western managers. They insist always on profits, the earlier the better. But our view is different and more long-term oriented. We enter the market with reasonable, well, let's say with low prices. We may even have a loss. But what is more important? If we become the market leader, one day our products will set the standards. Then we will drive the market and its prices. From my point of view, these contrasting time horizons are one of the main reasons why joint ventures of Western and Korean companies fail (Glowik, 2007a).

Concerning different work attitudes and language barriers, Mr. Kang further commented,

> When we had a problem with the customer, for example, it was sometimes hard to find a Western manager when it happened out of the ordinary daily working time. We Koreans cannot understand such customer treatment. For the Europeans, it seems more important to arrange the time with their private families. We Koreans work hard; we have a lot fewer holidays, but the Philips people had 2.5 times higher salaries than we had. How can a joint venture run like this in the long term? Moreover, I have to say, we had a communication problem. English was selected as the company language, but Koreans have weaknesses communicating in English (Glowik, 2007a).

The European view of the joint venture was different. A former senior manager at LG.Philips Displays, who preferred to remain anonymous, commented about the working atmosphere in the international joint venture like this,

> When we (Philips) had a meeting with LG people, sometimes they kept silent the whole time. Later, we recognized the Koreans arranged a separate meeting among themselves, where they discussed and fundamental decisions were made . . . without us. Moreover, I think the Koreans had very effective conversations among themselves in the 'smoker's room' more than during official meetings with us. It is hard to cooperate and get access to them. The Korean community is rather a closed shop (Glowik, 2004a).

Just two years after the establishment of the joint venture, on May 22, 2003, LG.Philips Displays announced the closure of its European production plants in Newport, Wales, and Southport, England, and that the management had started consultations with employees and trade union representatives (LG.PhilipsDisplays, 2005b, c). The corresponding press release said,

> The decision is based on business and economic conditions, which are characterized by an increasingly competitive and consolidating industry. The company's plant at Newport in South Wales produces color display tubes (CDT) for monitors and color picture tubes (CPT) for televisions as well as deflection yokes. A sharp decline in the market for CDTs due to increasing competition from other display technologies also supplying products for use in computer monitors

and severe downward pressure on prices for CDT and CPT are the primary reasons for the closure (LG.PhilipsDisplays, 2005c).

Phil Styles, general manager of manufacturing at Newport, commented,

> The decision to close was made with great regret and is based solely on the continuing adverse business situation. It in no way reflects on the performance of the employees at the plant, who have worked hard and demonstrated considerable commitment over these past five years (LG.PhilipsDisplays, 2005c).

Just a couple of months later, on December 2, 2003, LG.Philips Displays announced a decision to further restructure its industrial production infrastructure in Europe. As announced by the management,

> The measures, in line with the company's continuous drive for optimizing business performance, are necessary to remain competitive in a mature and consolidating industry. As a consequence, the company's cathode ray tube plants in Aachen, Germany, and a glass factory in Simonstone, UK, will be shut down. At all other sites in Europe, cost reduction will be realized by further optimizing the production infrastructure (LG.PhilipsDisplays, 2005e, f).

In the following years, LG.Philips continued the closing process, mainly of its European facilities. On March 2, 2005, LG.Philips Displays published the closure of its plant at Durham in North East England. As was stated in the press release,

> Crippling price erosion and a shift in demand from Europe to Asia Pacific are the main reasons for the decision, which has been made with great regret. Consultations with employees and trade union representatives have begun. Production is expected to cease towards the end of July 2005 and will result in the loss of 761 jobs (LG.PhilipsDisplays, 2005b).

Finally, in October 2005, Philips announced that it would stop television set manufacturing for the European market, which affected its major supplier LG.Philips Displays and particularly its brand new factory in Hranice, Czech Republic, as well as its R&D and manufacturing facilities in Angers, France. Nevertheless, major production operations in Asia and some in Brazil, representing 85 percent of total manufacturing capacity, as well as minor European component suppliers (Stadskanaal and Sittard, The Netherlands, and Blackburn, United Kingdom) continued activities (LG.PhilipsDisplays, 2005e, 2006, 2007a).

Three months later, on January 27, 2006, LG.Philips Displays Holding B.V. announced that due to worsening conditions in the cathode ray tube marketplace and unsustainable debt, the holding companies as well as one of the Dutch subsidiaries (LG.Philips Displays Netherlands B.V.) and its remaining legal German subsidiary in Aachen, Germany, had all filed for insolvency protection. The holding company of LG.Philips Displays in Hong Kong also announced that it would not be able to provide further financial support to certain loss making subsidiaries (in Europe) because it had been unable to obtain sustainable new or additional funding. As a result, approximately 350 employees at the company's operations in Eindhoven, the Netherlands, and 400 employees in Aachen, Germany, were dismissed (LG.Philips-Displays, 2006). Concerning the insolvency filings, LG.Philips Displays headquarters in Hong Kong officially declared in a corresponding press release,

> Over the past year, LG.Philips Displays and other CRT manufacturers have seen an unprecedented decline in the market for CRTs, especially in Europe. At the same time, the demand for new flat panel televisions, including liquid crystal display (LCD) and plasma televisions, has surged dramatically as these alternatives have dropped in price and become cost competitive faster than anticipated. Although demand for CRTs has dropped precipitously in mature markets, global demand for CRTs remains strong, especially in emerging markets. LG.Philips Displays has been in extensive discussions with the company's financiers and parent companies, Philips and LG Electronics, over the past several months to explore financial solutions to the market challenges, especially in Europe (LG.PhilipsDisplays, 2006).

The president and CEO of LG.Philips Displays, J.I. Son, commented,

> We deeply regret this outcome and the painful impact these filings will have on our valued employees and the communities that have supported us over the years. Unfortunately, market conditions and our financial situation have made this very difficult decision unavoidable. Having explored all possible restructuring options, we really have no choice but to take these actions. We are working to maintain employment for our remaining employees through our ongoing operations (LG.PhilipsDisplays, 2006).

In the course of its retrenchment strategy, additional subsidiaries of LG.Philips Displays in France, the Czech Republic, Slovakia, Mexico, and the US were liquidated. LG.Philips Displays emphasized that its plants in Brazil, China, Indonesia, South Korea, and Poland (component supplier) were, in principle, unaffected. The company's factories in the United Kingdom (Blackburn) and the Netherlands (Stadskanaal and Sittard, with support from some employees in Eindhoven) were economically viable and were expected to continue production, for which LG.Philips Displays would seek support and approval from the Dutch trustee and supervisory judge (LG.PhilipsDisplays, 2005e, 2006).

In fact, the LG.Philips Displays joint venture operations resulted in a loss just after the firm's foundation. The financial situation could not recover in the following years. What are the reasons? The European television set cathode ray tube market declined due to the fact that the CRT technology had reached the end of its product life cycle and had been replaced by flat panel technologies. Consequently, competition had become more and more price focussed. The remaining tube supplying manufacturers in Europe, such as large firms like Samsung, Thomson, and Matsushita but also small competitors like Ekranas (Lithuania) and Tesla (Czech Republic) operating in niche markets, were seriously competing for survival. Additionally, Chinese cathode ray tube manufacturers increased their shipments to Europe and worsened the attractiveness of the market. In parallel, the venture partners from contrasting cultural backgrounds could not solve internal communication problems, which had a negative impact on performance as illustrated below (LG.PhilipsDisplays, 2001a, 2007b).

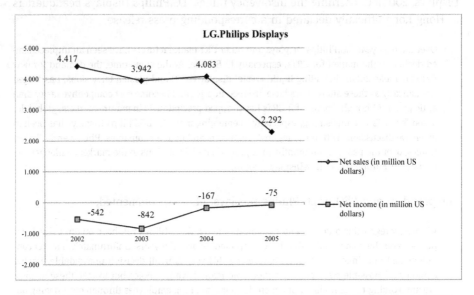

Figure 54. LG.Philips Displays' net sales and net income for the period 2002 to September 2005. Source: LG.Philips Displays (2005f, 2007a)

In 2001, when the joint venture with LG Electronics was established, the television set business unit of Philips had a turnover of USD 3 billion, ran twelve cathode ray tube production sites with 24,000 workers worldwide, and reached a profit of USD 157 million (Bondgenoten, 2001). Just a couple of years later, the former European market leader in consumer electronics, Philips, had disappeared with the joint venture bankruptcy and simultaneously disappeared from the cathode ray tube television set business (TheInquirer, 2006).

3.3.2.3.5 LG.Philips Displays gets a new name
Effective on April 1, 2007, LG.Philips Displays changed its name to LP Displays. The corresponding press release by the top management said,

> The new name and stylized logo are designed to reflect its new corporate status while saluting its roots as a joint venture between LG Electronics and Royal Philips Electronics. At the same time, it reinforces continuity in LP Displays' position as one of the world's leading global suppliers of picture tubes used for television sets and computer monitors. The new name and the logo act as an important step forward for LP Displays and reflect the management and financial stakeholders' confidence in both the future of the company and the CRT business (LG.PhilipsDisplays, 2007c).

LP Displays continued to focus its business on high performance CRTs and a growing demand for its 'SuperSlim' and 'UltraSlim' CRTs, particularly in emerging markets. The global demand for CRTs was expected to remain strong. LP Displays president and CEO, Mr. Jeong IL Son, commented,

> Of the countries with the largest populations, the majority will be CRT customers for the foreseeable future. Markets in Asia and South America offer the company an exciting challenge going forward, and the 'UltraSlim' and 'SuperSlim' series provide LP Displays the competitive advantage it needs to capture this tremendous opportunity (LG.PhilipsDisplays, 2007c).

LP Displays' management team remained in Hong Kong under the leadership of Mr. Son. The company continued to serve its global markets from its plants in Brazil, China, Indonesia, and South Korea and from its minor component operations in the Netherlands and the United Kingdom. LP Displays continued to employ around 11,000 people worldwide. The company's new name and logo reflected the change in ownership structure. Dutch representatives disappeared completely from the firm, which was originally established in 2001 as a fifty/fifty joint venture with a payment of USD 1.1 billion by Philips. A couple of years later, the top management consisted of Korean managers only: Mr. Jeong IL Son, president and chief executive officer; Mr. Deok Sik Moon, chief financial officer and deputy chief executive officer; Mr. J.M. Park, chief sales officer; and Mr. Soo Dyeog Han, executive vice president of New Business Development (LG.PhilipsDisplays, 2007c).

3.3.2.3.6 What happened next to the international joint venture terminations?

Without the financial involvement of Philips, it is questionable whether LG could have recovered and developed successfully after the Asian financial crisis as they have done in recent years. On the one hand, the management of Philips underestimated the sharp decline in conventional cathode ray tube TV demand when the company decided to invest in the joint venture with LG Electronics. On the other hand, the Philips' management obviously did not foresee that LCD/LED technology would drive the business at least for the next decade when they decided to leave the LG.Philips LCD joint venture in 2008. Moreover, the management of Philips did not pay attention to the absorptive and learning capabilities of LG Electronics' management. Meanwhile, the European joint venture partner, Philips, lost its vertical manufacturing integration in the consumer electronics business. Today (year 2016), we can still buy consumer electronics products such as television sets, audio, and others where the Philips brand is labelled on the outside of the product. Most customers believe the product is from Philips. However, the reality is that it is assembled by Taiwanese, Chinese, or other firms, usually based on a manufacturing contract with Philips.

During the international joint venture operations, LG Electronics gained access to the European distribution channels and learned about proper marketing instruments suitable for the European consumer. For instance, LG has changed the meaning of its initials to 'LG = Life is Good', hoping to get closer to its European customers. The strength of LG Electronics is its technology and research and development expertise. Through its new LCD module plant in Poland, the firm has become able to supply LCD modules to the factory of LG Electronics in Mlawa, Poland, which assembles final television sets and supplies them to the whole European market. Following the joint venture termination, LG Electronics could have significantly increased its net sales on the global markets. Nevertheless, net income has not increased over the years; but the Korean company has performed better than, for example, firms like Sony or Panasonic in terms of net income during recent years (compare Figure 55).

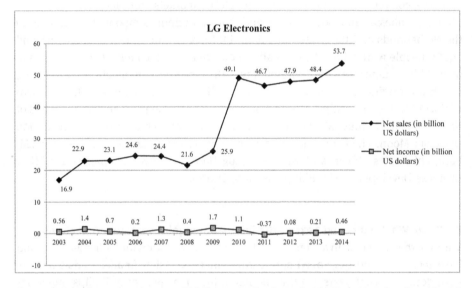

Figure 55. Net sales and net income of LG Electronics for the period 2003 to 2014. Developed based on various firm related sources (LG_Electronics, 2003, 2004, 2005a, 2006, 2007, 2008a, 2009a, 2010, 2011, 2012, 2013, 2014)

At present, LG Electronics makes use of its LCD/LED display technology expertise and expands into new business fields such as automotive. The Korean company develops innovative automotive infotainment devices, including monitors and navigation systems. Aside from in-vehicle infotainment, LG also offers safety, engineering, and electric vehicle solutions that target autonomous driving (LG_Electronics, 2015b). LG's new vehicle components division combines component-related business units by merging the car infotainment unit with the home entertainment division. LG Electronics' newly launched division called Energy Components develops motors for electric vehicles as well as inverters and compressors (LG_Electronics, 2015a, d). The home entertainment division, with its wide range of LCD/LED and OLED products, will remain one of the most important business units within LG Electronics for the coming years (compare Figure 56).

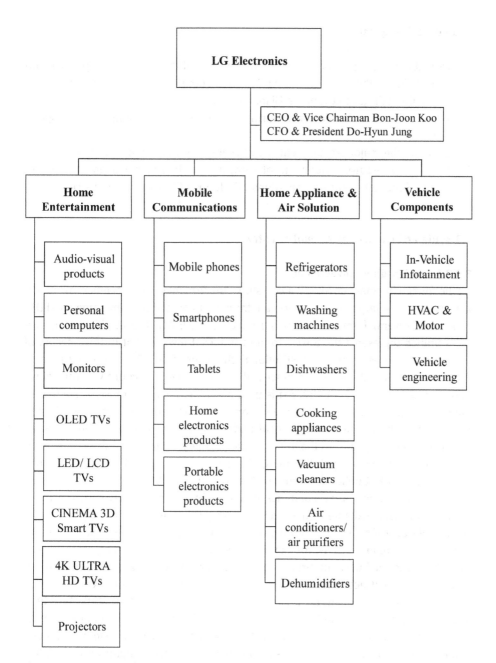

Figure 56. Organization (status 2015) of LG Electronics (LG_Electronics, 2015a, c, d)

Chapter review questions

1. Describe the resource strengths and weaknesses of the joint venture partners, LG Electronics on the one side and Philips on the other side, before they established LG.Philips LCD and LG.Philips Displays.
2. Explain the crucial milestones during the LG.Philips LCD joint venture operations.
3. Describe the major reasons that the LG.Philips Display joint venture failed.
4. What mistakes, from your point of view, did the Philips management make in terms of the joint venture operations LG.Philips LCD and LG.Philips Display?

3.3.3 Hierarchical modes of market entry

3.3.3.1 Foreign direct investment

As the foreign business develops successfully, the firm may consider enlarging its engagement in its target markets abroad through foreign direct investments (FDI), which has several forms (Rugman & Hodgetts, 2003: 41). The establishment of a sales branch represents the lowest form of financial involvement in the category of foreign direct investment. The institutional character of an FDI is mirrored by constant interaction and personal contact with actors in the host country in the course of day-to-day business activities. Aside from necessary resource transfers, such as financial, the issue of staff mobility and corresponding expatriate training arises in this context. The extent to which local and expatriate personnel are employed in the host country depends on the target market business volume, the size of the facilities, and the degree to which the foreign branches are embedded in a sales and distribution network (Duelfer & Joestingmeier, 2011: 152–153).

A firm investing abroad combines firm-specific advantages developed at home with other assets available in the foreign country (Hennart & Park, 1993: 1055). The term *wholly owned subsidiary* (WOS) describes an enterprise that owns all of the capital invested abroad, such as, for example, research and development, sales, and/or manufacturing facilities. The firm either sets up an entirely new operation (start-up or greenfield) or it acquires partial share (equity participation) or takes over completely an established firm in the target foreign country (Hitt et al., 2015: 197–198). The firm's resource availability and the firm-specific objectives determine whether the market entry will be either through firm-specific resources or external, through acquisitions. Firm-specific resources may consist of superior organizational ability, market knowledge, or technological expertise. Acquisitions come along with the advantage that the firm can combine its own resource advantages with those of an acquired foreign firm. The firm can acquire technological knowledge, foreign market knowledge, and a skilled labor force. A valuable brand reputation can be obtained, which might have taken years to build up; and, thus, immediate pressure from competition may be substantially reduced (Penrose, 1995: 127).

There are two different types of acquisitions: An international horizontal acquisition is made in order to realize the firm's growth strategy through expanding in foreign markets. A firm acquires another organization positioned in the same location of the industry chain abroad. Horizontal acquisitions provide prerequisites to increase the overall market share of the firm and usually provide potential for cost reduction because of larger operational capacities resulting in economies of scale effects. In the case of an international vertical acquisition, a firm either acquires a foreign supplier (backward integration) or a distributor (forward integration) in the target market abroad (Hitt et al., 2015: 197–198). The new external knowledge from the acquired firm needs to be integrated and combined with the existing internal knowledge. By assimilating the acquisition partner's knowledge and best practices, acquiring firms can enlarge their knowledge base, which helps a firm to adapt itself to the foreign market environment. The *absorptive capacity* of the acquiring firm influences the performance and effectiveness of its business operations in the foreign market (Zou & Ghauri, 2008: 212).

Nevertheless, in spite of all the advantages, an acquisition is by no means a universally available strategy for international market entry nor does it allow a firm automatically to escape from limited resources. More autonomy for the acquired business organization may provoke the risk of conflicts with the acquiring company's policies and activities and result in increased difficulties of working out an appropriate subsidiary-headquarters relationship. In consequence, there is a limit to the rate of expansion by acquisitions because consistent general policies have to be worked out and integrated between the acquired firm and its new headquarters. Operations, marketing, and accounting procedures need to be coordinated; and personnel policies and numerous other challenges need to be managed. For example, talented and highly skilled employees may leave the acquired firm. These challenges may offset the benefits derived from the acquisition of an established operation (Hill, 2012: 413) Therefore, financial, managerial, and organizational resource limits on the rate of expansion imply that no company can acquire every likely firm in sight in any given period of time. A firm has to choose carefully; and since mistakes may be costly and not always reparable, those target firms should be selected that seem most likely to complement or supplement existing resources. Acquisition decisions are influenced by the predilections and experience of the management and the expected profitability input of the acquired firm, which depends on the price paid compared with the expected contribution to the earnings of the acquiring firm (Penrose, 1995: 129).

An alternative to an acquisition is a greenfield investment, where the firm newly develops and builds up facilities. Necessary resources to start up a new business in the target foreign market have to be make available by the internal efforts of the firm (Brouthers, Brouthers, & Wilson, 2001: 27). In contrast to an acquisition, the establishment of a firm through a greenfield investment (foreign start-up) entails building an entirely new organization. Companies often establish start-ups by sending expatriates, who select and hire local employees and gradually build up the business.

Through its expatriates, the parent firm can train the new labor force, which makes it possible to better incorporate the company culture compared to with an acquisition, particularly in the case of a hostile takeover (Barkema & Vermeulen, 1998: 9). Brouthers and Brouthers (2000: 96) claim that firms that have developed strong capabilities, especially in the areas of technology and international operations, tend to favor greenfield investments instead of acquiring existing facilities.

Another entry mode through an FDI, called a merger, is where two firms amalgamate their resources to form a new company. International mergers typically involve firms of similar size with different national origins. Mergers are sometimes preferred to an acquisition in order to minimize the mental reservations of the national governments that may be involved, depending on the strategic importance to the local economy (Grant, 2013: 396–397). Figure 57 provides an overview of FDI alternatives.

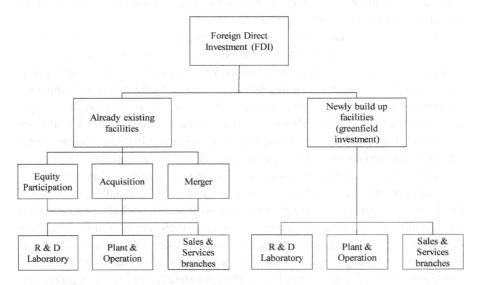

Figure 57. Decision tree of foreign direct investment (FDI) alternatives

The main advantage of market entry through the establishment of a wholly owned subsidiary is hierarchical control over decision making, which is important, for example, regarding quality assurance and the protection of intellectual property rights. Further advantages of FDI derive from the closeness to the market and its customers. This proximity improves the local product development and increases cultural sensitivity in marketing communication. A wholly owned subsidiary can be integrated (and controlled) in the firm's overall strategy when approaching diverse regional foreign markets (Deresky, 2014: 221–222). Additionally, some nations – for example, central and eastern European countries that joined the European Union in 2004 – support foreign investments with tax benefits and infrastructure developments in the case of greenfield projects. Assuming that quality and production efficiency is equal relative to the home country, the firm may enjoy additional cost savings due to low labor expenses.

Challenges that come up with the establishment of wholly owned subsidiaries arise from the increased planning and coordination complexity of foreign and local operations. The firm may underestimate culturally biased differences reflected in work ethics, quality consciousness of the employees, and loyalty toward the enterprise. Subsidiary operations have to be prepared to accept centrally determined decisions concerning production output, product portfolio, service mission, human resources, and price policy for the incoming and outgoing units (Hill, 2012: 498). The wholly owned subsidiary in a foreign country entails, among all market entry concepts, the highest uncertainty and investment risk (Hitt et al., 2015: 246).

Arora and Fosfuri (2000: 569) concluded from their research that managerial learning curve effects influence the choice of the firm's foreign operations. Prior experience in the host country increases the odds that the project will be carried out through a wholly owned operation rather than through, for example, licensing. Similarly, Barkema et al. (1996: 164) argue that firms entering foreign markets face cultural adjustment costs. The management takes advantage of the learning curve, especially when it chooses the expansion path in such a way that it can exploit previous experience in the same country or other nations with similar cultural characteristics.

3.3.3.2 The case study of Lenovo: Growth through acquisitions

In 1984, Legend Holdings was founded with USD 25,000 in China. In general, Lenovo is the result of the merger between Legend Holdings, at that time the most important technology company in the Chinese market, and the former Personal Computer Division of IBM. Consequently, the IBM product line ThinkPad was also acquired. Following the acquisition, the company changed its name to Lenovo in 2004 (Lenovo, 2013).

After acquiring the German consumer electronics company Medion in 2011 and the Brazilian CCE in 2013, Lenovo became the largest global PC company (Rhally, 2014). Moreover, the enterprise acquired the mobile phone assembler Motorola from Google for USD 2.91 billion in 2014 in order to benefit from Motorola's relationships with several telecommunication partners, its 8000 US patents, and an additional 15,000 patents related to other foreign countries (Osawa, 2014a; Rhally, 2014). In recent years, Lenovo completed additional important acquisitions and agreed to two international joint ventures (Lenovo, 2013a, 2014b):

- 2011 Joint venture of Lenovo and NEC (became largest PC company in Japan)
- 2012 Joint venture of Lenovo and EMC (took advantage of server and enterprise solutions)
- 2012 Acquisition of Stoneware (cloud-specialized software company)

Lenovo expanded its position in the global PC, tablet, and smartphone market behind well-known competitors like Apple and Samsung. In 2014, Lenovo PCs, tablets, and mobile smart phones reached around 45 percent of the world's population. Lenovo aims to become a multinational corporation instead of appearing to be a pure Chinese company. The management is made up of six different nationalities. Although the management leadership is based in China and the company is listed in Hong Kong, additional top executives are from Raleigh, Silicon Valley, Singapore, and Tokyo (Rhally, 2014).

Currently (status September 2015), Lenovo is led by chairman and CEO, Yang Yuanqing. The Chinese electronics firm employs 33.000 people in 60 countries, serving customers in more than 160 countries. Because of Lenovo's progress in global expansion, the locations of administration and sales branches, research centers, and manufacturing factories are distributed all over the world. Headquarters are located in Beijing and Raleigh, with research centers in several cities of Japan, China, and the USA. Manufacturing factories are located in the USA and China as well as in Mexico, India, and Brazil (Lenovo, 2013a, b).

Lenovo's product line consists of 'Think' branded PCs; 'Idea' branded PCs, servers, and workstations; and 'Yoga' branded tablets and smartphones. The major goal of Lenovo is to become number one in 'Smart Connected Devices', combining PCs, tablets, and smartphones (Lenovo, 2013a). As far as the company's internal structures are concerned, four business groups were created, including PC, mobile, enterprise, and ecosystem/cloud divisions as illustrated in Figure 58 (Lenovo, 2014c; Osawa, 2014b).

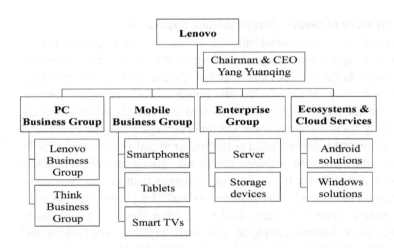

Figure 58. Organization [status 2014] of Lenovo (Lenovo, 2014c)

Lenovo sharply increased its net sales beginning in 2010 from USD 16.6 billion up to USD 38.7 billion in 2014 (compare Figure 59). Except for the year 2009 (loss of USD 0.23 billion), Lenovo continuously generated profits over the last years, although the profits were rather marginal (average around 2 percent of net sales) (Lenovo, 2014a, 2015). On one hand, Lenovo is operating in highly competitive markets (e.g., PC, tablets, etc.). On the other hand, Lenovo's own innovative capabilities – which were not gained through acquisitions such as IBM PC division, Motorola, and others – are still questionable (Lenovo, 2014d).

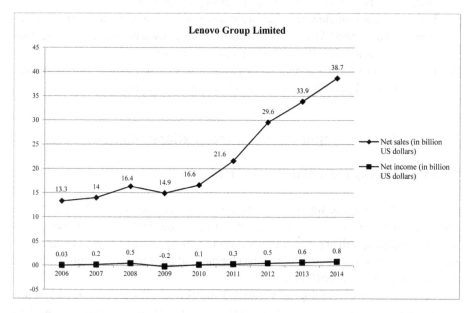

Figure 59. Net sales and net income development of Lenovo Group Limited from 2006 to 2014 (Lenovo, 2007, 2008, 2009, 2010, 2011, 2012, 2013b, 2014a, 2015)

And how good is Lenovo's global brand reputation?

In 2005, the company became positioned among leading enterprise-solution products with its ThinkPad. Then Lenovo tried to attract the customer's attention to consumer-centric products, such as the Yoga tablet (Rhally, 2014). In order to improve its brand awareness and reputation, Lenovo developed a comprehensive marketing strategy by advertising Lenovo as a global brand. Ever since Lenovo bought Motorola, there has been a lot of speculation as to what it would do with its existing mobile division. Lenovo has recently provided more details, saying it would run all of its smartphone operations under the Motorola umbrella and eventually shut down its business unit, Lenovo Mobile. Lenovo commented in a statement that 'effective immediately, Rick Osterloh, formerly president of Motorola, will be the leader of the combined global smartphone business unit'. Mobile employees will join Motorola; and, as reported earlier, Motorola will take over all design chores (Dent, 2015). In the course of its efforts to become a global player, Lenovo should take care not to lose its customers in China, a large and still very important domestic market (Rhally, 2014).

Chapter review questions

1. Applying your theoretical knowledge to the Lenovo case, describe the advantages and disadvantages of market entry through acquisitions.
2. From your point of view, describe what it would be like to be in the shoes of Lenovo's management. What resource strengths and weaknesses did Lenovo have in the past, and what should be done in the future?
3. Reflecting on Lenovo's global strategy ambitions, describe and discuss the opportunities and potential risks for the firm's management.

3.4 Decision Determinants of an International Market Entry

3.4.1 Entry rapidity and proximity to the market

The strategic concept of international market entry requires a clear formulation of the firm's objectives in the target foreign market. Objectives are a statement as to what the company will achieve within a certain period of time in terms of market position, return on investment, and the development of key business sectors in the target countries (Hibbert, 1997: 137).

An innovator's (technologically leading) strategy linked with skim pricing offers the opportunity to sell the products at a relatively high price level to the innovation-seeking customers in the target market abroad. Because of the product and/or service novelty, competitors are rather few (first-mover advantages of the innovator). Disadvantages derive from delayed market penetration and the risk that competitors appear in the course of time and take advantage of higher sales volumes. If fast market penetration is desired, the firm decides on a pricing strategy that attempts to accelerate market penetration and offers the foreign firm the opportunity to expand the target market share and make use of experience curve effects in order to further lower the price and finally dominate the industry (Wheelen & Hunger, 2010: 241). Potential risks arise from the defensive strategies of local firms, which may range from severe price competition to lobbying their local governments for support.

Market entry timing targets significantly influence the selection of the firm's entry strategies. Consequently, the length of time it takes to implement an international market activity represents an important decision-making criterion. On the one hand, a firm may be trying to achieve foreign market entry as rapidly as possible. For example, a firm might have developed a new product in a market where the technology is changing rapidly, such as in high-technology industries or where the product development can readily be copied by competitors, so as rapid an exploitation as possible is required. In such cases, export or licensing activities are more desirable than, for example, greenfield manufacturing investments, which are likely to be inappropriate because of the complexity of the project abroad and the corresponding time delay. On the other hand, if exporting is impeded through non-tariff barriers by the foreign government, contract manufacturing or licensing arrangements may be the fastest means of market entry. In operations through which the manufacturing function is internationalized and relocated to the foreign market, such as contract manufacturing and wholly owned foreign production, the international business in the foreign target market is not affected negatively because the operations take place inside those barriers. The firm secures a closer proximity to the target market abroad, which provides first-hand information to the firm (Luostarinen & Welch, 1997: 240). The less standardized the product and service and the more different the customer expectations in terms of quality, design, and purchasing attitudes, the more desirable it is for the firm to be as close as possible to the market.

3.4.2 Degree of hierarchical control and financial risk

The choice of entry modes comprises the essential decision of locating the firm's value-added activities and the level of operational control. Manufacturing resources might be either located domestically and are completely controlled by the firm or shifted partially or completely abroad (Hollensen et al., 2011: 8). The degree of hierarchical control of operations and the associated financial risk differ depending on the selected entry mode (Zhao, Luo, & Suh, 2004: 540). The degree of control and financial risk can be divided into four categories.

First, indirect and direct exports are market entry modes providing very low control mechanisms. Exports allow the producer to control its value-added functions at home and the product flow from the firm's warehouse facilities to the carrier, who delivers the cargo to the importer. Consequently, the exporter has no control over the conditions under which the product or service is marketed abroad (Hollensen et al., 2011: 8–9). The management involvement is concentrated in the exporter's home country (Meissner, 1995: 51). As a result, export implies a minimal resource commitment abroad, which comes along with low financial risks. A letter of credit (LC) serves as a common instrument for securing the importer's payment. Credit insurance protects the exporter from payment defaults by the importer in the context of an open account payment term. The premium paid by the exporter to the insurer depends on the importing firm's credit worthiness and the economic conditions of the importer's country of residence.

Second, contractual agreements, such as OEM, licensing, and franchising, are market entry modes indicating rather low control mechanisms. The major reason is that the contract partner in the target foreign country takes over the major part of the value-added activities, which entails the risk that the contractor's reputation can be easily harmed if quality, safety, labor, or hygiene standards are not met appropriately by the contract partner abroad. The financial risk for the OEM, licensor and franchisor is also relatively low because they do not invest in their own property for manufacturing and operations abroad.

Third, intermediate control modes include mainly strategic alliances and IJVs, where the partners agree to share resources such as knowledge and equity (in the case of an IJV) with the aim of supplementing each other's needs (Hollensen et al., 2011: 8). Cooperative modes of market entry, such as IJVs, are categorized as hybrid forms because cross-border activities, such as management involvement, financial flow, and the corresponding investment risk, are balanced between the partners, depending on equity, majority, or minority IJV capital-share structures (Meissner, 1995: 51).

Fourth, high-control modes comprise FDIs in the form of wholly owned subsidiaries (WOS), which involves full control over operations in the foreign market (Hollensen et al., 2011: 8–9). The WOS (hierarchical market entry mode) provide the most control but, in parallel, also require a substantial commitment of resources abroad with a corresponding increase of financial risk (Sanchez-Peinado, Pla-Barber, & Hébert, 2007: 84). Examples of WOS are research and development laboratories, sales and distributions branches, and manufacturing plants in the target foreign country.

FDIs, such as greenfield investment in the target foreign market, route the management efforts and the flow of financial capital from the home country to the foreign country. The investment volume becomes concentrated in the foreign market, and the corresponding risk increases due to the regional distance and environmental circumstances that are naturally unfamiliar compared to the home market surroundings. The foreign market environment has a direct impact on a firm's entry mode strategy in terms of the desired control and the perceived financial risk. Political uncertainties are not conducive to the establishment of WOS. Uncertainties in a country regarding the protection of intellectual property rights, for example, reduce the attractiveness of license agreements (Delios & Beamish, 1999: 917).

3.4.3 A two-step decision process approach towards an international market entry

The decision about how foreign markets should be entered naturally depends on the firm's resource availability. Additionally, in light of globalized value-added activities and trade patterns, the management's preference concerning target foreign markets and relevant market entry modes is often influenced by external stakeholders. For example, if an important customer of the firm establishes a factory in a foreign country, it may lead the supplying firm to 'follow the customer' in order to avoid another competitor's entrance into the business relationship.

Foreign governments may insist for several reasons, such as control or access to modern technologies, on the establishment of an 'equal joint venture' with a local firm. In many Asian countries usually due to a lack of personal network relationships with relevant business stakeholders, it is difficult to initiate local business operations as a foreign firm. In these cases, it is advisable to search for a local partner. Once a partner is found and, for example, an international joint venture is agreed upon, the firm is confronted with the challenge of sharing technological and managerial knowledge. As time goes by, through assimilation and learning, the local partner may become a serious competitor – as many multinationals have experienced to their regret. As a consequence of the discussion above, a firm that seeks international business should carefully evaluate beforehand the possible outcomes of its selected market entry mode, which is a very complex management task. In order to facilitate the challenging decision-making process for an international market entry, a two-step approach is introduced in the following section.

3.4.3.1 Step one – setting strategic priorities

As a first step, the management sets its *strategic priorities* in terms of the (1) *degree of hierarchical control,* (2) *market entry timing,* (3) *proximity to the market,* and (4) *financial risk.*

(1) *Degree of hierarchical control of firm operations*

The management should evaluate whether rather tight or loose control mechanisms concerning its operations in the target foreign country are required. The decisional process should consider elementary issues from the management's perspective such as the following.
- Necessity to protect advanced technological or managerial knowledge
  - → *If yes, tight control mechanisms, such as a WOS, are recommended, while cooperative (hybrid) forms, such as IJVs, are less appropriate.*
- Strategic market importance in terms of volume and growth rates
  - → *The more important these considerations are, the more desirable it is to be in the market through a WOS instead of serving the market from a distance (e.g., exports).*
- Degree of the firm's international market experience
  - → *The less experienced the management in international business, the higher the risk that, for example, an IJV partner may take advantage of the firm (opportunistic behavior).*
- Foreign government regulation
  - → *The foreign government may favor (e.g., an FDI) or restrict (e.g., export-related non-tariff barriers) a certain market entry mode. Environmental analysis of the target foreign country is of vital importance to make the most favorable decision.*
- The firm's resources (e.g., financial, human)
  - → *The choice of a market entry strategy naturally depends on the firm's resource assets. Building up and running a wholly owned sales and distribution network in the target foreign market comes along with the advantage of direct hierarchical control of the firm's operations, which, however, requires considerable resource cushions.*

(2) *Market entry timing*

The management needs to decide whether a fast or delayed foreign market entry is favorable to the firm. The decisional process on timing of the market entry should consider issues such as these.
- The need to follow an important customer or competitor abroad
  - → *The decision depends on the firm's integration in industry networks. The more important a bilateral relationship—for example, to a customer— the more desirable for the firm to follow the customer abroad.*
- The threat of fast technological product substitution

→ *The shorter the product and technology life cycles, the more advisable it is for the firm to enter various foreign countries simultaneously instead of an incremental (country by country) market entry, which is time consuming.*

– First mover (technological leader) or latecomer advantages
→ *Fast entry in the global markets is desirable for firms offering technologically advanced products. It helps to develop a technological leadership positioning. Technological latecomers (for example, targeting a cost leadership positioning) may take advantage of a delayed market entry, using the time to learn from the mistakes of the first movers and make things better.*

– Intensity of industry competition
→ *Competitive global markets may require fast market entry activities in order not to leave foreign market shares to the firm's competitors.*

– Investment volume
→ *Large investments—for example, in product developments or operations—naturally demand higher sales volumes, which can be realized through global market entries that help reduce the return-on-investment time framework.*

– Monitoring
→ *The management needs to evaluate the risk of losing control due to hasty entry activity or poor partner selection against the potential advantages and drawbacks related to a delayed market entry.*

(3) **Proximity to the market**

Concerning the firm's market proximity, the management should evaluate whether its foreign engagements should be located rather close or distant to its customers abroad. The decision is influenced by the following.

– Product and service
→ *Standardized products and services favor contractual market entry modes, such as exports. Different customer expectations in the target foreign market in terms of product features, design, and service often require a local presence of the firm (e.g., its own distribution and sales network). Particularly in markets where customers' behavior and attitudes are difficult to evaluate from a distance, the firm may prefer FDI.*

– Strategic importance of the foreign target market
→ *Attractive forecasts for a foreign market, identified by market volumes and promising growth rates, recommend a local presence instead of serving the market from a distance.*

– Logistics
→ *Flexible order management, transportation lead times, and logistics costs influence the firm's market entry. For example, heavy and bulky products may favor local assembly activities in the target foreign market.*

- Reputation
  - → *A firm may want to build up a local brand in the target foreign market, which helps to attract customers. Particularly in markets where customers favor domestic companies, the management may decide to launch its own operations in order to develop a local image.*
- Foreign government
  - → *Export-related trade barriers are avoided if, instead, the management considers local assembly activities (e. g., OEM or joint venture partners). The management may also consider whether there are FDI incentives granted in the target local market.*

(4) **Financial risk**

Concerning the financial risk, the firm's decisional process should consider the following facets.

- Financial cash and debt-to-equity ratio
  - → *Market entry through FDI is naturally more costly than contractual market entry modes (e. g., licensing). Firms with low debt-to-equity ratios and available financial cushions can better manage FDI -related uncertainties, which usually happen in the course of time. Smaller firms and firms with less financial potential should favor market entry strategies through contracting or cooperation.*
- Product and industry margins
  - → *In industries indicating rather low margins, the firm's management may favor contractual forms, such as franchising, licensing or OEM, because fixed costs are lower than with FDIs.*
- Time horizon of expected return on investment
  - → *The longer the time period needed for the investment to be paid back, the higher the firm's uncertainty and corresponding financial risk. Cooperative forms of market entry, such as joint ventures, may serve as an alternative to reduce the financial burden of the firm.*
- Expected reactions of local competitors
  - → *Local competitors may reduce the average prices in their home market hoping to create an entry barrier for foreign firms. Cooperative forms of market entry, such as a strategic alliance with a local partner, help to gain better access to information about local competitors' activities in the target foreign market.*

After reviewing the discussion above, the next step for the management is to make the decision about which of the *market entry strategy* alternatives should be selected.

3.4.3.2 Step two – selection of the appropriate market entry mode

Each foreign market entry mode has different implications for a firm's degree of hierarchical control, the financial resources the management has to commit, its market proximity, and the market entry timing framework (compare Figure 60).

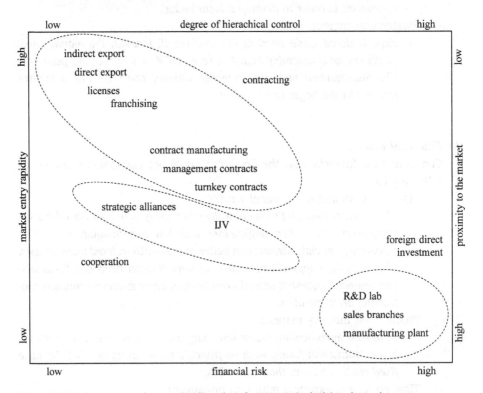

Figure 60. Market entry mode grouping based on four strategic decision determinants

It is of vital importance that the firm's management be aware of the opportunities and challenges of business expansion into a foreign country. Advantages and drawbacks result from the selection of the market entry mode, taking into account the firm's internal resources and external environmental conditions. The firm's management chooses its market entry mode, which depends on the strategic priorities outlined in phase one (setting strategic priorities), and are categorized as (1) contracting modes (market mechanisms), (2) cooperative modes (hybrid forms), and (3) FDI (hierarchical organization).

3.4.3.2.1 Contracting modes (market mechanisms)

Generally, a market transaction through contracting (for example, indirect exports via a commissioner) allows a fast foreign market entry but does not provide the management with sufficient hierarchical control mechanisms. From a historical perspective, exports belong to the most common entry mode, practiced by merchants and later by manufacturing firms. Firms with less international business experience or limited resources may choose contracting forms such as exports because the financial risk tends to be relatively lower than, for example, in the case of FDI. Figure 61 summarizes the relevant contracting forms for an international market entry and the corresponding suitable business categories.

Contractual market entry mode	Business category
Indirect exports	goods and services
Direct exports	goods and services
Licensing	services (technologically advanced knowledge)
Franchising	services (implementation of an entire business concept)
OEM	goods and services
Management contract	services (delivering administrative, technological, and managerial knowledge)
Turnkey contract	goods and services, such as large investment projects that include resource tangibles (e. g., plants) and intangibles (e. g., engineering and management knowhow)

Figure 61. Relevant contracting forms of international market entry and corresponding product categories

Within the group of contracting modes, indirect exports tend to be realized faster than, as an example, OEM because of the necessity of increased local involvement for OEM (e. g., search for suitable firm abroad, quality assurance activities). The main disadvantages derive from the distance to the foreign markets and their customers. Figure 62 summarizes relevant strategic decision determinants in terms of market entry rapidity, the degree of hierarchical control, financial risk, and proximity to the market from the exporter's point of view. The illustration also provides checkpoints that indicate when an export strategy is advisable and what potential strategic risks – from the exporter's perspective – are involved.

Market entry through contractual forms, such as license and franchising agreements, can be also realized within a relatively short period of time compared to FDI. Worldwide markets can be penetrated efficiently through the transfer of knowledge (license) or an entire business concept (franchising) to local contract partners. Both methods are suitable for firms with limited resources (e. g., to build up manufacturing or service network facilities) because the major part of investments in operations is done by the contracted firm (e. g., franchisee), which also takes on the entrepreneurial risk of running the business in the foreign markets. Licensing is often desirable in industries driven by rapidly changing technologies. The major disadvantage of licensing and franchising derives from limited hierarchical control of the contracted firm, which involves the potential risks of harming the business concept or damaging the reputation of the licensor or franchisor. Moreover, the contracted partner abroad may develop its own knowledge and expertise through learning and collect-

Market entry strategy	Entry rapidity	Hierarchical control	Financial risk	Proximity to the market	Strategy recommended if	Potential strategic risks
Indirect export	high	low	low	very low	no experience of the management in foreign trade	dependency on ntermediator (commissioner)
					rather standardized products with rudimentary after-sales services	commission costs often divided loyalties of the commissioner
					promising demand abroad	trade barriers
					saturated home markets	transportation risk and costs (e.g., bulky products)
Direct export	high	low	low	low	less experience in foreign trade	negotiation skills and language barriers
					rather standardized products with rudimentary after-sales services sold	trade barriers unfamiliar market environment
					promising demand abroad	transportation risk and costs (e.g.,
					saturated home markets	bulky products)

Figure 62. Overview of the strategic decision determinants and potential risks related to the market entry modes indirect and direct exports

ing experiences during the course of the contractual relationship. Efficient absorptive capabilities of the contract partner may result in the development of a new competitor.

Figure 63 summarizes relevant strategic decision determinants in terms of market entry rapidity, the degree of hierarchical control, financial risk, and proximity to the market from the licensor's and franchisor's point of view. The illustration also provides checkpoints that indicate when a licensing and franchising strategy is desirable and what potential strategic risks – from the licensor's and franchisor's perspective – is involved.

The contractual market entry strategy of original equipment manufacturing (OEM) is particularly applied by larger firms and multinational enterprises (MNEs) aiming to increase their global capacities, which usually comes along with the attempt to reduce production costs. Major drawbacks of OEM come from the limited hierarchical control of the contracted partner firm abroad, which produces the product in its own facilities under the name of the OEM brand. Through managerial

Market entry strategy	Entry rapidity	Hierarchical control	Financial risk	Proximity to the market	Strategy recommended if	Potential strategic risks
Licensing	high	low	low	low	lack of financial or organizational resources	licensee may damage reputation
					technologically fast developing industries	risk of technology copy by licensee
					shortened product life cycles	royalty fees lower than value of technology transfer
					fast market entry and penetration desired	limited experience curve and economies of scale effects
					FDI tends to be too risky	licensee may become competitor
					competing industry standards	
Franchising	high	low	low	low	fast market entry and penetration desired	franchisee may harm reputation
					realization of economies of scale	partner's disagreement over objectives and franchise fees
					limited financial resources	foreign partner selection
					sales of proven business concept	entrepreneurial capability of the franchisee

Figure 63. Overview of the strategic decision determinants and potential risks related to the market entry modes licensing and franchising

learning and technological assimilation from the OEM, there is a risk that a new competitor is developed abroad. Figure 64 summarizes relevant strategic decision determinants in terms of market entry rapidity, the degree of hierarchical control, financial risk, and the market proximity from OEM's point of view. The illustration also provides checkpoints that indicate when an OEM strategy is advisable and what potential strategic risks – from the OEM's perspective – are involved.

Management contracts mainly target the delivery of services to a business partner located in the target foreign country. Due to the fact that consulting, training, and education are naturally connected with the language capabilities, communication skills, behaviors, and attitudes of the people involved, a management contract busi-

Market entry strategy	Entry rapidity	Hierarchical control	Financial risk	Proximity to the market	Strategy recommended if	Potential strategic risks
OEM	medium	low-medium	low	medium	expansion of capacities necessary limited financial resources seeking to reduce operational costs more flexible order management	loss of manufacturing involvement and quality control reputation damage (e.g., quality, working conditions) knowledge transfer may foster a new competitor

Figure 64. Overview of the strategic decision determinants and potential risks related to the market entry mode original equipment manufacturing (OEM)

ness can be challenging. The more diversified the socio-cultural environment in the target foreign country relative to the home market, the more efforts are necessary to make sure that activities are done as planned and processes are implemented appropriately and efficiently.

Turnkey contracts serve as a suitable entry mode for firms with a specific technology, project management, and engineering expertise. On the one hand, turnkey contracts provide an opportunity to enter rather fragile political-legal markets that simultaneously contain a risky momentum. On the other hand, margins can be above average because competition in these emerging target markets is often marginal. The right partner selection – which, in many larger projects, is the government – is of vital importance and requires appropriate international business experience for the management. The direct involvement abroad (e. g., construction and start-up of a plant, education of local staff) during the course of incrementally transferring the operations to locals usually requires considerable firm resources to be reserved over a longer period time. Figure 65 summarizes relevant strategic decision determinants in terms of market entry rapidity, the degree of hierarchical control, financial risk, and proximity to the market from the perspective of the firm providing the management and turnkey contract. The illustration also provides checkpoints that indicate when a management contract and a turnkey contract strategy is desirable and what potential strategic risks are involved.

3.4.3.2.2 Cooperation (hybrid forms of foreign market entry)
Cooperative market entry modes – realized, for example, in an international equity joint venture – share the financial risk and earnings as well as the hierarchical control of operations between the cooperating partners. Firms sometimes are also confronted with foreign government regulations that require the establishment of a joint

Market entry strategy	Entry rapidity	Hierarchical control	Financial risk	Proximity to the market	Strategy recommended if	Potential strategic risks
Management contracts	medium	medium	medium	medium	specified managerial and/or technological expertise sales of services, such as training and consultation project expertise available	foster potential competitor lack of educated staff in the target country disputes about fees organizational misfit
Turnkey contracts	medium-low	medium	medium-high	medium-high	project expertise required specific engineering and complex technological process knowledge available business opportunity in emerging or less developed countries	infrastructure challenges political-legal and economically rather fragile countries lack of qualified personnel in the target country organizational misfit project complexity

Figure 65. Overview of the strategic decision determinants and potential risks related to the market entry modes management contracts and turnkey contracts

venture with a local firm in the target foreign country. Both international joint ventures and international strategic alliances with a local organization usually increase the proximity to the market due to the partner's local presence. However, considerable time should be reserved for the right partner selection and organization of the bundled activities. As many firms experienced to their regret, synergy effects tend to be overestimated in the course of running the bilateral cooperation. The realization of cooperative market entry activities tends to be more time consuming than in the case of license agreements, but entry usually is realized faster than in cases of establishing wholly owned operations.

Figure 66 summarizes relevant strategic decision determinants in terms of market entry rapidity, the degree of hierarchical control, financial risk, and proximity to the market from the perspective of the management seeking to establish an international strategic alliance or an international joint venture. The illustration also provides checkpoints that indicate when a cooperative strategy is advisable and what potential strategic risks are involved.

Market entry strategy	Entry rapidity	Hierarchical control	Financial risk	Proximity to the market	Strategy recommended if	Potential strategic risks
International Strategic alliance	medium	low-medium	low-medium	medium	exchange of information concerning target client groups, research, and development set of technological industry standards mutual strengthening of competitive positioning through complementary partner resources (e.g., distribution channels)	partner selection knowledge transfer opportunistic behavior of the partner reputation damage caused by the partner (e.g., working conditions) synergy effects below expectation partner is (often) also competitor
International joint venture	medium	medium	medium	medium	bundle of mutual strategic resources combined global market entry sharing of risks (and earnings) joint activities in research and development, manufacturing, marketing market penetration of innovative products	partner selection risk of opportunistic behavior of the partner knowledge transfer unclear ownership structures and decision power minor synergy effects partner is (often) also competitor

Figure 66. Overview of the strategic decision determinants and potential risks related to the market entry modes international strategic alliance and international joint venture

3.4.3.2.3 Wholly owned subsidiary (hierarchical forms of foreign market entry)

The foundation of a wholly owned subsidiary through FDI represents one of the most challenging market entry modes. Time is needed for the evaluation and selection of a suitable location (e. g., infrastructure, availability and qualification of staff, operational costs, etc.). Therefore, FDI is rather recommended for internationally experienced firms. The proximity to the market provides direct communication channels to the local customers, which is an important advantage. The integration into the firm's organization provides direct hierarchical control mechanisms and avoids loss of often strategically valuable knowledge to another firm. Major forms of FDI – whether realized through greenfield investment, equity participation, merger or acquisitions – are either the establishment of a sales branch and distribution network and/or research and development labs and/or wholly owned manufacturing subsidiaries. Figure 67 summarizes relevant strategic decision determinants in terms of market entry rapidity, the degree of hierarchical control, financial risk, and market proximity from the investor's point of view. The illustration also provides checkpoints that indicate when a FDI strategy is advisable and what potential strategic risks – from the investor's perspective – are involved.

Resource-rich firms may take advantage of market proximity through the establishment of a sales and distribution network, which is of particular value for a service-oriented pre- and after sales where prompt reactions to the customers' requirements are required. Heavy and bulky products, the regional availability of raw materials, trade barriers, culturally diverse customer behaviors, or long transportation lead times encourage direct investment in a foreign target market instead of distant-to-the-market business forms, such as exports. However, in some countries foreign acquisitions are banned in some sectors or are made difficult by legal restrictions on voting rights or a firm's cross-holdings – as is the case in Japan (Hennart & Reddy, 1997: 3).

On the other hand, Japanese firms, when they go abroad, tend to opt for high-control modes when the risk of doing business in the host country is perceived as high or the quality consciousness of the partner is perceived as less strict. Instead of attempting to reduce the resource commitment by using a lower control mode (e. g., OEM or franchising), which firms in the western hemisphere often opt for (e. g., Philips, Apple, DELL), Japanese firms favor long-term orientated engagements that secure hierarchical control of their operations (Taylor, Zou, & Osland, 2000: 146, 158 – 159).

In various cases, we can witness in high-technology industries that Chinese firms also follow the market entry pattern indicating high control mechanisms as practiced by Japanese and Korean firms. Therefore, in the next chapter, the case study of TCL (China) is introduced with the aim of figuring out how the Chinese firm organized, particularly in terms of their control mechanisms, when entering Western markets.

Market entry strategy	Entry rapidity	Hierarchical control	Financial risk	Proximity to the market	Strategy recommended if	Potential strategic risks
FDI	low	high	high	high	advanced experience in international business	unfamiliar environment and work ethics increase uncertainty
					attractive target markets (volume, growth rates)	often different legal systems
					follow the competitor and/or customer	investment volume
						language barriers
					bulky products, highly specialized products and services	socio-cultural challenges
						response of local firms
					avoid trade barriers	
					local cost advantage	protection of property
					subsidies or tax incentives	availability of supplier and service provider (e. g., logistics)
					building up a local brand reputation	
					availability of resources	relation to local authorities
						organizational complexity

Figure 67. Overview of the strategic decision determinants and potential risks related to the FDI market entry mode

Chapter review questions

1. What motivates a firm to internationalize?
2. Describe contractual market entry modes.
3. Explain the mutual commitment expectations of the relevant stakeholders in the case of direct exports.
4. Explain the characteristics of an international market entry through franchising, and mention the relevant advantages and risks from the franchisor's perspective.
5. Concerning a firm's market entry strategy decisional process, what issues should be evaluated by the management related to the degree of hierarchical control, market entry timing, the proximity to the market, and the financial risk?

6. How would you categorize 'cooperative strategies'?
7. What are the similarities and main differences between an international strategic alliance and an international joint venture?
8. Provide arguments that explain why firms agree to establish an IJV.
9. What are the main reasons for IJV failures, and how can the IJV failure risk be reduced, from your point of view?
10. Explain the characteristics of international market entry through original equipment manufacturing (OEM). Provide arguments that explain why a firm should favor an OEM strategy and what potentials risks are involved.
11. What alternatives does the management have concerning the realization of its FDI strategy?
12. What are the potential opportunities and drawbacks of FDI?

3.5 Case Study: Market Entry Strategies of TCL (China)

3.5.1 About the company

Over the past two decades, China's internationally embedded manufacturing industry has experienced a major transition (Chen, 2004: 216). The origins of this tremendous development occurred in the mid-1970s, when the Chinese government began to
realize that it might be advantageous for the national economy if foreign enterprises
were attracted to investment in the domestic markets. As a result of their engagement, these foreign firms would transfer technology and know-how to Chinese enterprises. In December 1978, the Chinese government initiated an opening of the local
economy to foreign investors through a so-called open-door policy. Just six months
later, in July 1979, the enactment of the 'Law of the People's Republic of China on
Joint Ventures Using Chinese and Foreign Investment' provided a legal status for foreign direct investments in China (Alon, 2003: 101).

Around two decades later, the Chinese government changed its policy. Instead of
attracting foreign investors to China, the political decision makers in Peking began to
encourage local firms to enter foreign markets around the globe. In October 2000, the
Chinese government announced its 'go global' strategy as a part of its long-term business growth efforts, giving encouragement and support to key firms to strengthen
their competitive positions outside their home market. As a result of the actions of
the government, many Chinese companies have increasingly searched for investment
opportunities outside their neighbor territories. They have focused on well-developed
countries such as Europe because of the stable political-legal environment, infrastructure, and technology. This investment behavior is exemplified by TCL, China's
largest television set manufacturer. The internationalization efforts of Chinese
firms such as TCL are based on a political vision declared by the Chinese government. TCL developed its international market entry strategies primarily by establishing majority-owned joint ventures with incumbent firms located in advanced European countries (ChinaBusiness, 2005; Deng, 2006: 76).

On the one hand, Chinese firms – for example, relative to their Japanese competitors – are rather latecomers in the electronics industry (Deng, 2006: 74; Mathews,
2002: 24). On the other hand, through market entries via various forms such as inter-

national joint ventures with Western firms, they attempt to 'balance' their previous competitive disadvantages with regards to technology, marketing, and brand reputation and speed worldwide market penetration. Chinese enterprises are active in establishing networks of distributors and research and development centers as well as product design units in various countries. For the strategic purpose of control of the desired resources, they tend to become either fully owned or the majority shareholder in the course of their venture operations (Deng, 2006: 72, 74).

How did TCL develop its business?

Established in 1981 and headquartered in Huizhou of Guangdong Province, TCL has become one of the largest Chinese electronics manufacturers within the last decades (TCL, 2006c, d). This development goes back to 1990, when TCL entered the television set industry through the acquisition of a relatively small Hong Kong-based firm. Following this acquisition, television sets became the core product of the group. TCL's business operations and product model portfolio have been expanded, but sales were focused geographically on China.

Today, TCL is organized into four strategic business units called multimedia, communication, home appliances, and lighting. Multimedia (e.g., television sets) and communication (e.g., smartphones and broadband) are the most important business units within the group. The lighting division, founded in 2000, has increased its importance within TCL group in recent years and specializes in lighting product development, production, and sales. Sales activities are further divided into traditional lighting and LED lighting, which covers engineering lighting, home furnishing lighting, road lighting, landscape lighting, and special lighting (TCL Lighting Electric Co., 2014). The complete organization of TCL (status 2014) is illustrated in Figure 68 (Alcatel_One_Touch, 2014; TCL, 2014a, b, c; Tonly_Electronics_Holdings_Limited, 2013).

TCL's 'going abroad' strategy was declared by its chairman, Li Dongsheng, who announced his vision for the Chinese firm in 2003.

> In the next three to five years, we want to see TCL's television and telecom business become one of the top five manufacturers globally. Our main challenge is we must improve our research and development (R&D) level. Most Chinese firms lack intellectual property rights. We want to focus on business in international markets. We must upgrade our technology and R&D. This is a big challenge for all Chinese companies. I believe our competitive advantage over international companies is in two areas: one is the efficiency of our supply chain; the second is that, in terms of the Chinese market, we are particularly good at knowing what the customer needs (Businessweek_Beijing, 2003).

Regarding TCL's internationalization strategy and market entry efforts for the future, Li Dongsheng further declared,

> We have three strategies overseas. First, we fully use our advantage in manufacturing when working with our partners. Our second strategy we have followed in Southeast Asia, India, Russia, and the Middle East. In these regions, we have sold our branded product (TCL and Rowa). Our third strategy is adapted to the European and US markets, the largest overseas markets.

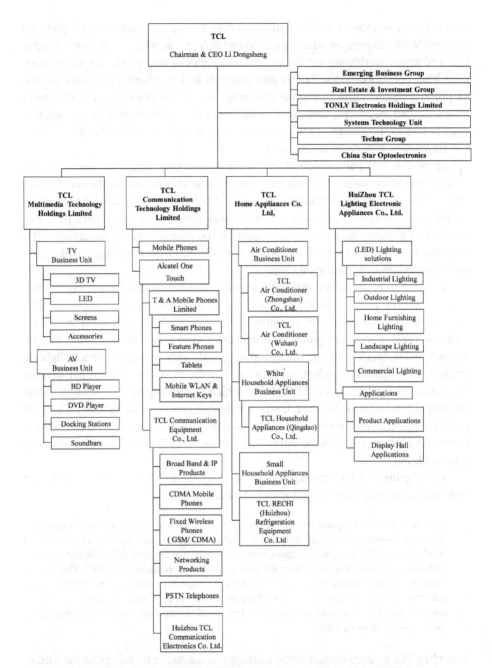

Figure 68. TCL Organization [status 2014]. Developed based on various firm related sources (Alcatel_One_Touch, 2014; TCL, 2014a, b, c; Tonly_Electronics_Holdings_Limited, 2013)

These markets are more mature and are already dominated by other brands. To develop our brands (TCL and Rowa) there involves higher investment and more risk. That's why we have acquired companies. This has lowered our cost, and the risk is lower. Whether the third model will be successful, we do not know yet. But we have seen other companies from Taiwan and South Korea that have not been very successful. Two examples are Acer and LG, both of which lost a lot of money going overseas. There are really successful examples like Samsung, but most companies are not like them. TCL's strategy is that we want to find strategic partners. We do not want to work alone and have to bear all the risk. That's because in these mature countries, the growth is relatively stable; and entry barriers are higher. Being the No. 1 player in TVs is very important in reaching our goal of being a global company (Businessweek_Beijing, 2003).

The international expansion started in September 2002, when TCL China purchased the traditional German firm that went bankrupt, Schneider Electronics GmbH, at a price of Euro 8.2 million. At the time, besides audio and conventional television set production, Schneider had a particular technological expertise in the laser technology used for television sets. Unfortunately, the laser technology standard later failed in the markets. Commenting on the acquisition, Mr. Tomson Li, at that time chairman of TCL International said,

> The acquisition of assets from Schneider marks an important step in TCL International's overseas expansion. It will accelerate our access to the European market. The Tuerkheim plant will be our first production base in Europe for televisions and other home entertainment products targeting the European market. While various brand names under Schneider are well established, we will initially focus on the SCHNEIDER and DUAL brands, particularly for the high-end market, as we see enormous market potential in the European consumer electronics market. We have full confidence in our overseas business in the years ahead (TCL, 2002).

Through the purchase, in addition to obtaining a well-established but only regionally (mainly in Germany) known brand such as Schneider and production facilities in Bavaria, TCL gained access to management knowledge concerning the European markets. Dr. Michael Jaffe, the insolvency administrator of Schneider, said,

> The acquisition marked an important step for both TCL and us. TCL has not only acquired the production facilities, but also the trademarks and distribution network as well as the technical know-how of the former employees of Schneider. This will form a solid base for TCL's entry into the European market. As for us, in addition to the renewed employment for some former staff of Schneider, new job opportunities will be created along with TCL's business expansion (Schneider, 2003; TCL, 2002).

The bright future for Schneider, as forecast after its acquisition, did not turn out to be true. Of course, TCL used the newly acquired trademark rights of Schneider as well as Dual and learned, through the former Schneider management, about local market conditions. However, in November 2004, Schneider announced the shutdown of the factory in Tuerkheim, Germany, and further restructuring activities. The offices of Schneider moved to Mindelheim, where distribution, marketing, and service activities were continued. Finally, all operations at Mindelheim were stopped; and the location shut down in December 2005, just two years after TCL became the owner. Manufacturing has continued at TCL's facilities in Asia, and the products are sold under the Schneider brand in Europe (Schneider, 2005a, b).

3.5.2 TCL-Thomson Electronics (TTE) international joint venture

The acquisition of Schneider in 2002 was not the first and only market entry activity of TCL China in Europe. The Schneider brand was well known in Germany but comparatively unknown in other European countries. Additionally, Schneider's manufacturing and research capacities were limited relative to the size and the strategic plans of TCL for its European market entry.

The traditional French company, Thomson, along with Philips one of the leading European brands in the 1990s and owner of several patents plus exclusive brands, also aroused the interest of the Chinese firm. On the one hand, TCL had production cost advantages due to reasonable labor costs and relatively less social security standards in China compared to France. On the other hand, TCL's weaknesses were its almost unknown brand name outside Asia, limited access to the European market, and the lack of patents and advanced technological know-how. In 2003, Thomson faced increasing difficulties regarding competitive manufacturing of television sets in comparison to firms from Turkey (e. g., Vestel, Beko) and the Far East, which resulted in the television set operations realizing a loss. Moreover, Thomson did not pay enough attention to the development of flat panel technologies, which enjoyed a significant market breakthrough in 2004 and provoked an even higher price competition in Europe in conventional television set sales. Finally, TCL China and Thomson, France, seemed to be ideal joint venture partners with significant mutual synergy potentials (Thomson, 2003, 2004).

In June 2004, TCL and Thomson agreed to combine their activities in order to establish a major player in the television set business with an annual production capacity of approximately 21 million units. The international joint venture of TCL-Thomson Electronics (TTE) started its operations in July 2004 (TCL, 2004b). TTE represented the largest agreement ever made until that time in which a Chinese company had taken control of a Western counterpart in an international joint venture (Deng, 2006: 76). The newly created firm, TTE, enabled TCL to access Thomson's distribution channels in the US and Europe; research and development laboratories (Singapore, Mexico, Germany, and France); and the main manufacturing capacities in France, Poland, Mexico, China, and Thailand. From the Chinese point of view, the brands of 'RCA' (American market) and 'Thomson' (European market) were of particular interest for TCL's marketing and sales in order to compensate for its own almost unknown brand initials 'TCL' in its overseas markets. The development of the Chinese brand 'TCL' would have been difficult and time consuming and consequently costly due to its unfamiliar initials in the minds of European and North American customers. As a TCL senior manager described the venture benefit for the Chinese,

> Leveraging the strengths of Thomson, we have a firm foothold in the R&D of main stream TV products and strong capabilities in high-end digital offerings. We deploy a multi-brand product

strategy, spearheaded by established household brands, including TCL, Thomson, and RCA, which are immediately recognizable to consumers worldwide (Deng, 2006).

At the beginning of the negotiations in 2003, before the final joint venture contract was signed, it was announced that TCL and Thomson would each invest 33 percent (for a total of 66 percent), and the remaining 34 percent would be launched at the Hong Kong stock exchange (Glowik, 2004b). This smart approach, initiated by the Chinese, was psychologically, with respect to French public opinion, well conceived. It did not appear to be a takeover by the Chinese firm but rather a partnership. The promotion of a joint venture transaction was easier to launch than, for example, an acquisition; and it avoided unfriendly reactions in the French public as well as potential barriers from French politicians, who tend to protect 'their industry'. If desired, Thomson had the chance to buy shares at the Hong Kong stock exchange in order to increase its joint venture decision power. Theoretically, the company ranked as an equal partner. However, industry insiders were convinced that Thomson might not have the financial resources to buy additional shares via the Hong Kong stock exchange.

Therefore, even though it was officially called an equal partnership at the beginning, TCL secured the majority control; and it can be assumed that a gradual takeover of the Thomson television set business by TCL may have been planned from the beginning of the joint venture operation. In January 2004, it was discussed that in the initial phase of the venture, TCL would hold 67 percent (and not 1/3 as proposed in 2003) and Thomson only 33 percent of the shares of TCL-Thomson Electronics (TTE). Thomson agreed to the venture because its television set division faced increasing financial difficulties before it was transferred to the joint venture. Finally, the French firm contributed the following TV manufacturing units to the venture (TCL, 2004a):

- RCA components SA de CV, Manufactures Avanzadas SA de CV, and Thomson Televisions de Mexico SA de CV [all in Mexico];
- Thomson Multimedia Operations Company Limited [Thailand];
- Thomson Zhao Wei Multimedia Co. Ltd. [China];
- Thomson Multimedia India Private Ltd. [India]; and
- Thomson Multimedia Polska Zyrardow [Poland].

In addition to the manufacturing capacities mentioned above, three research and development centers located in Villingen (Germany), Indianapolis (USA), and India were contributed to the TTE joint venture by the French partner Thomson (TCL, 2004a). Thus, through the venture with Thomson, TCL absorbed technological know-how, research and development resources, a wide range of patents, and valuable brands. Since the start of international venture operations, the television sets have been sold globally under three key brands: 'TCL' (Asia, Australia, Russia, and South America), 'THOMSON' (Europe, Russia, Ukraine, and Kazakhstan), and 'RCA' (North America) (TCL, 2007b, 2008a). According to the final 'Shareholders Covenants Agreement' with Thomson, TCL secured the position of the 'ultimate, controlling shareholding', with 38.74 percent of TTE's capital. The remaining share portion of 31.94 percent was placed before the public at the Hong Kong stock exchange. Thomson was entitled to nominate two out of eleven directors to the board as long as it held at least a 13.25 percent interest in TTE. Thomson finally decided to invest 29.32 percent of the issued share capital of TCL-Thomson Electronics. The Chinese venture parent partner, TCL, guaranteed its control of the board (TCL, 2005).

The newly formed venture TTE helped to expand the turnover and the international ambitions of TCL. However, the operating activities of TCL's strategic business, called TCL Multimedia, which included the joint venture operations of TEE, resulted in a loss in the subsequent years 2005 through 2008 as illustrated in Figure 69 (TCL_China, 2004, 2006, 2008, 2010, 2012, 2013a).

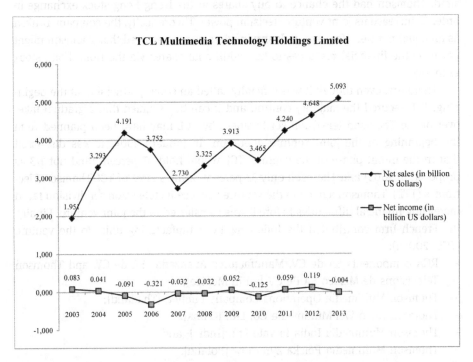

Figure 69. Financial performance of the strategic business unit TCL Multimedia between 2003 and 2013. Developed based on various firm related sources (TCL_China, 2004, 2006, 2008, 2010, 2012, 2013a)

During the course of worsening business, the joint venture partner Thomson decided to incrementally reduce its engagement of the issued venture capital share. In parallel, the Chinese venture parent, TCL, strengthened its alliance network with other firms. In February 2006, a memorandum of understanding was signed with LG.Philips LCD. Under its framework, it was agreed that LG.Philips LCD would supply LCD-

TFT panels to TCL, which guaranteed a stable purchase demand. Mr. Gary Yu, president of TTE Global Operation Center, commented concerning this partnership,

> TTE intends to increase the sales of LCD TVs globally. As LG.Philips LCD will take into consideration TTE's product designs in developing high-quality TFT-LCD products, this cooperation will enable both companies to boost their presence in the fast-growing LCD TV market with fruitful results (TCL, 2006e).

In 2008, after the decision of Philips' top management to outsource 70 percent of its LCD television set operations, the Dutch company further intensified its business relations with TCL, based on an original equipment manufacturing (OEM) agreement that was signed for the first time in 2007. TTE became one of the major OEM partners for Philips. The OEM contract, from the perspective of Philips, had the goal of lower manufacturing costs relative to its European operations. The television sets were manufactured, with attention to technical specifications and quality standards approved by Philips, at TCL factories in the Far East. These TV sets were globally distributed and labelled with the Philips brand in the European market, among other markets (Digitimes.com, 2008).

On April 15, 2008, TCL started construction of its own liquid crystal display (LCD) module plant in China's southern Guangdong province. The commencement of operations strengthened TCL's competitiveness in the LCD television set sector. The project was financed by TCL Corporation, with LCD panels and major technological support provided by TCL's project partner, Samsung (TCL, 2008b). Samsung intended to subcontract parts of its LCD manufacturing to the Chinese television maker after the plant's opening in 2009 (TCL, 2008c).

3.5.3 The gradual process towards the liquidation of TTE Europe

In Paris on November 3, 2006, the French joint venture partner, Thomson, announced that it would reduce its stake in TCL Multimedia from 29.3 percent to 19.3 percent of its share capital. Thomson's management said it intended to continue its business relationship with TCL. However, following the divestment, Thomson's interest in TTE would no longer have the status of a joint venture partner. The residual stake of Thomson in the TTE joint venture would be rather a financial participation (TCL, 2006b; Thomson, 2006).

In Hong Kong on May 24, 2007, approximately six months later, the chairman of TCL, Li Dongsheng, announced on behalf of the board the insolvency of all European operations. At the time of this announcement, who had the managerial decision power at TTE? Besides Li Dongsheng, the board was comprised of Lu Zhongli, Wang Kangping, Shi Wanwen, and Yuan Bing as executive directors. Albert Thomas da Rosa, Jr., ranked as nonexecutive director and Tang Guliang, Wang Bing, and Robert Maarten Westerhof as independent nonexecutive directors of the board (TCL, 2007a, c, d). According to the corresponding press release,

> The company expects that the French court will appoint a judicial liquidator to take control of TTE Europe. TTE Europe still faces a number of outstanding claims that it is unable to settle. As the operations of TTE Europe have caused significant losses for the Group in recent years, TTE Europe's insolvency filing will provide closure to the Group's involvement in TTE Europe, especially with respect to the settlement of claims (TCL, 2007c).

To maintain the European business from that time onward, TTE was organized as a platform for all television set-related activities and became a wholly owned subsidiary of TCL. It was agreed with Thomson that the OEM business would be expanded (assembly of television sets in China that are sold with the Thomson label around the world). Under the trademark license agreement, Thomson granted a twenty-year license to use Thomson's registered trademarks (RCA, RCA Scenium, and Thomson) for manufacture and sales of television products in certain countries in North America, Europe, and other regions in return for a royalty fee based on net sales. According to the agreement, TCL was allowed to use the Thomson trademark in Europe until 2008 without paying a royalty fee. In Russia, Ukraine, and Kazakhstan, TCL's subsidiary TTE could use the Thomson trademark until 2013 with payment of a royalty fee (TCL, 2006a; Thomson, 2007a, b).

As stated in TCL's official press release with respect to President Li Dongsheng's participation at the 'Caijing Chinese Business Forum on the road to internationalization' held in June 2008 in London,

> In January 2004, TCL acquired the color TV business of the French company Thomson; three months later, TCL also acquired mobile phone businesses operating under the Alcatel brand, causing unprecedented overseas interest in Chinese firms' international mergers and acquisitions. However, TCL's road to internationalization has been far from smooth as the restructuring of the company's European business in 2006 led to the company incurring losses.
>
> I hope that the international community will maintain an objective and tolerant attitude towards Chinese businesses that 'step outside China', viewing them as colleagues in areas such as market access, investment and mergers, and acquisitions, and that it will not overly politicize the economic vitality of Chinese business (TCL, 2008d).

TCL strengthened its international expertise and access to overseas operations with the TTE joint venture. The competitive advantage of the Chinese firm still remained in its Asian cost manufacturing platform. Consequently, its television manufacturing plants have been expanded in China (Huizhou, Henan, Wuxi), Mongolia, Thailand, and Vietnam. These plants produce a full range of products covering CRT, LCD, plasma, and projection TVs. Minor manufacturing locations (previously contributed by Thomson) survived in Poland (Zyrardow) and Mexico (Juarez). TCL's manufacturing activities for audio-visual products are based in China (Shenzhen) and include, for example, DVD player assembly. Research and development activities are concentrated in Shenzhen as well. Meanwhile, TCL belongs to the world's largest TV companies, with a relatively broad line of TV products as well as a growing AV (audio-video) line of business. In 2007, the Chinese firm launched an image campaign to strengthen its brand value from TCL China to 'TCL'—'The Creative Life' (TCL, 2007a, 2008a).

Are there any drawbacks, from the Chinese point of view, when considering the joint venture operations with Thomson? First of all, there were operating losses between 2005 and 2008 that had a significant negative impact on the overall firm records. At the time that the joint venture contract was signed in 2004, Thomson's cost competitiveness in the television set market was comparatively weak; and its potential might have been overestimated by TCL's management. Instead of paying attention to the new flat technologies like LCD and plasma, Thomson concentrated its efforts on projection TV products, which were in 2004 significantly cheaper to produce and, therefore, price attractive on the markets. However, the picture performance of projection TVs was relatively poor in comparison with the upcoming LCD and plasma television sets. Consequently, the forecast for the European market regarding projection TVs was rather pessimistic. Quality issues and increasing price competition in the cathode ray tube-based segments caused an even more difficult situation for Thomson, particularly in its core market, Europe.

The weakness of Thomson was temporarily ameliorated by TCL's main and most important strength: its low-cost production facilities for conventional CRT-based television sets in China. However, both TCL and Thomson so far had not gained significant technological expertise in flat panel technology nor did they have LCD or plasma module production capacities built up. Thus, the TTE main business segment had to focus on the mature and price competitive CRT markets, which were increasingly being replaced by LCD and plasma TVs in Europe.

No doubt, Chinese firms such as TCL have strong learning and absorptive capabilities. Thus, the tendency for them to continue their investments to acquire strategic resources around the globe is very high. The case study of TCL illustrates the firm's efforts to gain, within the shortest possible time period, resources in areas where the company has current weaknesses (Bacani, 2005; Deng, 2006: 77). Trademarks such as Schneider, Thomson, and REA, used for its European and US market entry, as well as intellectual property rights (RCA patents), R&D centers (e. g., Villingen in Germany), and access to European distribution channels were the most important resources TCL gained through the joint venture with Thomson. These acquired resources helped overcome market entry barriers for TCL in Europe. The management of TCL, until recent times relatively inexperienced in business operations outside China, gained stepwise managerial, technological, and cultural experience from its global business networks (TCL, 2004b).

3.5.4 TCL and Alcatel international joint venture

The case of TTE demonstrates that international joint ventures indicate a high rate of failure, which is in many cases not narrowly caused by 'cultural reasons' of the venture partners. The mobile phone joint venture between TCL and Alcatel developed in a pattern similar to that of TTE. In 2005, TCL acquired a 55 percent share in the French Alcatel's mobile phone manufacturing enterprise in order to establish TCL and Alcatel Mobile Phone Limited (T&A), which was worth 1 billion yuan (USD 121 million) in assets. By the end of the first quarter of 2005, T&A had lost over 660 million yuan (USD 79.71 million), more than TCL's original investment of USD 68.15 million (Yuxin, 2005). The development of the joint venture negatively contributed to a loss for TCL's strategic business unit, called TCL Communication Technology Holdings Limited, in 2005. Despite a sharp increase since 2009, profits have remained at a relatively marginal level (compare Figure 70) (TCL_China, 2005, 2007, 2011, 2014).

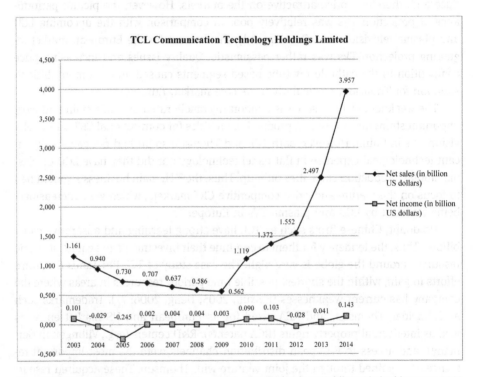

Figure 70. Financial performance of TCL Communication Technology Holdings Limited between 2003 and 2014. Developed based on various firm related sources (TCL_China, 2004, 2005, 2007, 2009, 2011, 2013b, 2014)

Within just a couple of months after the establishment of the joint venture, TCL was under pressure to undertake a substantial restructuring of its mobile phone venture with Alcatel of France, after admitting the business had failed to keep up with competitors on pricing and new technology. The restructuring included the transfer of research and development resources from France to China. French research and development staff were redeployed within Alcatel's organization. In May 2005, Alcatel announced it would switch its 45 percent holding in the joint venture to a 5 percent holding in TCL Communication Technology, listed separately on the Hong Kong stock exchange. Li Dongsheng, chairman of TCL, said,

> The company had originally planned to combine the two businesses within three years but now realized it needed to act more quickly. He further commented he was confident the changes would result in a 'major improvement' in the fourth quarter. TCL Group, has been dragged into a loss by the ailing mobile phone business and a similarly troubled TV venture (Palmer, 2005).

The international market entry strategy of TCL, as indicated by Schneider, TTE, and T&A, followed a certain pattern: first, in the case Schneider, it was announced at the beginning (when TCL acquired the firm) that the German facilities would continue operations. However, after a relatively short time, Schneider activities were terminated; and manufacturing as well as the complete research and development operation, including several patents and the trademark rights, had been transferred to China. Second, in the case of the joint venture with Thomson, agreed to as a 'venture of equals', TCL secured majority control right after the joint venture was established. And in the third case, TCL took over Alcatel's joint venture shares within just one year. However, these market entry strategies were costly for TCL. According to TCL's former and current chairman, Li Dongsheng, TCL's relationship with Alcatel and Thomson remained good; but he admitted working with the company's new foreign acquisitions had been more difficult than anticipated.

> TCL was the first Chinese company to make a major European acquisition, so we are facing a lot of new difficulties and problems. The overall integration will take longer than expected (Palmer, 2005).

Chapter review questions

1. Considering the case study, describe the strengths and weaknesses of TCL according to the resource-based view.
2. Explain TCL's strategic market entry concepts in Europe.
3. Thomson and TCL seemed to be ideal joint venture partners at the beginning of the venture, so why did the joint venture fail in the end?
4. Describe the possible reasons that international joint ventures fail.

Bibliography

Agence_France (2014) Foxconn sees net profit grow in 2013 on iPhone demand. Retrieved January 12, 2015 from http://gadgets.ndtv.com/mobiles/news/foxconn-sees-net-profit-grow-in-2013-on-iphone-demand-502407

Alcatel_One_Touch (2014) Alcatel One Touch. Retrieved November 26, 2014 from http://www.alcate lonetouch.com/de/

Alon, I. (2003) *Chinese culture, organizational behavior, and international business management.* Westport: Praeger Publishers.

Andersen, O., & Buvik, A. (2002) Firm's internationalization and alternative approaches to the international customer/market selection. *International Business Review,* 11 (3): 347–363.

Andrews, K. R. (2003) The concept of corporate strategy. In H. Mintzberg, J. Lampel, J. B. Quinn, & S. Ghoshal (Eds.), *The Strategy Process.* Essex: Pearson Education Limited.

Arora, A., & Fosfuri, A. (2000) Wholly owned subsidiary versus technology licensing in the worldwide chemical industry. *Journal of International Business Studies,* 31(4): 555–572.

Aulakh, P. S., Jiang, M. S., & Li, S. (2013) Licensee technological potential and exclusive rights in international licensing: A multilevel model. *Journal of International Business Studies,* 44(7): 699–718.

Bacani, C. (2005) China's new globalizers. Retrieved February 20, 2006 from http://www.cfoasia.com/archives/200505–03.html

Barkema, H. G., Bell, J. H. J., & Pennings, J. M. (1996) Foreign entry, cultural barriers, and learning. *Strategic Management Journal,* 17: 151–166.

Barkema, H. G., & Vermeulen, F. (1998) International expansion through start-up or acquisition: a learning perspective. *Academy of Management Journal,* 41(1): 7–26.

BBC (2008) Samsung HQ raided in bribes probe. Retrieved October 16, 2008 from http://news.bbc.co.uk/2/hi/business/7188712.stm

Bertrand, O., & Mol, M. J. (2013) The antecedents and innovation effects of domestic and offshore R&D outsourcing: The contingent impact of cognitive distance and absorptive capacity. *Strategic Management Journal,* 34(6): 751–760.

bfai_Bundesagentur_für_Außenwirtschaft (2007) Nicht mehr nur Glanz in Koreas Flachbildschirmbranche. Retrieved April 08, 2008 from http://www.bfai.de/nsc_true/DE/Navigation/Metanavigation/Suche/sucheUebergreifendGT.html

Blomstermo, A., Sharma, D. D., & Sallis, J. (2006) Choice of foreign market entry mode in service firms. *International Marketing Review,* 23: 211–229.

Bondgenoten, F. (2001) Philips. On the way into the third millenium. Retrieved July 26, 2004 from http://www.imfmetal.org/main/files/philips_english_2001.pdf

Brouthers, K. D., & Brouthers, L. E. (2000) Acquisition or greenfield start-up? Institutional, cultural and transaction cost influences. *Strategic Management Journal,* 21(1): 89–97.

Brouthers, K. D., Brouthers, L. E., & Wilson, B. J. (2001) Start-up versus acquisition: making the right diversification mode choice. *Global Focus,* 13 (1): 27–35.

Brouthers, K. D., & Hennart, J.-F. (2007) Boundaries of the firm: Insights from international entry mode research. *Journal of Management,* 33(3): 395–425.

Businessweek_Beijing (2003) TCL's boss talks strategy. Retrieved April 08, 2008 from http://www.businessweek.com/magazine/content703_46/b3858086.htm

Cai, S. (2012) Industrial organization in China: a case study of Foxconn's factory relocations. Retrieved April 2014 from https://escholarship.org/uc/item/57z9v7v7

Caruth, D. L., Pane Haden, S. S., & Caruth, G. D. (2012) Critical factors in human resource outsourcing. *Journal of Management Research,* 13(4): 187–195.

CDRinf (2007) LG Samsung form the world's largest display alliance. Retrieved August 14, 2008 from http://www.cdrinfo.com/sections/news/Details.aspx?NewsId=20430

Chandler, A. D. (1962) *Strategy and structure. Chapters in the history of industrial enterprise.* Cambridge: MA.

Chang, C. S., & Chang, N. J. (1994) *The Korean management system. Cultural, political, economic foundations.* London: CT: Quorum Books.

Chang, S.-J. (2003) *Financial crisis and transformation of Korean business groups. The rise and fall of Chaebols.* Cambridge: Cambridge University Press.

Chen, M. (2004) *Asian management systems.* London: Thomson Learning.

Chen, R., & Li, Z. (2007) A synthesis of interviews with executives of Samsung Electronics. *Journal of Asia Business Studies*, Spring 2007: 77–78.

Cheng, L. C. V., Cantor, D. E., Dresner, M., & Grimm, C. M. (2012) The impact of contract manufacturing on inventory performance: An examination of U.S. manufacturing industries. *Decision Sciences*, 43(5): 889–928.

Cherry, J. (2001) *Korean multinationals in Europe.* Mitcham, Surrey: Curzon Press.

ChinaBusiness (2005) Chinese TV makers pressure foreign rivals. Retrieved April 08, 2008 from http://www.atimes.com/atimes/China_Business/GK23Cb02.html

Cole, M., Mason, S., Hau, T.-C., & Yan, L. (2001) The manufacture/outsource decision in electronics manufacturing, final report. Fayetteville, Arkansas: The Logistics Institute, University of Arkansas.

Combs, J. G., Michael, S. C., & G.J., C. (2004) Franchising: A review and avenues to greater theoretical diversity. *Journal of Management* 30 (6): 907–931.

Contractor, F. J., & Lorange, P. (1988) *Cooperative strategies in international business. Joint ventures and technology partnerships between firms.* Lexington, Toronto: Lexington Books.

Corning (2013) Corning and Samsung strengthen strategic collaborations. Retrieved July 26, 2015 from https://www.corning.com/worldwide/en/about-us/news-events/news-releases/2013/10/news_center_news_releases_2013_2013102201.html

Das, T. K., & Teng, B.-S. (2000) Instabilities of strategic alliances: An internal tensions perspective. *Organization Science*, 11(1): 77–101.

Delios, A., & Beamish, P. W. (1999) Ownership strategy of Japanese firms: transactional, institutional, and experience influences. *Strategic Management Journal*, 20: 915–933.

Deng, P. (2006) Investing for strategic resources and its rationale: the case of outward FDI from Chinese companies. *Business Horizon*, 50: 71–80.

Dent, S. (2015) Lenovo's folding its own smartphone division into Motorola. Retrieved September 12, 2015 from http://www.engadget.com/2015/08/27/motorola-absorbing-lenovo-mobile/

Deresky, H. (2014) *International management: Managing across borders and cultures. Text and cases.* Boston et al. : Pearson.

Digitimes.com (2008) Philips said to be outsourcing 70 % of its LCD TVs to OEM makers in 2008. Retrieved April 17, 2008 from http://www.digitimes.com/news/a20080123VL200.html

DisplaySearch (2008a) 2008–2009 TFT LCD production will be enabled by plentiful supply of glass substrates. Retrieved September 05, 2008 from http://now.eloqua.com/es.asp?s=488&e=03dbde1d599646329aac8d7b705e9f60&elq=92DE11 A7D26642EDBC49F566F5641188

DisplaySearch (2008b) The influence of Sony's investment in Sharp's LCD TV panel factory. Retrieved September 10, 2008 from http://www.displaysearchblog.com/2008/03/the-influ ence-of-sonys-investment-in-sharp%e2%80%99 s-lcd-tv-panel-factory

Duelfer, E., & Joestingmeier, B. (2011) *Internationales Management in unterschiedlichen Kulturbereichen.* Munich: De Gruyter Oldenbourg.

Dunning, J. H., Pak, Y. S., & Beldona, S. (2007) Foreign ownership strategies of UK and US international franchisors: An exploratory application of Dunning's envelope paradigm. *International Business Review*, 16(5): 531–548.

Dutton, J. (2014) Samsung employees treat their 72-year-old chairman like a god. Retrieved November 26, 2014 from http://www.businessinsider.com/samsung-lee-kun-hee-and-lee-jae-yong-2014-8

Ellis, P. (2000) Social ties and foreign market entry. *Journal of International Business Studies*, 31: 443–469.

Emphasize_Emerging_Markets (2007) Philips will bei LG.Philips LCD aussteigen. Retrieved May 26, 2007 from http://www.emfis.de/funktionen-features/drucken/id/Philips_will_bei_LGPhilips_LCD_aussteigen_ID52049.html?L=78cHash%3D2de540bddc&print=1&cHash=b649f9e8db

Foscht, T., & Podmenik, H. (2005) Management-Verträge als Kooperationsform im Dienstleistungsbereich. In J. Zentes, B. Swoboda, & D. Morschett (Eds.), *Kooperationen, Allianzen und Netzwerke*. Wiesbaden: Gabler Verlag.

Frayne, C. A., & Geringer, J. M. (2000) Challenges facing general managers of international joint ventures. In M. Mendenhall, & G. Oddou (Eds.), *Readings and Cases in International Human Resource Management*, Vol. Vol. 3. Toronto: Southwestern College Publishing.

Gastelu, G. (2015) Apple might build a car, but Samsung already has. Retrieved June 1, 2015 from http://www.foxnews.com/leisure/2015/02/23/apple-may-be-building-car-but-samsung-already-has/

Genser. (2005) Samsung Electronics. As good as it gets?, *The Economist*.

GfK (2007) Gesellschaft für Konsumgütermarktforschung. Report: TV display sales in Europe 2004–2006. Nürnberg.

Glaister, K. W., Husan, R., & Buckley, P. J. (2003) Learning to manage international joint ventures. *International Business Review*, 12: 83–108.

Glowik, M. (2004a) Interview with a former senior manager of LG.Philips Displays during a conference in 2004, Brussels, Belgium.

Glowik, M. (2004b) Meeting with Thomson TV in Boulogne-Brillancourt, France, May 2004.

Glowik, M. (2007a) Interview with Mr. David Kang [Manager LG Electronics] Location: LG Twin Towers, Seoul, South Korea, Date: 2007, September, 19th.

Glowik, M. (2007b) Interview with Mr. M.B. Choi [Director LP Displays] Location: LG Twin Towers, Seoul, South Korea, Date: 2007, September 19th.

Glowik, M. (2007c) Interview with Ms. Nana Park [Market Research Analyst at Samsung SDI Korea], Location: Suwon, South-Korea, Date: 2007, September 30th.

Grant, R. M. (2013) *Contemporary strategy analysis* (7th ed. ed.). Chichester: John Wiley & Sons.

Hammerschmidt, C. (2012) Bosch withdraws from battery joint venture with Samsung. Retrieved July 26th, 2015 from http://automotive-eetimes.com/en/bosch-withdraws-from-battery-jv-with-samsung.html?cmp_id=7&news_id=222902458

Han, J., Liem, W.-s., & Lee, Y. (2013) In the belly of the Beast: Samsung Electronics' supply chain and workforce in South Korea

Hendrikse, G., & Jiang, T. (2007) Plural form of franchising: An incomplete contracting approach. In G. Cliquet, G. Hendrikse, M. Tuunanen, & J. Windsperger (Eds.), *Economics and Management of Networks*. Heidelberg: Physica-Verlag.

Hennart, J.-F., & Park, Y.-R. (1993) Greenfield vs. acquisition: The strategy of Japanese investors in the United States. *Management Science*, 39(9): 1054–1070.

Hennart, J.-F., & Reddy, S. (1997) The choice between mergers/acquisitions and joint ventures: the case of Japanese investors in the United States. *Strategic Management Journal*, 18 (1): 1–12.

Henning, G. (2013) Choosing between turnkey and consignment manufacturing. *Surface Mount Technology*, 28(1): 18–24.

Hibbert, E. P. (1997) *International business, strategy and operations*. Hampshire: Macmillan Press Ltd.

Hill, C. W. L. (2012) *International business: Competing in the global marketplace* (5th ed. ed.). Boston: McGraw-Hill/Irwin.

Hitt, M. A., Ireland, R. D., & Hoskisson, R. E. (2015) *Strategic management. Competitiveness and globalization* (11. Ed. ed.). Stamford, Conn.: Cengage Learning.

Hofstede, G. (2001) *Culture's consequences – comparing values, behaviours, institutions and organization across nations* (2nd ed. ed.). California: Sage Publications Inc.

Hollensen, S. (2014) *Global marketing. A decision-oriented approach*. Harlow: Pearson Education Limited.

Hollensen, S., Boyd, B., & Ulrich, A. M. D. (2011) Choice of foreign entry modes in a control perspective. *IUP Journal of Business Strategy*, 8(4): 7–31.

Holtbrügge, D., & Baron, A. (2013) Market entry strategies in emerging markets: An institutional study in the BRIC countries. *Thunderbird International Business Review*, 55(3): 237 – 252.

Hon_Hai_Precision_Company_Ltd. (2013) Group profile. Retrieved January 12, 2015 from http://www.foxconn.com/GroupProfile_En/GroupProfile.html

Hon_Hai_Precision_Industry Co., L. (2013) Corporate governance. Retrieved April 14, 2015 from http://www.foxconn.com/Investors_En/Corporate_Governance.html?index=2

Inkpen, B., & Ramaswamy, K. (2006) *Global strategy-creating and sustaining advantage across borders*. New York: Oxford University Press.

Jacobs, S. (2006) Nachsitzen bei Samsung. Beschäftigte sollen Materialreste verarbeiten – Schließungsplan angeblich auch für das Werk in Ungarn, *Tagesspiegel*.

Johanson, J., & Vahlne, J.-E. (1977) The internationalization process of the firm: A model of knowledge development and increasing foreign market commitments. *Journal of International Business Studies*, 8(1): 23 – 32.

Johnston, R. (2006) Toshiba picks Poland for flat TV. Retrieved June 06, 2007 from http://www.cbw.cz/phprs/rservice.php?akce=tisk&cisloclanku=2006

Kan, M. (2012) Foxconn builds products for many vendors, but its mud sticks to Apple. Retrieved January 15, 2015 from http://www.macworld.com/article/2012972/foxconn-builds-products-for-many-vendors-but-its-mud-sticks-to-apple.html

Kim, D.-O., & Bae, J. (2004) *Employment relations and HRM in South Korea*. Hampshire: Ashgate Publishing Limited.

Kim, L. (1997) *Imitation to innovation. The dynamics of Korea's technological learning*. Boston: Harvard Business School Press.

Kita, M. (2001) How the electronics manufacturing service business model can help Japanese corporations revolutionize their factories? *Japan Bank for International Cooperation Review* 4: 1 – 24.

Korea_Associates. (2012) Global value chain analyis on Samsung Electronics (Report).

Kotabe, M., & Murray, J. Y. (2004) Global sourcing strategy and sustainable competitive advantage. *Industrial Marketing Management*, 33(1): 7 – 14.

Kovar, J. F. (1999) Philips and LG invest in joint LCD venture. Retrieved August 19, 2008 from http://www.crn.com/it-channel/18804858

Kutschker, M., & Schmid, S. (2006) *Internationales Management*. Munich: Oldenbourg Wissenschaftsverlag.

Lambe, C. J., Wittmann, C. M., & Spekman, R. E. (2001) Social exchange theory and research on business-to-business relational exchange. *Journal of Business-to-Business Marketing*, 8(3): 1 – 36.

Lane, P. J., Salk, J. E., & Lyles, M. A. (2001) Absorptive capacity, learning, and performance in international joint ventures. *Strategic Management Journal*, 22: 1139 – 1161.

Lenovo (2007) Annual report 2006/2007. Retrieved May 4, 2015 from http://www.lenovo.com/ww/lenovo/annual_interim_report.html

Lenovo (2008) Annual report 2007/2008. Retrieved May 4, 2015 from http://www.lenovo.com/ww/lenovo/annual_interim_report.html

Lenovo (2009) Annual report 2008/2009. Retrieved May 4, 2015 from http://www.lenovo.com/ww/lenovo/annual_interim_report.html

Lenovo (2010) Annual report 2009/2010. Retrieved May 4, 2015 from http://www.lenovo.com/ww/lenovo/annual_interim_report.html

Lenovo (2011) Annual report 2010/2011. Retrieved May 4, 2015 from http://www.lenovo.com/ww/lenovo/annual_interim_report.html

Lenovo (2012) Annual report 2011/2012. Retrieved May 4, 2015 from http://www.lenovo.com/ww/lenovo/annual_interim_report.html

Lenovo (2013a) About Lenovo. Retrieved January 12, 2015 from http://www.lenovo.com/lenovo/us/en/our_company.html

Lenovo (2013b) Annual report 2012/2013. Retrieved May 4, 2015 from http://www.lenovo.com/ww/lenovo/annual_interim_report.html

Lenovo (2014a) Annual report 2013/2014. Retrieved May 4, 2015 from http://www.lenovo.com/ww/lenovo/annual_interim_report.html

Lenovo (2014b) Annual report 2013/ 2014. Retrieved January 12, 2015 from http://www.lenovo.com/ww/lenovo/annual_interim_report.html

Lenovo (2014c) Lenovo statement on January 2014 reorganization. Retrieved November 15, 2014 from http://news.lenovo.com/article_display.cfm?article_id=1763

Lenovo (2014d) Lenovo to acquire Motorola mobility from Google. Retrieved January 12, 2015 from http://news.lenovo.com/article_display.cfm?article_id=1768

Lenovo (2015) Annual report 2014/2015. Retrieved May 4, 2015 from http://www.lenovo.com/ww/lenovo/annual_interim_report.html

LG.PhilipsDisplays (2001a) News archive, LG.Philips Displays posts annual sales over USD 4 billion in 2001. Retrieved November 25, 2005 from http://www.lgphilips-displays.com/english/newsroom/newsarchives.htm

LG.PhilipsDisplays (2001b) Philips and LG sign definitive agreement on joint venture. Retrieved November 23, 2005 from http://www.lgphilips-displays.com/english/newsroom/newsarchives.htm

LG.PhilipsDisplays (2005a) CRT continues to be dominant force in display technologies. Retrieved November 28, 2005 from http://www.lgphilips-displays.com/english/newsroom/newsarchives.htm

LG.PhilipsDisplays (2005b) LG.Philips Displays announces closure of its Durham plant. Retrieved November 02, 2005 from http://www.lgphilips-displays.com/english/newsroom/newsarchives.htm

LG.PhilipsDisplays (2005c) LG.Philips Displays announces closure of its plant in Newport, Wales and Southport, England. Retrieved November 25, 2005 from http://www.lgphilips-displays.com/english/newsroom/newsarchives.htm

LG.PhilipsDisplays (2005d) LG.Philips Displays plant in Durham gets 'Best Supplier Award'. Retrieved November 28, 2005 from http://www.lgphilips-displays.com/english/newsroom/newsarchives.htm

LG.PhilipsDisplays (2005e) LG.Philips Displays to restructure its European industrial production infrastructure. Retrieved November 28, 2005 from http://www.lgphilips-displays.com/english/newsroom/newsarchives.htm

LG.PhilipsDisplays (2005f) Mexico President Vincent Fox opens new LG.Philips Displays factory in Gomez Palacio, Mexico. Retrieved December 28, 2005 from http://www.lgphilips-displays.com/english/newsroom/newsarchives.htm

LG.PhilipsDisplays (2006) LG.Philips Displays operations in Eindhoven, Netherlands and two of its subsidiaries file for insolvency protection. Retrieved March 03, 2006 from http://www.lgphilips-displays.com/english/newsroom/newsarchives.htm

LG.PhilipsDisplays (2007a) Composition for LG.Philips Displays plant in Hranice approved. Retrieved September 05, 2006 from http://www.lgphilips-displays.com

LG.PhilipsDisplays (2007b) Corporate information. Retrieved May 19, 2007 from http://www.lgphilips-displays.com

LG.PhilipsDisplays (2007c) LG.Philips Displays gets a new name. Retrieved May 22, 2007 from http://www.lgphilips-displays.com/english/newsroom/news_16_03_2007.html

LG.PhilipsLCD (2001) Investor Relations, LG invited 1,6 billion USD foreign capital, sold 50% shares to Philips. Retrieved November 27, 2005 from http://www.lgphilips-lcd.com/home Contain/jsp/eng/inv/inv101_j_e.jsp?BOARD_IDX=146&languageSec=E

LG.PhilipsLCD. (2003) Annual Report 2003. Financial highlights: 3.

LG.PhilipsLCD (2005a) Newscenter, LG.Philips LCD announces exercise of option to purchase additional convertible bonds. Retrieved November 28, 2005 from http://www.lgphilips-lcd. com/homeContain/jsp/eng/pr/pr201_j_e.jsp?BOARD_IDX=850&languageSec=E

LG.PhilipsLCD (2005b) Newscenter, LG.Philips LCD announces pricing of USD 1,0 billion initial public offering of 33,600.000 primary shares. Retrieved November 28, 2005 from http://www. lgphilips-lcd.com/homeContain/jsp/eng/pr/pr201_j_e.jsp?BOARD_IDX=718&languageSec=E

LG.PhilipsLCD (2006a) Investor presentations. Retrieved January 06, 2006 from http://www.lgphi lips-lcd.com/homeContain/jsp/eng/inv/inv800_j_e.jsp?tabVal=IP2

LG.PhilipsLCD (2006b) Investor Relation, LG.Philips LCD reports fourth quarter 2005 results. Retrieved January 14, 2006 from URL:http://www.lgphilips-lcd.com/homeContain/jsp/eng/inv/ inv101_j_e.jsp?BOARD_IDX=1002&languageSec=E

LG.PhilipsLCD (2006c) LG.Philips LCD signs investment agreement with the Polish government. Retrieved January 05, 2006 from http://www.lgphilips-lcd.com/homeContain/jsp/eng/pr/ pr201_j_e.jsp?BOARD_IDX=941&languageSec=E

LG.PhilipsLCD (2006d) Management information. Retrieved January 05, 2006 from http://www. lgphilips-lcd.com/homeContain/jsp/eng/inv/inv310_j_e.jsp

LG.PhilipsLCD (2007a) LG.Philips LCD production network. Retrieved July 27, 2007 from http:// www.lgphilips-lcd.com/homeContain/jsp/eng/com/com600_j_e.jsp

LG.PhilipsLCD (2007b) LG.Philips LCD sales network. Retrieved July 27, 2007 from http://www.lgphi lips-lcd.com/homeContain/jsp/eng/com/com700_j_e.jsp

LG.PhilipsLCD (2007c) LG.Philips LCD's module plant in Poland begins mass production. Retrieved June 16, 2007 from http://www.lgphilips-lcd.com

LG.PhilipsLCD (2008a) Core competency. Retrieved April 17, 2008 from http://www.lgphilips-lcd. com/homeContain/jsp/eng/com/com340_j_e.jsp

LG.PhilipsLCD (2008b) LG.Philips LCD income statement. Retrieved June 11, 2008 from http://www. lgphilips-lcd.com/homeContain/jsp/eng/inv/inv400_j_e.jsp

LG.PhilipsLCD (2008c) Ownership structure. Retrieved April 17, 2008 from http://www.lgphilips-lcd. com/homeContain/jsp/eng/inv/inv520_j_e.jsp

LG_Electronics (2003) Annual report 2003. Retrieved May 4, 2015 from http://www.lg.com/global/ investor-relations/reports/annual-reports

LG_Electronics (2004) Annual report 2004. Retrieved May 4, 2015 from http://www.lg.com/global/ investor-relations/reports/annual-reports

LG_Electronics (2005a) Annual Report 2005. Retrieved May 4, 2015 from http://www.lg.com/glob al/investor-relations/reports/annual-reports

LG_Electronics (2005b) Corporate information. Retrieved November 21, 2005 from http://www.lge. com/about/corporate/corporateinfomation.jsp

LG_Electronics (2006) Annual report 2006. Retrieved May 4, 2015 from http://www.lg.com/global/ investor-relations/reports/annual-reports

LG_Electronics (2007) Annual report 2007. Retrieved May 4, 2015 from http://www.lg.com/global/ investor-relations/reports/annual-reports

LG_Electronics (2008a) Annual report 2008. Retrieved May 4, 2015 from http://www.lg.com/glob al/investor-relations/reports/annual-reports

LG_Electronics (2008b) History. Retrieved September 05, 2008 from http://www.lge.com/about/cor porate/history.jsp

LG_Electronics (2009a) Annual report 2009. Retrieved May 4, 2014 from http://www.lg.com/glob al/investor-relations/reports/annual-reports

LG_Electronics. (2009b) Annual Reports 2000–2009.

LG_Electronics (2010) Annual report 2010. Retrieved May 4, 2015 from http://www.lg.com/global/ investor-relations/reports/annual-reports

LG_Electronics (2011) Annual report 2011. Retrieved May 4, 2015 from http://www.lg.com/global/in
vestor-relations/reports/annual-reports

LG_Electronics (2012) Annual report 2012. Retrieved May 4, 2015 from http://www.lg.com/global/
investor-relations/reports/annual-reports

LG_Electronics (2013) Consolidated financial statement 2013. Retrieved May 4, 2015 from http://
www.lg.com/global/investor-relations/reports/financial-statements

LG_Electronics (2014) Consolidated financial statement 2014. Retrieved May 4, 2015 from http://
www.lg.com/global/investor-relations/reports/financial-statements

LG_Electronics (2015a) Business domains. Retrieved April 14, 2015 from http://www.lg.com/global/
about-lg/corporate-information/business-domains

LG_Electronics (2015b) Business overview. Retrieved June 1, 2015 from http://www.lg.com/global/
business/automotive/business-overview

LG_Electronics (2015c) Executives. Retrieved April 14, 2015 from http://www.lg.com/global/about-
lg/corporate-information/executives

LG_Electronics (2015d) Overview. Retrieved April 14, 2015 from http://www.lg.com/global/investor-
relations/company-info/overview

Li, J. (1995) Foreign entry and survival: Effects of strategic choices on performance in international
markets. *Strategic Management Journal*, 16: 333–351.

Li, Y., & He, H. (2013) Evaluation of international brand alliances: Brand order and consumer
ethnocentrism. *Journal of Business Research*, 66(1): 89–97.

Lorange, P., & Roos, J. (1995) *Strategiske allianser i globale strategier*. Oslo: Norges Eksportrad.

Love, J. H., & Ganotakis, P. (2013) Learning by exporting: Lessons from high-technology SMEs.
International Business Review, 22(1): 1–17.

Luostarinen, R. (1980) *Internationalization of the firm. An empirical study of the
internationalization of firms with small and open domestic markets with special emphasis on
lateral rigidity as a behavioral characteristic in strategic decision-making*. Helsinki: The
Helsinki School of Economics.

Luostarinen, R., & Welch, L. (1997) *International business operations*. Helsinki: Kyriiri Oy.

Lynskey, M. J., & Yonekura, S. (2002) The environment-creating mechanism of a firm: Sony and
Samsung. In D.-S. Cho (Ed.), *Entrepreneurship and Organization*. New York: Oxford University
Press.

Mahoney, J. (1992) The choice of organizational form: vertical ownership versus other methods of
vertical integration. *Strategic Management Journal*, 13: 559–584.

Mathews, J. A. (2002) *Dragon multinational. A new model for global growth*. New York: Oxford
University Press.

Matsushita (2003) Matsushita and Toshiba announce outline of new cathode ray tube joint
venture. Retrieved February 19, 2008 from http://ir-site.panasonic.com/relevant/
en030129-5/en030129-5.html

Matsushita (2005) Matsushita to close cathode ray tube operations in North America and Europe.
Retrieved February 19, 2008 from http://panasonic.co.jp/corp/news/official.data/data.dir/
en051130-3/en051130-3.html

Meissner, H. G. (1995) *Strategisches Internationales Marketing* (2. Ed. ed.). München: Oldenbourg
Wissenschaftsverlag.

Meschi, P.-X. (2005) Stock market valuation of joint venture sell-offs. *Journal of International
Business Studies*, 36: 688–700.

Mintzberg, H., Lampel, J., Quinn, J. B., & Ghoshal, S. (2003) *The strategy process. Concepts,
contexts, cases* (4th ed. ed.). Essex: Pearson Educaton Limited.

Morschett, D. (2005) Contract manufacturing. In J. Zentes, B. Swoboda, & D. Morschett (Eds.),
Kooperationen, Allianzen und Netzwerke. Grundlagen-Ansätze-Perspektiven. Wiesbaden:
Gabler Verlag.

Mozur, P., & Luk, L. (2012) Hon Hai hits obstacles in push to use robots. Retrieved January 12, 2015 from http://www.wsj.com/articles/SB10001424127887324024004578172022369346936

Müller, S., & Gelbrich, K. (2004) *Interkulturelles Marketing*. München: Verlag Franz Vahlen.

Naisbitt, J. (1996) *Megatrends Asia*. New York: Simon & Schuster.

O'Toole, J. (2013) Foxconn's worker hours still excessive – report. Retrieved January 12, 2015 from http://money.cnn.com/2013/12/12/technology/foxconn-labor/

one-blue. (2009) Panasonic, Philips and Sony to establish One Stop Shop product license for Blu-ray Disc™ (Report).

Osawa, J. (2014a) Lenovo completes Motorola acquisition *The Wall Street Journal*.

Osawa, J. (2014b) Lenovo to reorganize into four business groups. *The Wall Street Journal*.

Otani (2008) Sony, Sharp form joint venture for 10th-generation liquid crystal display fabrication. Retrieved May 05, 2008 from http://techon.nikkeibp.co.jp/article/HONSHI/20080327/149601/

Palmer, M. (2005) TCL to restructure mobile phone joint venture. Retrieved December 10, 2015 from http://www.ft.com/intl/cms/s/0/d02683f6 – 1af2 – 11da-a117 – 00000e2511c8. html#axzz3LVJELXTA

Pedersen, T., Petersen, B., & Benito, G. R. G. (2002) Change of foreign operation method: Impetus and switching costs. *International Business Review*, 11(3): 325 – 345.

Penrose, E. (1995) *The theory of the growth of the firm* (2nd ed.). Oxford: Oxford University Press.

Philips (2008) Company profile and history. Retrieved September 05, 2008 from http://www.phi lips.com/about/company/history/index.page

Plambeck, E. L., & Taylor, T. A. (2005) Sell the plant? The impact of contract manufacturing on innovation, capacity and profitability. *Management Science*, 51(1): 133 – 150.

Porter, M. E. (1999) *Wettbewerbsstrategie. Methoden zur Analyse von Branchen und Konkurrenten* (10. Ed. ed.). Frankfurt/M.: Campus Verlag.

Potkány, M. (2008) Personnel outsourcing processes. *Ekonomie a Management*, 11(4): 53 – 62.

Ramstad, E. (2009) Samsung's swelling size brings new challenges. *The Wall Street Journal*.

Rhally, C. (2014) Do not say you are a Chinese company: How Lenovo grew as a global brand. Retrieved January 15, 2015 from http://projourno.org/2014/04/dont-say-youre-a-chinese-com pany-how-lenovo-grew-as-a-global-brand/

Roberto, M. (2009) Vertical integration at Samsung Retrieved December 10, 2014 from http://mi chael-roberto.blogspot.de/2009/11/vertical-integration-at-samsung.html

Rowley, C., Sohn, T.-W., & Bae, J. (2002) *Managing Korean business: organization, culture, human resources and change*. London: Frank Cass Publishers.

Rugman, A. M., & Collinson, S. (2012) *International business* (3. ed. ed.). Essex: Pearson Education Limited.

Rugman, A. M., & Hodgetts, R. M. (2003) *International business*. Essex: Pearson Education.

Samsung. (2004) Company Presentation: Welcome to Samsung. Group Overview, History, Main Business and Global Operations: 45. Seoul: Samsung Electronics.

Samsung (2007) Samsung: The digital E-company. Retrieved April 16, 2008 from http://www.sam sung.de/about_history.asp

Samsung (2008a) Joint Venture von Bosch und Samsung. Retrieved July 18, 2008 from http:// www.beschaffungswelt.de/news-248-Joint%20Venture%20von%20Bosch%20und%20s am sung

Samsung (2008b) Strategische Allianzen. Retrieved July 18, 2008 from http://www.samsung.com/ at/aboutsamsung/companyprofile/majorstrategicalliances/C

Samsung (2014a) Affiliated companies. Retrieved October 19, 2014 from http://www.samsung. com/us/aboutsamsung/samsung_group/affiliated_companies/

Samsung (2014b) Research and development. Retrieved October 16, 2014 from http://www.sam sung.com/us/aboutsamsung/samsung_electronics/business_area/rd_page/

Samsung (2014c) Unternehmensführung. Retrieved October 16, 2014 from http://www.samsung.com/de/aboutsamsung/samsungelectronics/executives/executives_02.html

Samsung (2014d) Why integration matters: What Samsung's vertical integration means to you. Retrieved December 10, 2014 from http://www.samsung.com/global/business/semiconductor/minisite/SSD/global/html/about/whitepaper09.html

Samsung (2015) Samsung Profile 1995–2014. Retrieved January 18, 2015 from http://www.samsung.com/us/aboutsamsung/samsung_group/our_performance/

Samsung_Electronics (2004) Annual report 2003. Retrieved January 18, 2015 from http://www.samsung.com/us/aboutsamsung/investor_relations/financial_information/annual_reports.html

Samsung_Electronics (2005) Annual report 2004. Retrieved January 18, 2015 from http://www.samsung.com/us/aboutsamsung/investor_relations/financial_information/annual_reports.html

Samsung_Electronics (2006) Annual report 2005. Retrieved January 18, 2015 from http://www.samsung.com/us/aboutsamsung/investor_relations/financial_information/annual_reports.html

Samsung_Electronics (2007) Annual report 2006. Retrieved January 18, 2015 from http://www.samsung.com/us/aboutsamsung/investor_relations/financial_information/annual_reports.html

Samsung_Electronics (2008) Annual report 2007. Retrieved January 18, 2015 from http://www.samsung.com/us/aboutsamsung/investor_relations/financial_information/annual_reports.html

Samsung_Electronics (2009) Annual report 2008. Retrieved January 18, 2015 from http://www.samsung.com/us/aboutsamsung/investor_relations/financial_information/annual_reports.html

Samsung_Electronics (2010) Annual report 2009. Retrieved January 18, 2015 from http://www.samsung.com/us/aboutsamsung/investor_relations/financial_information/annual_reports.html

Samsung_Electronics (2011) Annual report 2010. Retrieved from http://www.samsung.com/us/aboutsamsung/investor_relations/financial_information/annual_reports.html

Samsung_Electronics (2012) Annual report 2011. Retrieved January 18. 2015 from http://www.samsung.com/us/aboutsamsung/investor_relations/financial_information/annual_reports.html

Samsung_Electronics (2013) Annual report 2012. Retrieved January 18, 2015 from http://www.samsung.com/us/aboutsamsung/investor_relations/financial_information/annual_reports.html

Samsung_Electronics (2014a) Annual report 2013. Retrieved January 18, 2015 from http://www.samsung.com/us/aboutsamsung/investor_relations/financial_information/annual_reports.html

Samsung_Electronics (2014b) Company reports. Retrieved November 26, 2014 from http://www.samsung.com/uk/aboutsamsung/samsungelectronics/companyReports/companyreports_02.html

Sanchez-Peinado, E., Pla-Barber, J., & Hébert, L. (2007) Strategic variables that influence entry mode choice in service firms. *Journal of International Marketing*, 15(1): 67–91.

Schneider (2003) Press-archive: TCL: A strong brand in Far East and a strong parent company for the traditional brand SCHNEIDER. Retrieved from http://www.schneider-electronics.de

Schneider (2005a) Press-archive: Schneider. Member of TTE Europe. Retrieved December 19, 2005 from http://www.schneider-electronics.de

Schneider (2005b) Press – current news: TCL Thomson Electronics (TTE) defines new sales structure for the brand SCHNEIDER. Retrieved November 12, 2005 from http://www.schneider-electronics.de

Schuler, R. S. (2001) Human resource issues and activities in international joint ventures. *International Journal of Human Resource Management*, 12(1): 1–52.

Sharp (2004) Loewe and Sharp agree on the enhancement of LCD TV collaboration and Sharp's additional investment. Retrieved August 13, 2008 from http://hiddenwires.co.uk/resourcesnews2004/news20041215–05.html

Shelton, S. (2015) Samsung SDI expands auto battery division Retrieved June 1, 2015 from http://www.hybridcars.com/samsung-sdi-expands-auto-battery-division/

Sony (2008) History. Retrieved July 18, 2008 from http://www.sony.net/Fun/SH/1–34/h4.html

Sony (2011) Sony and Samsung shift to new LCD panel business alliance. Retrieved July 26th, 2015 from https://www.corning.com/worldwide/en/about-us/news-events/news-releases/2013/10/news_center_news_releases_2013_2013102201.html

Taylor, C. R., Zou, S., & Osland, G. E. (2000) Foreign market entry strategies of Japanese MNCs. *International Marketing Review*, 17(2): 146–163.

TCL (2002) Press Release, TCL aquires assets of Schneider Electronics AG. Retrieved April 15, 2008 from http://www.tclhk.com/tclhk/admin/upload/ir/press/ep02919.pdf

TCL (2004a) Major and connected transaction combination agreement for establishment of TCL-Thomson Electronics Limited. Retrieved April 15, 2008 from http://www.tclhk.com/tclhk/admin/upload/ir/announcements/ec04130.pdf

TCL (2004b) Press Release, TCL and Thomson – Finalization of other definitive agreements and dispatch of shareholders' cicular relating to the establishment of TTE Corporation. Retrieved April 15, 2008 from http://www.tclhk.com/tclhk/admin/upload/ir/press/ep0462.pdf

TCL (2005) Exercise of exchange option by Thomson. Retrieved April 15, 2008 from http://www.tclhk.com/tclhk/admin/upload/ir/announcements/ec05810.pdf

TCL (2006a) Agreement made for the intended restructuring of the European operation of the group. Retrieved October 27, 2006 from http://www.tclhk.com/tclhk/admin/upload/ir/announcements/ec061027.pdf

TCL (2006b) Announcement of the agreement made for the indended restructuring of the European operation of the group. Retrieved April 08, 2008 from http://www.tclhk.com/tclhk/admin/upload/ir/press/ep06219.pdf

TCL (2006c) Corporate presentation 3rd quarter 2006. Retrieved April 08, 2008 from http://www.tclhk.com/tclhk/admin/upload/ir/presentation/cp061020.pdf

TCL (2006d) Corporate presentation fiscal year 2005. Retrieved April 08, 2008 from http://www.tclhk.com/tclhk/admin/upload/ir/presentation/cp060726.pdf

TCL (2006e) Press Release: TTE forges strategic alliance with LG.Philips LCD – growing liquid crystal display TV business with a global leader. Retrieved April 08, 2008 from http://www.tclhk.com/tclhk/admin/upload/ir/press/ep06219.pdf

TCL (2007a) About us, company profile. Retrieved November 06, 2007 from http://www.tclhk.com/2007/en/aboutus/introduction.asp

TCL (2007b) About us, global sales network. Retrieved November 06, 2007 from http://www.tclhk.com/2007/en/aboutus/network.asp

TCL (2007c) Insolvency filing by a major subsidiary. Retrieved May 24, 2007 from http://www.tclhk.com/tclhk/admin/upload/ir/announcements/ec070524.pdf

TCL (2007d) Interim report 2007. Retrieved April 15, 2008 from http://www.tclhk.com/tclhk/admin/upload/ir/reports/ea07903.pdf

TCL (2008a) Global operations of TCL. Retrieved September 16, 2008 from http://www.tcl.com/main_en/About%20TCL/Company%20Profile/index.shtml?catalogId=13046

TCL (2008b) TCL achieves Q1 profits of RMB 449 Million, Major business operations show stable growth. Retrieved June 14, 2008 from http://www.tcl.com/main_en/News%20Center/Corporation%20News/2008042941587.shtml

TCL (2008c) TCL obtains OEM contract from Samsung. Retrieved September 14, 2008 from //http://www.chinasourcingnews.com/2008/05/07/22246-tcl-obtains-oem-contract-from-samsung/

TCL (2008d) TCL overseas business growth surpasses domestic trends. Retrieved September 14, 2008 from http://www.tcl.com/main_en/News%20Center/Corporation%20News/2008070142030.shtml

TCL (2014a) The creative life. Retrieved November 26, 2014 from http://www.tcl.com/About/index_en.html

TCL (2014b) TCL Air Conditioner (Zhongshan) Co., Ltd. Retrieved November 26, 2014 from http://hao.tcl.com/

TCL Home Appliances (HK) Co., Ltd. Retrieved November 26, 2014 from http://hao.tcl.com/

TCL (2014c) TCL Communication Technology Holdings Limited. Retrieved November 26, 2014 from http://tclcom.tcl.com/

TCL Lighting Electric Co., L. (2014) TCL. Retrieved December 14, 2014 from http://lighting.tcl.com/en/about.aspx?id=69

TCL_China (2004) Annual report 2004. Retrieved May 5, 2015 from http://www.google.de/url?sa=t&rct=j&q=&esrc=s&source=web&cd=2&ved=0CCkQFjAB&url=http%3 A%2F%2Fmultimedia.tcl.com%2FUserFiles%2FFile%2FIR%2FAnnual%2520Report%2F2004annual(eng).pdf&ei=QI2WVfmEGYr-UOP-hOAH&usg=AFQjCNEjo-Y8Nn1EEpZ_UCaf2vef7Kds1 A&sig2=P8kt_GqDLnUH3HzGdZuHUA

TCL_China (2005) Annual report 2005. Retrieved May 5, 2014 from http://www.tclcom.com/?page=financial_report

TCL_China (2006) Annual report 2006. Retrieved May 5, 2015 from http://www.google.de/url?sa=t&rct=j&q=&esrc=s&source=web&cd=3&ved=0CDIQFjAC&url=http%3 A%2F%2Fmultimedia.tcl.com%2FUserFiles%2FFile%2FIR%2FAnnual%2520Report%2F2006annual(eng).pdf&ei=QI2WVfmEGYr-UOP-hOAH&usg=AFQjCNEwifhzYPi-2paM8zc1RIzpzP7gpQ&sig2=MI AKWm9UiaBTMCX2wtHy8w

TCL_China (2007) Annual report 2007. Retrieved May 5, 2015 from http://www.tclcom.com/?page=financial_report

TCL_China (2008) Annual report 2008. Retrieved May 5, 2015 from http://www.google.de/url?sa=t&rct=j&q=&esrc=s&source=web&cd=1&ved=0CCEQFjAA&url=http%3 A%2F%2Fmultimedia.tcl.com%2FUserFiles%2FFile%2FIR%2FAnnual%2520Report%2F2008 %2520annual(eng).pdf&ei=-o-WVYGzCsnbUdnxpegN&usg=AFQjCNFrB-tKdQ2tePSjg_VfUXcpFm64Fg&sig2=WChGyHrmppsuCuyNcg7NOg

TCL_China (2009) Annual report 2009. Retrieved May 5, 2015 from http://www.tclcom.com/?page=financial_report

TCL_China (2010) Annual report 2010. Retrieved May 5, 2015 from http://www.google.de/url?sa=t&rct=j&q=&esrc=s&source=web&cd=1&ved=0CCEQFjAA&url=http%3 A%2F%2Fmultimedia.tcl.com%2FUserFiles%2FFile%2FIR%2FAnnual%2520Report%2F2010 %2520annual(eng).pdf&ei=8ZCWVdXGBYXxUOe6gdAE&usg=AFQjCNHQsxFCUv0 fLXGQHZ8CrWRi31e71Q&sig2=67YPmlxJ72wJ24Xoinur0 A

TCL_China (2011) Annual report 2011. Retrieved May 5, 2015 from http://www.tclcom.com/?page=financial_report

TCL_China (2012) Annual report 2012. Retrieved May 5, 2015 from http://www.google.de/url?sa=t&rct=j&q=&esrc=s&source=web&cd=1&ved=0CCEQFjAA&url=http%3 A%2F%2Fmultimedia.tcl.com%2FUserFiles%2FFile%2FIR%2FAnnual%2520Report%2F2012 %2520annual(eng).pdf&ei=P5GWVeyZIMOrU9vXrLAP&usg=AFQjCNEsAfSpCuY7YbCWnNsVjRO2_3AgYA&sig2=cS7OLXWHYDzod22P4cOfzw

TCL_China (2013a) Retrieved May 5, 2015 from http://www.google.de/url?sa=t&rct=j&q=&esrc=s&source=web&cd=3&ved=0CC0QFjAC&url=http%3 A%2F%2Fmultimedia.tcl.com%2FUserFiles%2FFile%2FIR%2FAnnual%2520Report%2F2013 %2520annual(eng).pdf&ei=-o-WVYGzCsnbUdnxpegN&usg=AFQjCNHivEkTwAAY2M8leKFdgMNMWVU0 mA&sig2=Y9hiuhVDaEqWJnjrrYERuQ

TCL_China (2013b) Annual report 2013. Retrieved May 5, 2015 from http://www.tclcom.com/?page=financial_report

TCL_China (2014) Annual report 2014. Retrieved May 5, 2015 from http://www.tclcom.com/?page=financial_report

TheInquirer (2006) LCD rise causes crash of two LG Philips CRT firms: CRT has had its day. Retrieved April 08, 2008 from http://www.theinquirer.net/gb/inquirer/news/2006/01/27/lcd-rise-causes-crash-of-two-lg-philips-crt-firms

Thomson (2003) Press Release, TCL and Thomson creating a new global leader in the TV industry. Retrieved November 03, 2003 from http://www.thomson.net/EN/Home/Press/Press+Details.htm?PressReleaseID=1346e56b-b16e-4aed-acde-2f4823c4f7dc

Thomson (2004) Press Release, TCL shareholders' meetings approve creation of TCL-Thomson Electronics. Retrieved July 02, 2004 from http://www.thomson.net/EN/Home/Press/Press+Details.htm?PressReleaseID=43f2ee5f-b909–42f3–9417-edd346d130c5

Thomson (2006) Press Release, Thomson sells down TCL Multimedia stake from 29.3% to 19.3%. Retrieved November 03, 2006 from http://www.thomson.net/EN/Home/Press/Press+Details.htm?PressReleaseID=585d8fec-16a7–4993–9bbb-6b7e420d8528

Thomson (2007a) Homepage I. Retrieved November 07, 2007 from http://www.thomson.net/EN/Home/Group/

Thomson (2007b) Homepage II. Retrieved November 07, 2007 from http://www.thomson.net/EN/Home/Group/timeline1.htm

Tonly_Electronics_Holdings_Limited (2013) Tonly Electronics Holdings Limited. Retrieved November 26, 2014 from http://www.tonlyele.com/EN/

Toshiba_Matsushita_DT (2008) About us. Retrieved May 21, 2008 from http://www.tmdisplay.com/tm_dsp/en/profile/outline.html

Tu, W.-M. (1984) *Confucian ethics today – the Singapore challenge:* Singapore Federal Publications.

Tung, A.-C., & Wan, H. (2012) Contract manufacturing in late industrialization. *Singapore Economic Review*, 57(4): 1–15.

Van den Oever, R. (2013) Philips exits consumer electronics. Retrieved June 18, 2015 from http://blogs.wsj.com/source/2013/01/29/philips-exits-consumer-electronics/

Vergara, R. A. G. (2012) Samsung Electronics and Apple, Inc.: A study in contrast in vertical integration in the 21st century. Retrieved December 10, 2014 from http://www.google.de/url?sa=t&rct=j&q=&esrc=s&source=web&cd=6&ved=0CFsQFjAF&url=http%3A%2F%2Fwww.aijcrnet.com%2Fjournals%2FVol_2_No_9_September_2012%2F9.pdf&ei=TlSIVJeHKsLzPLfTgYAG&usg=AFQjCNGQ71ajB9jU-o5Dh4xFjTgVWnco6 g&sig2=wieJsi4herk8xZRAKuPdwQ

Vollmann, T. E., Berry, W. L., Whybark, D. C., & Jacobs, F. R. (2005) *Manufacturing planning and control for supply chain management.* New York: McGraw-Hill/Irwin.

Welch, L. S., Benito, G. R. G., & Petersen, B. (2007) *Foreign operations methods: Theory, analysis, strategy.* Cheltenham: Edward Elgar.

Welge, K. M., & Holtbrügge, D. (2015) *Internationales Management* (5. Ed. ed.). Stuttgart: Schäffer-Poeschel Verlag.

WeltOnline (2008) Endlich darf auch Sony einmal triumphieren. Retrieved July 15, 2008 from http://www.welt.de/meinung/article1522979/Endlich_darf_auch_Sony_einmal_triumphieren.html

Wheelen, T. L., & Hunger, J. D. (2010) *Strategic management and business policy. Achieving sustainability* (12. Ed. ed.). Boston: Pearson Education Ltd.

Williamson, O. (1991) Comparative Economic Organization: The Analysis of Discrete Structural Alternatives. *Administrative Science Quarterly*, 269(36): 269–296.

Wohllaib, N. (2006) Licht aus. Das Ende der Kathodenstrahlröhre. Retrieved April 07, 2008 from http://www.nzz.ch/2006/02/03/em/articledi1k4_1.8356.html

Worstall, T. (2013) Why Samsung beats Apple or perhaps vice versa. *Forbes.*

Yan, A., & Gray, B. (2001) Antecedents and effects of parent control in international joint ventures. *Journal of Management Studies*, 38(3): 394–416.

Yan, A., & Zeng, M. (1999) International joint venture instability: A critique of previous research, a reconceptualization and directions for future research. *Journal of International Business Studies*, 30 (2): 397–414.

Yiwei, W. (2014) Foxconn: still stay OEM, still downstream the chain. Retrieved January 12, 2015 from http://huxiu.me/post/91434691946/foxconn-still-stay-oem-still-downstream-the

Yuxin, H. (2005) The disillusion of TCL and Alcatel. Retrieved December 10, 2014 from http://eng lish.caijing.com.cn/2005–05–30/100043203.html

Zeira, Y., & Newburry, W. (1999) Equity international joint ventures (EIJVs) and international acquisitions (IAs): Generic differences in the pre- and post- incorporation stages. *Management International Review*, 39(4): 323–352.

Zentes, J., Morschett, D., & Schramm-Klein, H. (2011) *Strategic retail management. Text and international cases*. Wiesbaden: Gabler Verlag.

Zhao, H., Luo, Y., & Suh, T. (2004) Transaction cost determinants and ownership-based entry mode choice: a meta-analytical review. *Journal of International Business Studies*, 35(6): 524–544.

Zou, H., & Ghauri, P. N. (2008) Learning through international acquisitions: the process of knowledge acquisition in China. *Management International Review*, 48(2): 207–226.

Zschiedrich, H., & Glowik, M. (2005) Opportunities and limitations of international production relocations: a case study of the television set industry in central and eastern European countries. In P. Chadraba, & R. Springer (Eds.), *Proceedings of the 13th Annual Conference on Marketing and Business Strategies for Central & Eastern Europe*. Vienna: Vienna University of Economics and Business Administration.

Subject index